Celebrating the Jewish Year

The Winter Holidays

Celebrating the Jewish Year

The Winter Holidays

Hanukkah ▲ Tu b'Shevat ▲ Purim

Paul Steinberg

Edited by Janet Greenstein Potter

2007 • 5767
The Jewish Publication Society
Philadelphia

JPS is a nonprofit educational association and the oldest and foremost publisher of Judaica in English in North America. The mission of JPS is to enhance Jewish culture by promoting the dissemination of religious and secular works, in the United States and abroad, to all individuals and institutions interested in past and contemporary Jewish life.

The Jewish Publication Society
2100 Arch Street
Philadelphia, PA 19103

Composition and design by Masters Group Design

Interior artwork by Adam Rhine, with permission from the artist, www.HebrewArt.com

Cover artwork by Adam Rhine, with permission from Sounds True, 413 S. Arthur Avenue, Louisville, CO 80027

Manufactured in the United States of America

07 08 09 10 11 10 9 8 7 6 5 4 3 2 1

ISBN 13: 978–0-8276–0876–9 (volume 1)
ISBN 13: 978–0-8276–0849–8 (volume 2)

Library of Congress Cataloging-in-Publication Data

Steinberg, Paul.
  Celebrating the Jewish year / Paul Steinberg; Janet Greenstein Potter, editor. — 1st ed.
    v. cm.
  Includes bibliographical references and index.
  Contents: v. 1. The fall holidays: Rosh Hashanah, Yom Kippur, Sukkot
  ISBN 978-0-8276-0842-9 (alk. paper)
  1. Fasts and feasts—Judaism. 2. Calendar, Jewish. I. Potter, Janet Greenstein. II. Title.
  BM690.S72 2007
  296.4'3—dc22
                                    2007010805

Publisher's Note:
With few exceptions, the essays taken from other sources are as they appear in the original.
As a result, there are variations in spelling and language from piece to piece.

JPS books are available at discounts for bulk purchases for reading groups, special sales, and fundraising purchases. Custom editions, including personalized covers, can be created in larger quantities for special needs. For more information, please contact us at marketing@jewishpub.org or at this address: 2100 Arch Street, Philadelphia, PA 19103.

For my parents

Which is the path of virtue a person should follow?
That which brings honor to one's Maker
As well as respect from one's fellow human beings.

—Rabbi Yehudah Ha-Nasi
Mishnah *Avot* 2:1

Contents

Part 4: Purim

Pathways Through the Sources

Interpretations of Sacred Texts

Significance of the Holiday: Some Modern Perspectives

Acknowledgments

This book has undergone several transformations. It began as one thing, and only because of the grace and guidance of Janet Greenstein Potter, the editor, does it arrive in its current form. I am indebted to her undying persistence in pursuit of excellence and her careful reading of the manuscript. If there are any errors, they are indeed my own.

I must also acknowledge all of my teachers who have helped and supported me in my learning from the American Jewish University and from the Ziegler School of Rabbinic Studies. The Ziegler School is a unique place of study, one that embodies the essence of both academic integrity and the true spirit of Torah learning. I am especially grateful to two of my rabbis there: Bradley Shavit Artson and Elliot Dorff. Thank you for being my models of *hokhmah, yirat Shamayim,* and *hesed.*

Furthermore, I am thankful to those who generously contributed original pieces for this volume, namely rabbis Bradley Shavit Artson, Robert Cabelli, Gail Diamond, Daniel Isaacson, Julie Pelc, Adam Raskin, David Seidenberg, Elie Kaplan Spitz, Alana Suskin, and Laurie Hahn Tapper.

Finally and most of all, I thank my wife, Maureen, and our children, Rina and Nili, for your patience and support. You are my greatest teachers of all.

I would also like to extend my gratitude for permission to use material from the following sources:

"The Baal Shem Tov about Joy on *Tu BeShvat,*" in *A Tu BeShvat Seder: The Feast of Fruits from the Tree of Life* by Yitzhak Buxbaum. New York: Jewish Spirit Publishing, 1998, 26.

"Purim Vision II," in *The Jewish Holidays: A Guide and Commentary* by Michael Strassfeld. New York: HarperCollins Publishers, 1985; HarperResources Quill, 2001, 197–8.

"Lights by Night," in *The Eternal Journey* by Jonathan Wittenberg. New York: Aviv Press, 2003, 105–7.

Introduction

WINTER AND THE HOLIDAYS OF HISTORY

Speculation starts with concepts, biblical religion starts with events. The life of religion is given not in the mental preservation of ideas but in events and insights, in something that happens in time.[1]
—Abraham Joshua Heschel

Why is the Torah, the most holy document in Judaism, in the form of a story? Because stories give us context and relevance. We need context and relevance to understand deep, complex concepts and how to apply them to everyday life. In fact, the ability to conceive and grasp stories may be a large part of what distinguishes our essence from that of machines. Anthropologist and linguist Gregory Bateson writes:

> There is a story which I have used before and shall use again: A man wanted to know about mind, not in nature but in his private large computer. He asked it, "Do you compute that you will ever think like a human being?" The machine then set to work to analyze its own computational habits. Finally, the machine printed its answer on a piece of paper, as such machines do. The man ran to the get the answer and found, neatly typed, the words: THAT REMINDS ME OF A STORY.[2]

Bateson's anecdote illustrates what makes us distinctly human. He compares how we think with how a computer computes. With a comical twist, the punch line points out that we humans, at our core, are storytellers. We think in stories. We communicate and convey ideas through the narrative and context of stories. We teach in the form of stories. As opposed to computers, which respond to problems by computing numerical data and following programmed formulas, we answer questions by drawing upon morals and principles from the stories that we learn and retell. Thus, the Torah—embedded with material that explains what being human is all about—naturally occurs in the form of a story.

Throughout time, stories have been the vehicle that people have used to deal with spiritual questions. Who are we? Why are we here? How should we live? Only stories can handle these questions, because only stories can convey the subtleties of life—its imperfections and shades of gray. Furthermore, stories are eternal, since they can be reinterpreted and reapplied to each generation. A story can continuously unfold. For Judaism, the prayers, rituals, and holidays all hearken back to the ever-emerging story of God, the world, and the Jews. Over many years, aspects of Judaism change, because events are constantly informing our collective narrative. When we use the expression "Torah," we are not necessarily referring solely to *the* Torah, but to all of the writings, teachings, and interpretations that have been derived from it over the course of Jewish history. The entire body of Torah is, therefore, not something static; it lives and evolves throughout time with all of humanity.

The specific book itself, the Torah, comprises the Five Books of Moses as the first section of the Bible. The other two sections are Nevi'im (The Prophets) and Kethuvim (The Writings). Many of the practices of Judaism, such as the observance of certain holidays (Sukkot in the fall and Passover in the spring, for example), originate within the stories of the Torah, in addition to growing out of the months or seasons as experienced in the ancient world. But the meaning and celebration of each winter holiday—Hanukkah, Tu b'Shevat, and Purim—originate somewhere outside of the Five Books of Moses. The story of Hanukkah comes initially from the Books of the Maccabees, which are not simply absent from the Torah—they are not in the Hebrew Bible (TANAKH) at all. They are found in the Apocrypha, a collection of Jewish literature that falls outside the canon. The holiday of Tu b'Shevat, although related to portions of the Torah that concern agriculture, emerges from Rabbinic literature rather than from the Bible. Purim is the only one drawn directly from the Bible. Even so, it is not found in the most sacred Five Books of Moses but rather in Kethuvim, considered to be the most recent part of the Bible.

These three holidays are wonderful examples of Judaism's integrative ability to acclimate to new places and times. Rabbi Nina Beth Cardin describes this adaptability when she says: "We Jews are a union of weavers. Interlacing our traditions and language, our rituals and laws, with fibers gathered from cultures around us...."[3] How, after all, could we possibly measure Jewish spirituality without the adaptations and advances of medieval Spain? Could we eliminate Maimonides (the renowned thinker and scholar of medieval Egypt and Spain) or Kabbalah (Jewish mysticism)? How could we celebrate our holidays without the now-familiar, ingrained traditions borrowed from the countries of Eastern Europe? How could we grasp the depth and complexity of modern Jewish life without the philosophical and legal discourse that took place in the United States over the past 150 years? Such absences would render Judaism, in many ways, unrecognizable.

Hanukkah, Tu b'Shevat, and Purim grew out of the historical story of Judaism—the development of Jewish context and pattern within the passage of time. These holidays occur in the dead of winter, but even in the damp darkness they contribute to the flow of life, as they are born once more with each of the earth's revolutions around the sun. They have been witnesses to the disappearance both of cultures and of peoples. All during this time, the Jews have survived, continuing to intertwine new threads of Torah with the old, creating the tapestry of Jewish spirituality as we know it today.

Framework of This Book

THE JEWISH TRADITIONS ARE ROOTED IN certain assumptions about the meaning of human existence and the world in which we live. Such assumptions play out in Jewish holiday observance and ideology. The first two parts of the book explore those foundational beliefs, particularly focusing on the relationship between the human spirit, the seasons, and the calendar. Then each of the three holiday sections includes a discussion of the holiday's biblical origins, followed by several explorations of its special ideology and customs. Although synagogue ritual is touched upon, the primary focus of the book is on personal and home customs and their rationales. These are often the clearest expression of the encounter between the spirit and the world.

Another one of the most significant forms of spiritual expression in Judaism is found in the study of texts. As Rabbi Louis Finkelstein of the Jewish Theological Seminary has said, "When I pray I talk to God, but when I study, God talks to me." To help us experience the diversity of viewpoints held and traditions practiced throughout time, each holiday section also includes four groups of writings. In the first group, "Pathways Through the Sources," we look at writings from some of the greatest Jewish thinkers in history, each of which reflects an ideological aspect of the holiday. The richness of these sources invites your own analysis to discover the many treasures each text possesses.

The Jewish tradition teaches that we learn sacred texts on different levels of understanding. Thus in the second group of selections, "Interpretations of Sacred Texts," are passages that I examine at three levels, the first two of which follow traditional patterns of commentary. The first level is *peshat*, the literal, most obvious meaning of the text. The second is *derash*, an interpretation that incorporates explanations of the text given over thousands of years of rabbinical and historical inquiry. The third is "Making It Personal," my own interpretation, which addresses new ways by which we today may identify with this sacred text and apply it to our lives. I hope that by following these three levels of interpretation you will be able to grow cognitively along with the development of ideas in the text. If you ease the integration of the text into your personal life, ultimately it may become a part of your self-knowledge. These three levels—two that are traditional and one that is more modern—reflect the ways we converse and build relationships with the voices of the past and how those voices live on through us.

The third group of selections, "Significance of the Holiday," comprises contributions, original to this book, from renowned scholars and rabbis of our time. These essays discuss the historical development of the holiday, as well as its theological, ethical, agricultural, and seasonal meanings. Also provided are additional essays on important themes and practices unique to that holiday.

Judaism has always recognized that the truth can be understood only in a multiplicity of voices and manners. The fourth group of selections for each holiday is "Alternative Meditations." These include essays, stories, poems, anecdotes, and rituals that add profound expression to a holiday in a nonclassical, innovative manner. The volume is rounded out in part 5, "Guidance along the Way," with two components: a discussion about the conversational style of Jewish learning and a series of sketches describing many traditional sources and scholars—guideposts on our spiritual journey through the holidays.

PART I

Eternal Moments of Jewish Time

נר תמיד

Before Creation shaped the world, God, eternal, reigned alone; but only with Creation done could God as Sovereign be known. When all is ended, God alone will reign in awesome majesty. God was, God is, always will be glorious in eternity. God is unique and without peer, with none at all to be compared. Without beginning, endlessly, God's vast dominion is not shared....

—*Adon Olam*[1]

▲ ▲ ▲ ▲ ▲ ▲ ▲ ▲ ▲ ▲ ▲ ▲

Time Defined

ONE OF THE MOST MYSTIFYING aspects of life is the concept of time. Philosophers, scientists, and mystics all discuss time and its role in the universe. They ask, Does time exist? Would it exist without us to notice it? Would it exist without space? These are perhaps the most awe-inspiring questions to ask. They are also among the most elusive and difficult to answer. Just when we provide ourselves answers and believe we have grasped the concept of time, it slithers away, demanding reexamination.

The modern world has been able to define, and thereby simplify, the notion of time by tying it to space: the physical universe and its history. We measure time—the day and the year—by calculating the earth's orbit around the sun and by comparing changes in the physical world, such as those in nature, including climate, decay, erosion, or even man-made structures come and gone. Time is also made comprehensible by identifying "points in time" that relate to places or events. We can understand the time of 1776 because we relate it to an event, the establishment of America's independence; and we can understand the time of 1948, the year the State of Israel declared its independence, when we contrast it to the events of 1776. Through the comparison of points in time and through their association with events in the story of human existence, we can better define the significance of those moments.

The only way to truly experience and understand the essence of time, however, is to separate it from objective relationships. We must consider time alone. Imagine for a moment, time without space or space without time. It is hard to do. Try to picture floating alone in deep outer space, in the darkness, where absolutely nothing seems to happen. To dwell there would mean dwelling in a moment beyond time, because we would have no physical markers against which to measure time. In the darkness of outer space, with no tangible matter or external observer to define existence, time is completely subjective.

Judaism conceives of time according to a similar concept: subjectivity without space. This model is inconsistent with modern and Western geometric concepts of time, which, as author Ole J. Thienhaus states, "are rooted in Greek philosophy which presumes space is the primary dimension.... The metaphors 'time line' and 'point in time' are directly derived from geometry."[2] For Judaism, on the other hand, time is truly beyond measurement, something that can only be experienced. It is by experience that Jews comprehend time: we remember, we encounter, and we ritualize time.

HESCHEL TIME

Abraham Joshua Heschel, the great 20th-century theologian and professor of ethics and mysticism, has been considered the foremost authority on the Jewish concept of time. He illustrated time and its meaning in Judaism through poetic nuance and metaphor. Explaining that time is not something measured, he established that it is a "realm in which we abide."[3] Time is more of a cosmic story—a story wherein events and experiences are the factors that distinguish change—than it is an objective instrument to measure distance in history. Heschel insisted we must acknowledge that time is boundless, continuously rolling along, carrying space and events along with it, as opposed to imagining that space and events are carrying time.

Heschel's description of time points directly to the profound importance of the Jewish holidays, specifically their role as moments marked in time. In fact, he coined a phrase, "the architecture of time,"[4] that represents the nature of our experience in celebrating the Sabbath and the holidays. According to this view, the holidays are not mere memorials of past events. They are the eternal "palaces," "sanctuaries," and "monuments" of time that make up the structure of Jewish sanctification. The celebration of any holiday represents something other than a dot on a timeline; each occasion is reinforced by the collective experience of our ancestors mingled with the observance of holidays throughout our own lifetimes—sanctification and re-sanctification. For us, time serves as the home of spirit and faith; space is the home of the corporeal.

HOLIDAY TIME

We witness Judaism's conception of time when we see how the religion transformed the agricultural holidays mentioned in the Torah—Sukkot, Passover, and Shavuot—into components of our spiritual history. Sukkot and Passover went from being merely fall and spring harvest festivals to being expressions of our freedom; and Shavuot went from being an early summer harvest festival to being a celebration of the giving of the Torah. This new perspective on holidays was a radical departure from that of pagan religions, which worshiped the physical: the human body, the seasons, and the earth.

The Jewish holidays that are historical in nature (only peripherally linked with the Torah) took their cues from the pilgrimage festivals; over the centuries, Hanukkah, Tu b'Shevat, and Purim have become infused with a more spiritual level of meaning. Thus these time-worn, historical holidays remain relevant, colored by our ever-evolving spirituality. At the same time, Judaism gives birth to modern, history-based holidays that have an intense measure of spirit right from their conception, such as Yom Ha-Shoah (Holocaust Remembrance Day) and Yom Ha-Atzmaut (Israel Independence Day).

TELLING TIME

Although Judaism counts years, it does not count them based on a certain point in history as, for example, the Christian world does with B.C. and A.D.[5] in reference to the birth of Jesus. Without an absolutely accurate way to identify when the universe began, Judaism uses the literal account of the Bible for a starting point. By doing so, Judaism creates a structure in which all moments are defined through their relationship to God as the source of the universe. In this "architecture of time," some moments may be more overtly eventful than others (holidays and major historical events), yet each one is a contributor to the unfolding of Creation. Furthermore, in this arrangement, all moments reverberate along the course of the spiritual plane, all the way back to Creation. Every one of our days is imbued with ultimate meaning as we reawaken to life. Then on each Shabbat (Sabbath) we relive the culminating moment when the universe began; and on each holiday we reexamine the spiritual principle that grew from that historical event. In affirming this architecture of time, and its continuous flow from Creation, we bless each day of our year and encounter the holiness of every moment.

PART 2

Hanukkah

They [the Jews] were so very glad at the revival of their customs, when, after a long time of intermission, they unexpectedly had regained the freedom of their worship, that they made it a law for their posterity, that they should keep a festival, on account of the restoration of their temple worship for eight days. And from that time to this we celebrate this festival, and call it Festival of Lights.

—Flavius Josephus[1]

From Darkness to Light

W E SAVOR AND CELEBRATE THE FIRST of the winter holidays with a warm rush of sensations: sounds from the crackling fry pan, as the scent of latkes wafts from the kitchen; voices uplifted in song, recalling the great warrior Judah Maccabee; each colorful spin of the dreidel, twirling with the beautiful Hebrew letters; and especially the spectacle of light—the light of the menorah that draws the family together to count the nights and remember the rededication of the Temple in Jerusalem more than 2,000 years ago. Hanukkah, the Festival of Lights, has evolved over recent centuries to become one of Judaism's most recognized and celebrated holidays. Its tremendous popularity within the yearly holiday cycle is actually a bit odd, if we consider that Hanukkah was born from a historical experience rather a biblical directive. In fact, Hanukkah ranks as only a minor festival from a religious point of view.

Because the holiday occurs in December,[2] the Hanukkah many people experience today began as a response to the massive shadow that Christmas[3] has cast over Europe and America in recent centuries. The commercial face of Hanukkah often presents itself—falsely—as the "Jewish Christmas." In truth, Hanukkah is something incongruously different: the first explicit observance to commemorate the triumph of religious freedom over totalitarianism. (Passover commemorates a different kind of freedom—national freedom.) Hanukkah is meant to represent the historic Jewish insistence on *not* assimilating.

The annals of history prove that Jews have been prepared to surrender political and economic freedoms, as long as religious freedom was guaranteed. Jews made that compromise many places and times throughout history, including Babylonia in the 6th century B.C.E., Europe in medieval times, and America in its formative years. Hanukkah commemorates the undeniable strength of will held by our Jewish forbearers who fought for religious freedom in a dominant, non-Jewish society, where no such freedom existed. These freedom fighters recognized the limits for subscribing to passivity and defined the far reaches of Jewish courage and integrity. Furthermore, even though it is a story about Jews, Hanukkah symbolizes the universal value of freedom from oppression—religious oppression, in particular— for all people.

Today, Hanukkah continues to grow in its significance. Israeli Jews see a natural connection between the 2nd-century B.C.E. victory of a clan called the Maccabees and the continuing struggle for peace and security in the modern State of Israel. Israeli sports teams are often named after the Maccabees, and the "Jewish Olympics," held every four years in Israel, are called the World Maccabiah Games. Hanukkah has also become more visible and significant in America, especially in the world of pop culture. Jewish celebrities and public personalities make a visible statement of their identity each December when they light a Hanukkah menorah (the nine-branched candelabra called a *hanukkiah*) rather than putting up a Christmas tree. Hanukkah now stands as a readily apparent marker in the Jewish year because it brings attention to our background and identity, regardless of our general level of religious observance. Historically, this holiday was established to commemorate an ancient battle, one that was fought to retain Jewish identity and religious practice in the midst of intense pressure to assimilate. Because we continue with this same struggle in modern times, the relevance of Hanukkah is further clarified and its role is strengthened.

A Young Holiday

The underpinnings of Hanukkah differ from those of the other Jewish holidays, because the origins of Hanukkah and the development of its practices are not drawn from the Bible and are only given slight mention in the Mishnah (Judaism's body of "oral" law written down in the 1st to 3rd centuries C.E.).[4] The first notable mention of Hanukkah appears circa the 6th century C.E. in the Gemara (a commentary on the Mishnah) with this question: "What is Hanukkah?"[5] Most likely, the question is rhetorical. We can surmise that the sages were already aware of Hanukkah, because its story was widely circulated within sources known to Jews. The talmudic Rabbis would have been familiar with the Books of the Maccabees, which we generally consider the primary historical sources for the story of Hanukkah. These are found in the "deuterocanonical"[6] books, most of which are in a 5th-century C.E. collection called Apocrypha. Although such books are not part of the canonized Hebrew Bible (the TANAKH), they were popular among Jews and early Christians and were set in the biblical canon of the Catholic Church, as well as the canons of Ethiopian, Oriental, and Eastern Orthodox churches.

SEPTUAGINT

Centuries earlier, however, the Books of the Maccabees had been part of the first Greek translation of what was then described as the Hebrew Bible. This translation was called the Septuagint (literally, "The Seventy"), and the story of its origin comes from a legend found in the fictional "Letter of Aristeas." Retold by Philo of Alexandria, the 1st-century C.E., assimilated Jewish philosopher, the legend says that the Greek king of Egypt in the 3rd century B.C.E. requested a Greek translation of the Bible for the magnificent library of Alexandria. The High Priest (*Kohen Gadol*) of the Jews commissioned six members from each of the Twelve Tribes of Israel, for a total of 72 (not 70, but close!),[7] who were taken to Alexandria and placed in separate chambers. Therein they transcribed their own translations. After exactly 72 days, each of the translators emerged with an identical translation of the Five Books of Moses (the Torah). This legend served to affirm the validity and sacred status of the books of the Septuagint as a legitimate Bible. A version of this legend would later appear in the Talmud itself (*Megillah* 9a–b).

The process of translating the remaining books of the Hebrew Bible (different in totality from today's TANAKH) into Greek continued gradually. Some of the newer books that were selected for inclusion, such as the Books of the Maccabees, were written centuries after the initial translation and often composed in Greek. These were placed in a separate category within the Septuagint called Anagignoskomena.

Within the Septuagint, there are four Books of the Maccabees. The first two of them, each written around the start of the 2nd century B.C.E., provide parallel accounts of the Maccabean history, spanning from approximately 180 B.C.E. to 160 B.C.E.. The Third Book of the Maccabees has nothing to do with the Maccabees and tells instead of an earlier Jewish persecution, under the ruling Ptolemy dynasty in Egypt, from 222 to 205 B.C.E. The Fourth Book of the Maccabees (circa 1st century C.E.), is about the Hanukkah story and Jewish martyrdom but seems to be a completely independent work from the other books in both style and philosophy.

JUDITH

The Book of Judith is a well-known deuterocanonical book in the Apocrypha that is related to Hanukkah. During the medieval period, especially after the 9th century, it became customary to recount this story during the holiday, even though it has no direct

A Scroll of Its Own

One of the lesser-known sources for Hanukkah is the Scroll of Antiochus. It was read communally during the Middle Ages, notably in Spain, Italy, Yemen, and Persia. The contents differ in certain details from those in the Apocrypha and in the books of historian Josephus. For example, it says that Judah Maccabee was killed in front of his father, Mattathias, at the beginning of the battle waged against the Greco-Syrians. According to other sources, Mattathias died before the war began. In addition, the scroll gives prominence to the miracle of the oil and the commandment to kindle lights on Hanukkah— not mentioned at all in the Books of Maccabees. Scholars disagree on a date for the scroll's creation, with estimates ranging from the 1st to 11th centuries,[12] and on a location for its author, anywhere from the Middle East to Europe. There is no religious mandate to read the scroll, and it has become largely absent from today's liturgy.

relation to the Maccabees or to the rededication of the Temple.[8] The setting and details, in fact, vary by storyteller and by era in which the story has been told. Judith (*Yehudit*, literally "Jewess" in Hebrew) is a wealthy, pious, and beautiful widow from a time earlier than the Maccabees. In one version, after the Assyrian[9] general Holofernes besieges a town in Israel, Judith single-handedly infiltrates the army encampment and, with her beguiling and seductive powers, succeeds in reaching the general's tent. She plies Holofernes with wine, and he soon dozes off. Judith seizes this opportunity to behead him. The Israelites are then able to defeat the invaders.

In several other biblical or apocryphal stories and proverbs of the same era, beautiful, non-Jewish, enemy women are depicted as a danger to the Jewish people, for example, the notorious Delilah.[10] Judith, however, is made into a heroine of Jewish redemption. The plot and theme of her story closely mirror that of an Israelite woman named Jael in the biblical Book of Judges.[11] During a time of war, Jael serves milk to the Canaanite general Sisera, who subsequently falls asleep. She then kills him by driving a tent pin through his head. Her action is followed by the Israelites' victory in battle. Most scholars identify the Book of Judith as fiction, perhaps because it is a copy of the biblical story of Jael. But whether fact or fiction, the Book of Judith conveys an historical portrait of the ancient Near East[13] and thus provides valuable insights into the story and meaning of Hanukkah.

JOSEPHUS

Perhaps of most significance to Hanukkah is the account written by the 1st-century C.E. author Josephus, an aristocratic Greek Jew known also as the Roman citizen "Flavius Josephus." As a military leader of the Jewish soldiers and later as an agent of the Romans, he was an eyewitness to the First Jewish-Roman war (66–73 C.E.) and to the destruction of the Second Temple (70 C.E.). The transition in his allegiance had occurred following a siege in the Galilee, when Josephus surrendered to Rome rather than commit suicide with his compatriots. Afterwards, he served two Roman generals as an informer and negotiator. Despite being regarded as a traitor to his people, he remained a loyal and law-observant Jew in his own eyes and those of most Rabbinical commentators. The works of Flavius Josephus, particularly *The Antiquities of the Jews* and *The War of the Jews,* are some of the only surviving historical material from that time and place. They provide invaluable records of Jewish history and practice, including an account of the Maccabean revolt.

Revolt against an Empire[14]

CONQUER AND DIVIDE

Hellas is "Greece" in Greek, and so we use the word hellenization to describe the expansion of Greek language, culture, and religion into other parts of the ancient world. Alexander the Great of Macedonia[15] was born in 356 B.C.E. He fostered the hellenization of the Near East, and consequently the Jews, as part of a monumental military campaign in which his army conquered most of the then-known civilizations. After Alexander died in 323 B.C.E., his empire was divided among four of his military officers. They warred with each other for years over the entirety of Alexander's empire until boundaries were clearly established in 281 B.C.E. to create four large territorial states. Two of Alexander's former officers, Ptolemy and Seleucus, had already established powerful dynasties. With the partition of the empire, Judea (Palestine) came under the control of the Ptolemy dynasty, which also ruled Egypt and Phoenicia. By approximately 198 B.C.E. the Ptolemies had lost their hold on the Judean region to the Seleucid dynasty, which also ruled Syria, Asia Minor, and Mesopotamia. It is during the reign of the Seleucids, under King Antiochus IV, that the story of Hanukkah is set.

As with most stories, this one begins well before the most obvious moment. Hellenization was a sweeping cultural influence that spread from the surrounding areas into Judea, where most of the people readily accepted the changes. It was not only a cultural phenomenon but also a social and economic one. Modern Greek agricultural techniques had helped bring abundance to the region. Spurred by that success, commerce flourished, travel and trade increased, and the population grew. Most Jews adopted the new Greek clothing, language, and overall culture just as their neighbors were doing. In major Hellenistic cities, such as Syrian Alexandria, Jews achieved great wealth and attained positions of nobility. They managed, however, to keep a distance from the Greek religion, even though it was a central component of hellenization.

Hellenism beyond Greece

The importance of Greece proper (the territory of modern Greece) declined after the death of Alexander the Great; the powerful centers of Hellenistic culture became Alexandria, the capital of Ptolemaic Egypt, and Antioch,[16] the capital of Seleucid Syria.

The political climate in the region was volatile, because Judea was in the middle of a constant, geopolitical tug-of-war between the two feuding dynasties: the Ptolemies of Egypt and the Seleucids of ancient Syria. Most Jews were inclined toward the Seleucids, because of the strong connection that existed between the Jews of regions then under Seleucid control—Persia and Babylonia—and the Jews of Judea, who had left those same countries anda returned to Israel after centuries of exile. Furthermore, Jews were primarily farmers, whose interests were very different from those of people in Ptolemy-controlled Alexandria—the greatest port in the Mediterranean region and a place where business and commerce flourished.

DECLINE OF THE PRIESTHOOD

About 230 B.C.E., the tension between the Ptolemy supporters and the Seleucid supporters reached a crisis level that affected Jerusalem and the Temple itself. Onias the Second, the *Kohen Gadol,* refused to pay his obligatory silver tribute to the Ptolemies, the dynasty in control of Judea at that time. The king of Egypt made plans to invade Jerusalem over this act of defiance. To stave off the assault, Onias's nephew, Joseph ben Tobias, convinced his uncle to relinquish the civil aspect of the High Priest's responsibilities, such as tax collecting, which he himself took over. Joseph reasoned that he could act as intermediary, appeasing the Egyptians, while Onias could concentrate on the religious part of his role and remain loyal to the Seleucids.

Splitting the duties of the priesthood had a tremendous social effect; it was, perhaps, the most important factor leading to the Maccabean revolt, around which the story of Hanukkah is centered. As the chief tax collector, Joseph ben Tobias proceeded to take advantage of his position, acting corruptly and administrating loosely, all for his own personal gain. These activities drew negative attention toward the Jews from outsiders and created discontent among the Jews themselves, particularly between the noble class and the peasantry. Furthermore, the actions of Joseph and the Tobiads (the term used by 1st-century historian Flavius Josephus for the descendants of ben Tobias) explicitly redefined the priesthood. From then on, the once sacrosanct, ancient tribe of priests was openly perceived as being capable of undignified and corrupt behavior, such as one finds in a typical bureaucracy.

Over the next 70 years, the Tobiads transformed the priesthood into an aristocracy that ruled over hellenized Jerusalem. They spoke Greek, wore Greek clothes, used Greek names, and were anxious to start the Olympic Games in Judea. Their passion for Judaism and its priestly code of moral conduct was apparently gone. Under Tobiad control, the holy city of Jerusalem was degrading into a mere hub for commerce, a bureaucratic seat for tax collectors, and a nest of scandal within the nobility. The Jewish peasants did not trust the priests, and the atmosphere of suspicion would tarnish the city of Jerusalem, the Temple, and priesthood until the onset of the Maccabean revolt in 166 B.C.E.

ANTIOCHUS "THE MADMAN"

In 175 B.C.E., amid this social-political unrest, a new ruler, Antiochus IV, ascended to the throne of Greco-Syria. As did many rulers, he appended the title Epiphanes ("God Manifest") to his name; but many people referred to him instead as Antiochus Epimames ("The Madman"). Immediately upon assuming power, he decided to pursue the conquest of Egypt, which no other Seleucid king had been able to accomplish. The Romans were advancing eastward and expanding their empire. If Antiochus could conquer and annex Egypt, his kingdom's size and power would be greatly increased and the Romans might be resisted. But before doing so, he would have to stabilize his own country and consolidate political support by uniting the disparate cultural, social, and religious elements. Under Alexander the Great, hellenization had been a movement that still allowed room for cultural variation; under Antiochus, hellenization was intended to take a big step further and become the agent of cultural totalitarianism.

The Jews were clearly targets of Antiochus's strategy of hellenization. He understood that to ultimately succeed in Egypt, he would need to disrupt the influence of the Jews within his own territories. He decided to tackle the priesthood in Jerusalem by replacing Onias the Third, the latest *Kohen Gadol*, with Onias's brother Joshua, who was loyal to the Greeks. Joshua became High Priest and immediately changed his name to Jason.

To a certain extent, Antiochus's plan worked. Jason submitted to the king's will and helped implement the new totalitarian doctrine. Jerusalem became a little version of Antioch, replete with a gymnasium where the Jewish *Kohanim* (Priests) often played Greek sports in the nude. Meanwhile, King Antiochus had access to the Temple treasury to help fund his military campaign to conquer Egypt. All these activities fueled the restless anger of the pious Jewish peasants, who became even more enraged when Antiochus allowed Menelaus, a Tobiad, to purchase the position of *Kohen Gadol*. They were incensed that this sacred position, for which Menelaus had outbid Jason, was for sale at all. But to make matters worse, Tobiads were not even descendants of Aaron, who was the brother of Moses and the traditional ancestor of all *Kohanim.*

As a condition of his appointment, Menelaus had promised he would increase the tax revenue. When he failed to do so, he was summoned to appear before the king. While away, Menalaus left his brother Lysimachus as High Priest in his stead. Lysimachus proceeded to rob the Temple of many of its sacred vessels, an action that led to riots in the streets, during which the supporters of Jason (even knowing all his faults) battled the supporters of Menelaus.

Meanwhile, after a decisive battle in 169–8 B.C.E., Antiochus was on the brink of annexing Egypt to Syria. The Roman army, however, was moving victoriously eastward. With its own sights set upon Egypt, Rome warned Antiochus not to expand his kingdom in that direction. Antiochus was not powerful enough to defy the mighty Roman Empire; and finding his ambitions for conquest thwarted, he would become even more aggressive toward the people he already ruled.

While Antiochus was away, Jason had managed to retake Jerusalem from Menelaus— a victory based on the rumor that Antiochus was dead. But he was not able to seize control of the government and was forced to flee. Antiochus, furious with the rebellion, returned to Jerusalem, slaughtered thousands of people, and reinstalled Menelaus. Once Antiochus departed and heard that a second rebellion had broken out, he outlawed Judaism. Among the now-forbidden practices were the rite of circumcision, the study of Torah, and the keeping of kashrut (Jewish dietary laws).

In the Jews's Holy Temple, he placed a statue of Zeus—the god he believed was manifest in his own royal being—and sacrificed swine on the altar. He stripped the Temple of its sacred vessels, including the seven-branched golden menorah, and stole the silver and gold coin.

THE HASIDIM

In Jerusalem, reactions to the new regulations were mixed. Many Jews enjoyed being freed from the restrictions of Jewish law, and Jews who had long been interested in Hellenistic life further welcomed Antiochus's decree. There were even Jews who helped persecute other Jews found disobeying the new laws. Antiochus himself seemed to believe that he was merely speeding up the inevitable transition: most Jews would peacefully yield to hellenization, and only a few would have to be forced. Many Jews, however, resisted with their lives and died as martyrs.

Groups of resisters known as Hasidim[17] (literally, "Loyal Ones") could be found throughout Judea. The most significant was a priestly family known as the Hasmoneans,[18] residing in the town of Modi'in. After the father, Mattathias, refused to take part in a pagan sacrifice, he and his five sons fled to the Gophna Hills. There they became the leaders of a guerilla army that would lead the Jews' revolt against the Greek-Syrians—one of the most remarkable revolts of all time.

Many different groups of Hasidim had risen up against the Seleucids. Two factors distinguished the Hasmoneans from the others: first, they were priests, which gave them prestige among the non-hellenized Jews; and second, they were willing to fight on the Sabbath (typically, Hasidim were easily captured on that day and then burned alive). After about a year of rebellion, Mattathias fell ill and died, leaving his son Judah to be the leader. Another son, Simon, acted as Judah's counsel.

JUDAH MACCABEE

Judah was nicknamed "the Maccabee." One tradition teaches that Maccabee is really an acrostic for the words in Exodus 15:11, "Who is like You O LORD, among the celestials;..." (*mi kamokha ba-elim Adonai*). Most scholars, however, prefer the explanation that Maccabee is derived from the Hebrew *maccaba*, meaning "hammerhead." It was quite common in Hellenistic times to nickname people according to their physical characteristics, and this tradition teaches that Judah was called "hammerhead" because of the shape of his skull. Whatever the origin of his nickname, it was certainly appropriate, considering his ferocity in battle.

At the start of the revolt, Judah had a small group of extremely dedicated guerillas, the Maccabees. At first, they did not attack the Greek-Syrians directly, but traveled throughout the countryside, where they destroyed pagan altars and circumcised Jewish children. The initial military test for Judah and his militia was against the Greco-Syrian governor of Judea and commander of its forces, Apollonius. Judah surprised the troops at Nahal el-Haramiah and completely crushed them. Appolonius was killed. Antiochus, busy with a rebellion in another kingdom, then sent an even larger force to attack the Maccabees. This time Judah was accompanied by new recruits who had been stirred into action by the earlier victory. His band of resistors had become a small, but resolute and well-organized, army. With their leader a man of exceptional strategic and inspirational abilities, the outnumbered Jewish rebels again defeated the Greco-Syrian force.

The next miraculous victory for Judah Maccabee was against the viceroy of the Seleucid empire, Lysias, who was the temporary ruler of Syria while Antiochus was away. In 165 B.C.E., outraged by the recent defeat, Lysias mustered an army of 60,000 infantry, 5,000 cavalry, and a massive number of troops on elephants to crush the rebellion. In the First Book of the Maccabees,[19] we learn that 5,000 Syrians were slain, but this figure hardly explains how Judah and his army (albeit formidable by this time) could leave the battlefield victorious. Scholars have put forth various explanations, particularly ones that relate to political distractions on the Greco-Syrian side; but, truly, this victory was a testament to the undeniable will of the Maccabees and the Jewish people.

REGAINING THE TEMPLE

The Hebrew word *hanukkah* means "dedication." On the 25th of the Hebrew month of Kislev in 165 B.C.E., exactly three years to the day that Antiochus humiliated the Jewish people with the statue of Zeus, the victorious Jewish army formally rededicated the Temple. Judah stationed soldiers to guard the area, while others cleaned the Temple and replaced and purified its vessels for a celebration. Singing songs and hymns, they celebrated for eight days. Psalm 30, which explicitly mentions the Temple dedication, was probably composed at this time, along with others. The celebration also took to the streets with a parade of torches that is likely the origin of the name "Festival of Lights," as Flavius Josephus refers to it more than 100 years later.[20]

It is important to remember that the Temple rededication was not the end of the Maccabean revolt. For years, the Maccabees continued to battle the Greco-Syrian troops throughout the hill country surrounding Jerusalem and in the Galilee (northern Israel)—even defeating Nicanor, the great general of the elephant corps. In 160 B.C.E., in reaction to that loss, the Syrian king Demetrius sent his friend General Bacchides to attack the Jews. He besieged Jerusalem and trapped the Maccabean forces. According to the First Book of the Maccabees, Judah's soldiers were terrified by the size of Bacchides's force, and two thirds of them deserted. Left with less than 1,000 soldiers against more than 20,000, Judah managed to escape from Jerusalem to confront the enemy in the rough terrain surrounding the city. At a place called Eleasa, Judah Maccabee died in battle. His brothers buried him in Modi'in near their father. Resistance continued under the leadership of Judah's brothers Simon and Jonathan, who finally broke the Greco-Syrian control of Judea. Jonathan proved to be an excellent leader and politician and, by 152 B.C.E., had become the High Priest of the Jews. The Hasmonean dynasty would rule Judea for the more than 100 years—a notable, but relatively short, period of history.

Why Eight Days?

IT'S MIRACULOUS

> *When the Greeks entered the Temple they defiled all the oils, and when the Hasmoneans prevailed and defeated them, they searched and found only one cruse of oil which lay with the seal of the* Kohen Gadol. *It contained only enough oil to light for one day, yet a miracle happened and they used it to light for eight days.*
> —B. Talmud, *Shabbat* 21b

This aspect of the Hanukkah story, learned from the Talmud, is commonly taught to Jewish children in Hebrew and Sunday schools across America; and it is surely the most remembered part of the holiday narrative, told and retold throughout the world. Perhaps this miracle-centered version occurs so often because Jews are more familiar

The Miracle Number

The number eight, in and of itself, has a symbolic relationship to the miracle of Hanukkah. The preceding number—seven—represents nature: for example, the seven days of Creation, the seven days of the week, and the *shemitah* (every seventh year, when agricultural lands are rested). Eight, by being one more than seven, is a transcendent number. It takes us to the next level beyond time and nature. The eight-day Hanukkah miracle violates our understanding of what we call "the laws of nature." The extension of "burn time" from one day to eight, as an event that defies explanation in the physical world, is on a par with the miraculous dividing of the Red Sea. By contrast, in the story of Purim (see part 4 of this volume) the miracle comprises an accumulation of occurrences that are not outside the usual workings of nature but instead form a miracle in their totality.

with the Talmud than with the Apocrypha, where the historical Books of the Maccabees are found. Or perhaps the frequency is inspired by the emphasis on the oil and the *hanukkiah* (Hanukkah menorah); they offer something tangible with which to express our deep connection to and appreciation for the valor of our ancestors. Most likely though, the recounting of the miracle is so dominant and popular because it focuses on the role of God in this story, as opposed to the Maccabees' military accomplishments—a focus echoing a phrase from the biblical Book of Zechariah that is always chanted during Hanukkah: "Not by might, nor by power, but by My spirit...."[21]

Whatever the reason, the talmudic legend remains the account of Hanukkah that most Jews know. Within it, however, are layers of items to ponder and criticize and questions to answer. For example, even people who seem to accept the legend and not question the miraculous nature will ask why we must celebrate for eight days; after all, if there was enough oil for one day, then the duration of the miracle was only seven days not eight![22] The common response from the tradition is that the oil burned extraordinarily slowly, diminishing only a bit for each of the eight days, and therein lies the miracle.

Beyond any symbolic explanations for the number eight lie some more practical, concrete, or commemorative explanations. One Rabbinic tradition says that the Hasmoneans may have needed eight days to become purified after being in contact with the dead on the battlefield. Purification consisted of being sprinkled with clean water that had been mixed with the ashes of an unblemished, sacrificial red heifer. The sprinkling would have occurred on days number three and seven, and only the next day could the Hasmoneans, now ritually cleansed, produce a new batch of purified oil.[23] Another explanation, the one heard more often, claims simply that it took eight days to obtain olives and crush them into oil.[24]

A lesser-heard explanation for the commemorative number eight and the lighting of candles on Hanukkah is found in *Pesikta Rabbati,* a collection of midrashim compiled in the 9th to 13th centuries. It says that when the Hasmoneans entered the Temple, they discovered eight iron rods. Into these, they carved grooves, filled the grooves with oil, and then kindled wicks in the oil.[25] According to this tradition, the eight days of Hanukkah honor that specific moment when the Hasmoneans officially took control of the Temple.

It's Historical

The questions surrounding the eight-day miracle of the oil are fascinating, and Rabbinic literature discusses them at length. When we look at the purely historical sources, however, such questions are not part of the discussion. Flavius Josephus, the most significant historian living in the ancient Near East, makes no mention of a miracle in his account of the Hasmoneans and the rededication of the Temple. Nor is there any mention in the Apocrypha, which provides a basic narrative about Hanukkah. The First Book of the Maccabees (c. 100 B.C.E.), believed to have been written in Israel, simply refers to Hanukkah as a holiday of thanksgiving and joy to be annually observed.[26] The Second Book of the Maccabees ("second," but slightly earlier, c. 124 B.C.E.),[27] written in Egypt, gives a plausible historical reason why Hanukkah is celebrated for eight days, yet clearly lacks any reference to a miracle:

> *The sanctuary was purified on the twenty-fifth of Kislev, the same day of the same month as that on which foreigners had profaned it. The joyful celebration lasted for eight days, like the Feast of Tabernacles [i.e., Sukkot], and then they recalled how, only a short time before they had kept that feast while living like wild animals in the mountains and caves. So carrying garlanded wands and flowering branches, as well as palm fronds [i.e., the ritual symbols of Sukkot], they chanted hymns to the One who so triumphantly achieved the purification of his own temple.*
> —2 Macc. 10:5–7[28]

This version explains that Hanukkah was a belated celebration of the fall festival of Sukkot, because the Jews had not been able to celebrate that holiday during wartime. In the next verse of the same chapter, the text says that the celebration should be repeated every year to commemorate what happened in the Hasmonean era. Having eight days

The *Lulav* of Freedom

In approximately 137 B.C.E., the Hasmonean dynasty began to mint its own coins, a process that continued for nearly 200 years. Minting coins was a clear sign of strength and independence; the country had enough stature to engage in international trade with its own currency. Among the different images that appeared on the coins was the *lulav* (palm branch), a symbol of military victory,[30] just as it was in ancient Rome. During the holiday of Sukkot, the ritual use of the *lulav* is symbolic of another kind of triumph, that of spiritual freedom, when we rejoice in our clean slate after Rosh Hashanah and Yom Kippur. If Hanukkah was originally a delayed celebration of Sukkot, perhaps the *lulav* on the Hasmonean coins also symbolizes freedom. It hearkens back to the first Hanukkah as an act of national independence.

of Hanukkah is as a parallel to the eight days of Sukkot (including Shemini Atzeret). This connection may also inform two related matters. One is a passage in the First Book of the Maccabees that refers to Sukkot as the holiday of independence, thus mirroring itself back onto Hanukkah. The other is the selection of the *lulav* (one of the four species used during Sukkot) as the symbol that was imprinted on Hasmonean coins of the period.[29]

The December Connection

Pagan ideology and ancient religious festivals grew from precivilized experiences of celestial bodies and of the natural world. A separate deity represented each element: sun, moon, stars, wind, rain, land, oceans, plants, animals, or the seasons. Judaism's great gift to spirituality and religion was the new understanding that these elements do not stand alone but are unified in a profound way by one Creator; and each aspect of the universe is connected to and influenced by the other. Although Jews continued to experience certain natural occurrences as markers in the yearly cycle of holy days, for example, the coming of a new moon or the events surrounding the harvest, they expressed their spirituality and concentrated their devotion in ways very different from those of pagans.

WINTER SOLSTICE

Pagans regarded the time of year when days begin to grow longer as the rebirth of their various sun gods. The occurrence represented the triumph of light over the forces of darkness and was a time of celebration. For example, in pre-Islamic Persia, the eve of the winter solstice (the day of the year with the least amount of daylight) was a holiday called Yalda ("Birth"). It honored the birth of the sun god Mithra, who symbolized light, goodness, and strength. Later, Ancient Rome imported this holiday and celebrated it as a week-long pagan festival, *Sol Invictus,* or "Day of the Invincible Sun."

In Judaism, the holiday of Hanukkah takes place around the time of the winter solstice; but of course our holiday has nothing to do with pagan sun gods. It celebrates the Jewish spiritual rebirth that occurred during the rededication of the Temple in Jerusalem. According to traditional sources, the date for the first night of Hanukkah was chosen intentionally as a sign of scorn and mockery directed at *Sol Invictus.*[31] Three years earlier, during that December festival, Antiochus IV had dedicated the Temple to Zeus. Yet, in the following excerpt from the Talmud, we see that the Rabbis did not want people to think that Hanukkah, or in effect any Jewish holiday, was conceived from the spiritual basis, or in the manner of, a pagan holiday:

The Rabbis taught: When Adam, the first human, witnessed that the daylight waned [after his creation in September (Tishrei)], he said, "Woe is me! Perhaps it is because I sinned that the world grows darker and is slowly returning to a state null and void. This is what the heavens decreed upon me." So, Adam stood, fasted, and prayed for eight days. Then Adam saw that the month of Tevet [the month following Kislev and Hanukkah] arrived and the days began to grow longer. He said to himself: "This is the natural way of the world" [i.e., the days grow shorter and longer throughout the yearly cycle]. Therefore he celebrated for eight days and the following year he set it as an annual eight-day festivity. Adam set it as a celebration in honor of God in Heaven; they [the pagans] established it as a time of idolatry.
—B. Talmud, *Avodah Zarah* 8a[32]

At the same time, Christianity had its own concerns about the popularity of rites in late December that were associated with the rebirth of pagan gods; and it reinterpreted many of the pagan symbols to suit its own god and savior, Jesus. In fact, early iconography and artwork dating to the 3rd century portray Jesus with sun-like attributes such as a radiated crown and a solar chariot.[33] Even the date of Christmas bears overtones of proselytization. The original celebration of the birth of Jesus was held on January 6; but as early as 273 C.E., the Roman Catholic Church had moved it to December 25.[34] For historians, the rationale is clear. Because of the overwhelming popularity of *Sol Invictus* in

Cultural Adaptation

Religions and societies have crossed currents over the ages by borrowing from and synchronizing with one another. Despite the unique faith, history, and ritual beauty expressed by each Jewish holiday, Judaism undoubtedly borrowed and reinterpreted many symbols, ideas, and festivities from its neighbors, including the Babylonians. Thus we see a cross-pollination of religious ideology and other celebrations at this winter season, especially involving the concept of spiritual rebirth and the ritual of candle lighting. Such appropriation continued into the 20th century, when, in 1966, Dr. Maulana Karenga created the holiday of Kwanzaa to provide an alternative to Christmas and to celebrate black unity. Kwanzaa shares certain characteristics with other December holidays: it lasts for multiple days, and its rituals include lighting one candle each day, exchanging gifts, and eating a feast.

the Roman Empire, the Church fathers chose to synchronize the celebration of Jesus' birth with a day in the week-long pagan festival.[35] In this way, people could convert to Christianity without losing the joyous flavor of the pagan festivities.[36]

Lights, Dreidel, Action

Kindling Lights

Light has symbolically sparked the imagination of Jews throughout the millennia. It is, after all, God's first creation; and according to Jewish mysticism, vessels of light are the containers of the universe. In much of Rabbinic literature, light is synonymous with goodness, peace, redemption, wisdom, God, and the soul; while the flame—the conveyer of the light—has always represented that which is sacred. For these reasons, the candlelighting ceremony serves as one of the primary rites in Judaism, performed to recognize and frame the moments that are holy and eternal. We light candles and say a blessing on every Sabbath, on many of the holidays, and on the occasions when we honor the memory of people who have died. At Hanukkah, which is also known as *Hag Ha-Urim* ("Festival of Lights"), we bring all of the symbolic meaning of light to each night's ceremony. The flames transform the holiday from one that commemorates a military victory and subsequent miracle to one that celebrates the eternal triumph of the Jewish spirit.

The ritual object that holds the Hanukkah lights is a special candelabra called a *hanukkiah* (often referred to as a Hanukkah menorah).[37] A *hanukkiah* has nine branches: one for each of the eight days and one for holding the *shamash*, which is used to light the other lights. Two principles guide all of the customs associated with lighting the wicks floating in oil or the candles that fill the *hanukkiah*. The first one is *pirsumei nissah*, to publicize the miracle of the oil.[38] This concept underlies the tradition of placing the *hanukkiah* in a place where it is visible to passersby. It should be positioned, if possible, near a window, facing the public thoroughfare. In ancient times, Jews put their *hanukkiot* outside for all to see, except when living in the midst of religious persecution.[39] Only recently have we seen a reemergence of lighting *hanukkiot* outside homes and a new practice of lighting large ones in public places, such as shopping centers and office buildings. The most usual time for lighting is right after sundown, but in some communities it occurs at nightfall (about 20 to 30 minutes after sundown). The wicks should remain burning for at least half an hour, to span the traditional time when people walking home from the marketplace would have viewed the lights.[40] On Friday night, the Hanukkah lights must be kindled early, before the Shabbat lights, because lighting a fire is not permitted once the Sabbath has arrived.[41]

The principle of *pirsumei nissah* also extends to the material that is burned in the *hanukkiah*. Although any oil may be used, olive oil is preferable because it was used by the Maccabees during the rededication of the Temple in Jerusalem.[42] Today, however, most people use wax candles rather than using oil with floating wicks. Electric *hanukkiot* are considered unacceptable by the vast majority of rabbis, unless the person is in a place where a flame is not permitted, such as a hospital room, and the only alternative would be to not observe the ritual.[43]

The second principle guiding our candlelighting tradition is *l'shem mitzvah*, which means "for the sake of the commandment itself." The lights should be solely for

Judaism and the Number Eight

Jews distinguish what is sacred by elevating moments and objects to holy status. Numbers have meaning, and eight represents a reaching toward the divine. The ceremony of male circumcision (*brit milah*) happens on the eighth day of life; some scholars say the number eight symbolizes the Maccabees' joy at restoring freedom to perform the ceremony prohibited by the Greco-Syrians. The tzizit—the knotted fringes on the tallit (prayer shawl)—are eight in number. The Talmud speaks of a harp with seven strings and teaches that in the time of the messiah it will have eight, representing an elevated state of perfection.[44] In the days of the Temple in Jerusalem, there were eight holy vestments worn by the High Priest, eight poles for carrying the holy vessels of the sanctuary, and eight instruments accompanying the Psalms. On Hanukkah we take in the light from the eight main branches of the *hanukkiah* and strive toward achieving our spiritual potential.

Left to Right or Right to Left?

In the 18th century, talmudist Israel Isserlin described two customs for lighting Hanukkah candles.[46] Jews in the Rhineland lit the candles starting with the one at the farthest left position, a practice he said was consistent with a statement in the Talmud about sprinkling blood in a Yom Kippur purification rite: "All turns should be to the right" (Yoma 58b). Isserlin said that Jews in Austria lit in a direction opposite that of the Rhinelanders: they lit from right to left. The Austrians argued that the Talmud is referring to turns made after a required first step in the sprinkling. But since the candles represent a situation where we choose the first step, we should choose the right-to-left direction used in writing the sacred language, Hebrew. Ultimately, the Rhinelanders' practice won out, because the Shulchan Arukh, the code we follow today, favored lighting left to right.[47] Halakhic authority Moses Sofer provided the justification.[48] He explained that although we write Hebrew from right to left on the page, we draw each letter with a stroke from left to right.

celebrating the festival and not for any personal benefit, such as lighting a room. For this reason the shamash—the extra candle used each day to light the main Hanukkah candles—is placed distinctly apart from the others. In that way, any benefit we might gain from the light is understood to be from the shamash, not from the ritual lights themselves.

On the first night of the holiday, one candle is placed on the far right of the hanukkiah. Each succeeding night, one more candle is added, placed in the branch to the left of the preceding candle. Even though we place the candles in the hanukkiah from right to left (from first to last), we light them from left to right (from last to first). We say the blessings before we light the candles, sing Ha-Nerot Hallelu ("We Kindle These Candles") while lighting them, followed by the hymn Ma'oz Tzur ("O Mighty Stronghold").[45]

Reading the Directions

Rabbinic scholars pondered how many lights should be kindled each night of Hanukkah. The question stemmed from imprecise directions in the Talmud, which says, "One light for a man and his household and the mehadrin min ha-mehadrin light for each member of the household."[49] The Hebrew word mehadrin (literally, "beautify") is understood to convey being conscientious or zealous. Mehadrin min ha-mehadrin are very zealous people—the most mehadrin of the mehadrin. The revered medieval philosopher Maimonides gives the clearest explanation of what the Talmud might mean by its directions.[50] He describes four approaches that may be taken:

1. *Basic Mitzvah.* A single candle [not necessarily in a *hanukkiah*] is lit for the entire household each night. (In other words, by the end of Hanukkah, the total number of candles lit during the entire holiday would be only 8.)

2. *The Zealous.*[51] A single candle is lit for each member of the household each night. (In a family of five, for example, the total number of candles lit during the entire holiday would be 40, excluding the *shamash.*)

3. *The Very Zealous.*[52] Each member of the household lights a separate *hanukkiah,* and one candle is added for each successive night of the holiday. (In that same five-member family, 5 candles would be lit on the first night, 10 candles on the second night, 15 candles on the third night, and so on; the total number of candles lit during the entire holiday would be 180.)[53]

4. *Sephardic*[54] *Custom.* A single *hanukkiah* is used for the entire household, and one candle is added for each successive night of the holiday.[55] (The total number of candles lit during the entire holiday would be 36.)

We might wonder if the most rigorous approach, that of the very zealous, has become obligatory. The answer is no, because the act of gazing at the lights, not necessarily lighting the candles oneself, is enough to satisfy the principle of *pirsumei nissah,* publicizing the miracle of the oil. That is why the fourth custom Maimonides describes, in which a single *hanukkiah* is lit for the entire family, is as prevalent today as the third one, in which each member of the family, without regard to generation or gender, prepares and lights an individual *hanukkiah.*

GAMBLING ON THE HOLIDAY

The dreidel (known as *sevivon* in Hebrew) is a four-sided spinning top. Aside from the *hanukkiah,* it is the most recognized symbol of Hanukkah and is used to play a betting game (referred to merely as "playing dreidel") that is popular during the holiday. A dreidel is adorned with four Hebrew letters, one per side: *nun, gimel, heh,* and *shin.* Every player puts money (or candy, raisins, matchsticks, etc.) into the pot and then each takes a turn spinning the dreidel. When the dreidel falls over, the letter that is facing up decides the outcome for that turn.

Smoke Screen

According to legend, when the Greco-Syrian king Antiochus IV outlawed Judaism, Jews would gather secretly to study Torah. While they were studying, their children played dreidel nearby. When the children saw soldiers coming, they would run and warn the adults to stop studying. In another version of that legend, the adults would play dreidel themselves while simultaneously discussing Torah. If soldiers arrived, they would find only a busy bunch of Jewish gamblers, instead of Jewish scholars who were learning the forbidden text.

Why Those Letters?

The Hebrew language provides alpha characters, but not numerical characters. Instead, each letter of the alphabet is assigned a numerical equivalent. In the ancient system called *gematria*, mystics found the hidden meaning of Hebrew words and interpreted connections among them by studying the numerical values of the letters. The total numerical equivalent of the letters on a dreidel is the same as that of the letters in the word *Mashiach* ("Messiah"). For some people, this *gematria* implies that the Hanukkah symbol of redemption is found in the game.

Other people find spiritual reward in playing dreidel because they see each letter as the beginning of a word pertaining to the powers within us—four different facets of our souls: *nefesh* ("spirit"); *guf* ("body"); *sekhel* ("mind"); and *hakol* ("all encompassing"). From a different perspective, other seekers of meaning believe that each letter is an allusion to the four kingdoms that attempted to destroy the Jewish people: *nun* for Nebuchadnezzar of 6th-century Babylon; *gimel* for Gog, who is associated through genealogy to ancient Greece; *heh* for Haman of Persia in the story of Purim; and *shin* for the mountainous land of Seir, which is identified with Esau (the earliest ancestor of Roman civilization). The most common symbolic explanation for the letters, however, describes them as the initial sounds of the four-word phrase *nes gadol haya sham*, "a great miracle happened there," referring to the miracle of the oil. In Israel, the letter *shin* for the word *sham* ("there") is replaced with the letter *pay*, for the word *po* ("here").

Although such explanations are very interesting, it is not likely that the game originated in ancient history.[56] Dreidel, first mentioned in Jewish literature about 1500, has a precedent in a popular English and Irish Christmastime game called *Teetotum* or *Totum* ("Take All"). The four letters on the English spinning top were N (nothing), T (take all), H (half), and P (put down). The Eastern European[57] Jewish game is modeled directly on the German version called *Trundl* or *Torrel* ("Spinning Top"), and the Yiddish word dreidel comes from the German word *drehen* ("to turn").[58] The letters on the German top were N (*Nichts* or nothing), G (*Ganz* or all, H (*Halb* or half), and S (*Stell Ein* or put in). Transliterated into Yiddish (which is written in the Hebrew alphabet), these letters are the *nun, gimel, heh,* and *shin* we use today; and they obviously represent the same dividends.

To Bet or Not to Bet

The prevalence of gambling during Hanukkah was a source of frustration for medieval rabbis, particularly betting when playing cards.[59] As it was, rabbis railed against card playing in general but could only contain it rather than completely stop it. In Frankfurt, Germany, for example, rabbis prohibited card playing at all times except on the holidays of Hanukkah and Purim—and when attending to the mother of a newborn![60] One night was especially popular with Jews for playing cards, a night that often coincided with Hanukkah—Christmas Eve. Jews had a nickname for the evening, *Nital Nacht,* a play on *natoli dominicus*—night of the birth of "the Lord" (Jesus). Kabbalists believe that on this night evil forces penetrate the world, and even the most holy activities, such as studyng Torah or getting married, are forbidden. Because Jews did not permit themselves to learn on that night,[61] time was spent playing cards, an activity jokingly referred to as *klein shas* ("little Talmud").

One might ask whether it is permissible for Jews to gamble at all. It is clear that rabbis have not been favorably disposed toward gambling, but does gambling actually go against *halakhah* (Jewish law)? There is not much that explicitly addresses casual gambling; however, the Mishnah says that professional gamblers should not be trusted in court as witnesses.[62] The Gemara expands upon the Mishnah's position by giving two opinions about gambling. One determines that gambling is a form of stealing, because it is assumed that the loser never concedes psychologically that the money is really gone; and the other says that gambling equals poor citizenship, because even though legal it makes no positive contribution to society.[63]

Maimonides marries these two opinions and forms the strictest point of view: professional gambling [meaning by a person with no other profession] is an altogether bad thing, because the winning is akin to thievery and the losing is a failure to contribute to the world [a waste of time].[64] Maimonides is apparently not speaking of casual gamblers, such as those who play cards on Hanukkah. Therefore, even though the bulk of halakhic literature portrays gambling in negative terms, the majority of the sources argue that the prohibitions on gambling pertain only to professional gamblers.[65]

In societies that celebrate Christmas and New Year's Day—particularly British and American societies—sporting events and gambling have long been quite common and intense during the "holiday season," even on Christmas Day itself. Against that backdrop, Rabbi David Golinkin, president of the Schechter Institute of Jewish Studies in Jerusalem and a professor of Jewish law, describes the matter of gambling and the dreidel from an interesting perspective: "The dreidel game represents an irony of Jewish history. In order to celebrate the holiday of Hanukkah, which celebrates our victory over assimilation, we play the dreidel game, which is an excellent example of cultural assimilation! Of course there is a world of difference between imitating non-Jewish games and worshiping idols, but the irony remains nonetheless."[66]

Hanukkah Foods

The only food mentioned in the classic sources about Hanukkah is cheese. Accordingly, it is customary to eat a cheese dish during the holiday to commemorate the story of Judith (see "A Young Holiday," earlier in this part), wherein the "miracle occurs through milk which Judith feeds the enemy."[67] This custom has been upheld for centuries, particularly among the Ashkenazim (Jews whose ancestors migrated from Germany and France to Eastern Europe).

Oddities appear when examining the rationale for this custom. Only in one commonly known version of the Book of Judith (there are as many as three) called *Megillat Yehudit* ("The Scroll of Judith") is cheese explicitly mentioned.[68] It says that Judith asks her maidservant to prepare two pancakes (*levivot* in Hebrew; "latkes" in Yiddish). She makes the fried cakes very salty and adds "slices of cheese." Judith feeds them to Holofernes, who then drinks enough wine to become intoxicated and fall asleep. In this case, we can at least ascribe cheese a role as contributor to Holofernes's thirst and Judith's opportunity to kill him. But there is a further curiosity: the Book of Judith has nothing to do with the miracle of Hanukkah from a historical or narrative perspective. Holofernes, an Assyrian, was the commander-in-chief for the Babylonian king Nebuchadnezzar, who reigned from 605 to 561 B.C.E. His military assault caused the destruction of the First Temple, an event that occurred 400 years before the Maccabees came to power! Thus we realize that the story of Judith is customarily recounted during Hanukkah because of thematic parallels, not because Judith actually helped in the Maccabean victory or the miracle of Hanukkah.

The latkes with cheese, as described in *Megillat Yehudit*, may be the forerunner of the wildly popular potato latkes of today.[69] This sequence seems likely, especially when we learn that potatoes were not widely cultivated in Eastern Europe, the birthplace of this culinary delight, until the mid-18th century. Potato latkes, fried in oil, were probably introduced as an inexpensive, appetite-satisfying way to celebrate the miracle of Hanukkah and its story of the oil that lasted for eight days.

Cooking with Oil

Through the centuries Hanukkah has developed into a celebration not merely of resistance to tyranny, but also of foods cooked in oil; indeed, it is difficult to imagine a more festive holiday, or one to be more happily observed, than that which prescribes the eating of fried foods.[70]
—Matthew Goodman

Latkes are not the only tasty Hanukkah treat cooked in very hot oil. *Sufganiyot*,[71] small Israeli doughnuts, are first deep-fried, then filled with jelly or custard and dusted with sugar. Early Zionists brought the doughnut recipes to Israel where this holiday fare now reflects the melding of East and West: the fritter is of Sephardic origin, and the jelly filling comes most likely from the Germans, who ate apricot-glazed doughnuts on Hanukkah. *Sufganiyot* are Israel's most popular Hanukkah food, prominently displayed in the windows of every bakery. They are beginning to be seen in America where jelly-filled doughnuts are served at Hanukkah events in synagogues and schools.

From Gelt to Gifts

Gelt is the Yiddish word for "money." The giving of gelt at Hanukkah—associated today with gifts to children—is a relatively recent custom. The origins are unclear, but perhaps the Hanukkah custom is associated with the older Purim custom (see part 4 of this volume) of sending gifts to the poor.[72] Another possible association is found in Joseph Karo's Shulchan Arukh, a 16th-century code of Jewish law, which specifically mentions that we should derive no benefit from the *hanukkiah*, "even to use the light to count your money."[73] In contrast, relinquishing money by giving it away may remind us that the purpose of the lights is not practical but spiritual—to recall the miracle and to deepen our relationship with Hanukkah. The most likely origin for the gelt-giving custom comes from 18th-century Eastern Europe and is based on the close etymological relationship that exists between the words *hanukkah* ("dedication") and *hinukh* ("education").[74] Tradition tells us that the founder of Hasidism, the Baal Shem Tov ("Master of the Good Name"),[75] traveled at this time of year from village to village—dressed as a simple wayfarer—where he would tell inspirational stories to the children and teach them how to pray. Other teachers continued this practice; and over time, parents began giving money to these rabbis. People believed that any one of the teachers could actually be the Prophet Elijah, who was expected to arrive in the guise of a common person from a neighboring town. According to the understanding of these righteous gift-givers, their financial show of commitment would inspire Elijah—whichever teacher he might be—to hasten the longed-for coming of the Messiah.

Before long, the custom expanded. Instead of giving gelt to teachers alone, parents began giving money to their children to honor and reward them for learning Torah.[76] Then in the 19th century, when Jews started manufacturing chocolate, the tradition developed into giving chocolate coins instead of, or in addition to, real money. Chocolate gelt adds to the fun and taste of the holiday and also provides something innocent to wager when playing dreidel.

POSITIVE IS POWERFUL

In light of the Christmas gift-giving frenzy that takes place in the United States around the time of Hanukkah, the simple, old custom of giving gelt has, for many people, erupted into a competition of materialistic excess. Hanukkah was never meant to be a major gift-giving holiday, yet often American Jews feel as through they do not want to deprive their children of what their Christian neighbors receive each December. As a countermeasure, Jewish leaders try to help parents understand that measuring Hanukkah against Christmas actually creates a negative situation, when, in fact, a positive response would be something truly effective for the spirituality of their children. Here Dr. Ron Wolfson, professor of education at the American Jewish University, expands upon the common answer given to the question many children ask, "Why don't we have Christmas?"

> The answer to the child is incomplete. "We're Jewish—we have Hanukkah" is only the beginning of the response. "We're Jewish, and we have Hanukkah, Sukkot, Passover, Shavuot, Purim, Simchat Torah, Rosh Hashanah, Yom Kippur, Lag B'Omer, Yom Ha'atzma'ut, Tu B'Shvat[77]—and, most importantly, Shabbat every week." The child who has experienced the building

of a sukkah will not feel deprived of trimming a tree. The child who has participated in a meaningful Passover seder will not feel deprived of Christmas dinner. The child who has paraded with the Torah on Simchat Torah, planted trees at Tu B'Shvat, brought first fruits at Shavuot, given *mishloach manot* at Purim, and welcomed the Shabbat weekly with candles and wine and challah by the time she or he is three years old will understand that to be Jewish is to be enriched by a calendar brimming with joyous celebration.[78]

THE COMEBACK COINS

More than 22 years after the Maccabees recaptured the Temple in Jerusalem, Simon the Maccabee (surviving son of Mattathias) finally brought full independence to Judea. The Hasmonean dynasty minted the first Jewish coins in history, most of which depicted cornucopia, symbols of the prosperity in the Land of Israel during those years. One of the coins minted by the last of the Hasmonean kings, Mattathias Antigonos (40–37 B.C.E.), portrayed the seven-branched menorah on one side and the Table of Shew Bread[79] on the other; both were symbols of the restored Temple. Scholars conjecture that these designs may have been intended to remind people about Hanukkah, because the commemorative holiday was being neglected during the waning years of the Hasmonean dynasty.

After the Second Temple was destroyed in 70 C.E., and except during a revolt against the Romans in the 2nd century,[80] no Jewish coins were minted for nearly 2,000 years—not until the founding of the State of Israel in 1948. Ten years later, the Bank of Israel began striking special commemorative coins for use as Hanukkah gelt. The first annual Hanukkah coin portrayed the same seven-branched menorah that had appeared on the last of the Maccabean coins. Most year's since then (except 1964–71), the Hanukkah coin has honored a different Jewish community from around the world.[81] The giving of coins on this holiday has come to reflect a hearty remembrance of the high point of Jewish political and religious freedom in ancient times.

·◆— Hanukkah —◆·
Pathways Through the Sources

1 Maccabees
The Totalitarian Experience

In Genesis 11, the story of the Tower of Babel cautions us that the actions of a totalitarian regime go against God's will. Outside of Scripture, in the First Book of the Maccabees, we find the historical accounting of the despot Antiochus IV, in a narrative that brings this caution into clear view. The decrees and events described in this reading are all too familiar, as we know from overwhelming events that have followed: the expulsions of Jews from England (1290) and Spain (1492) and the near-annihilation of European Jewry during the Holocaust.

> On his return from the conquest of Egypt in the year 143 [169 B.C.E.],[82] Antiochus marched up with a strong force against Israel and Jerusalem. In his arrogance he entered the Temple and carried off the gold altar, the lampstand with all its fittings … and whatever secret treasures he found, and carried them all away when he left for his own country. He had caused much bloodshed, and he boasted arrogantly of what he had done….

> [Two years later] the king issued an edict throughout his empire: his subjects were all to become one people and abandon their own customs. Everywhere the nations complied with the royal command, and many in Israel willingly adopted the foreign cult, sacrificing to idols and profaning the Sabbath. The king sent agents to Jerusalem and the towns of Judea with written orders that ways and customs foreign to the country should be introduced….

> Pagan altars, idols, and sacred precincts were to be established, swine and other unclean beasts to be offered in sacrifice. The Jews were to leave their sons uncircumcised; abominable, unclean and profane, and so forget the law and change all their statutes. The penalty for disobeying the royal command was death. Such were the terms of the edict issued by the king throughout his realm….

Every scroll of the law that was found was torn up and consigned to the flames, and anyone discovered in possession of the Book of the Covenant or conforming to the law was to die.

—I Macc. 1:20–4, 41–57[83]

2 Maccabees
Phinehas-Mattathias Connection

Zeal for one's religion either can be inspiring or can be frightening. Phinehas, grandson of the High Priest Aaron, is lauded in the Bible (Num. 25) for his use of violence; and he is spoken of as a model of faith and courage in this passage from the extra-canonical First Book of the Maccabees. Yet later, the Rabbinic sages would become worried about such a level of zeal, and many of them would denounce Phinehas's actions.[84] Today, in a world that suffers from suicide bombings and other acts of terrorism done in the name of heaven, we, too, question zealousness. Yet, although we may not necessarily condone times when religious zeal leads to violence, we must consider times when it is the inspiration for admirable results. In this reading, which compares Mattathias to Phinehas, we learn about the need to maintain loyalty, dedication, and passion for our beliefs.

At that time Mattathias, son of Johanan, son of Simon, a priest of the family of Joarib, moved away from Jerusalem, and settled in Modi'in. He had five sons: Johanan surnamed Gaddi, Simon called Thassi, Judah called Maccabee, Eleazer called Auaran, and Jonathan called Apphus. When he saw the blasphemous things that were taking place in Judah and Jerusalem, he said:

"Yea, behold, our sanctuary and our beauty,
And our glory have been laid waste!
The heathen have profaned them.
Why then should life continue for us?"

Mattathias and his sons stored their clothes, put on sackcloth, and mourned bitterly.

Then the king's officers who were compelling the people to renounce God came to the town of Modi'in to force them to sacrifice. Many Israelites came forward to them; even Mattathias and his sons were there. The officers of the king said to Mattathias: "You are a leader, a prominent and great man in this town. You are firmly supported with sons and brothers. Come forward first, and carry out the order of the king, as all the heathen, the men of Judah, and those left in Jerusalem have done; then you and your sons will be honored with silver and gold and many gifts."

Mattathias answered and replied in a loud voice: "Though all the heathen within the bounds of the royal domain obey him, and each one forsake the worship of his fathers, and show preference for his commands, yet will I, my sons, and my brothers walk in the covenant of our fathers. Far be it from us to forsake the Law and the testaments. We will not listen to the decree of the king by going astray from our worship, either to the right or to the left."

When he stopped speaking these words, a Jew came forward in sight of all to sacrifice upon the altar in Modi'in, in accordance with the decree of the king. When Mattathias saw him, he was filled with zeal, and his soul was stirred up. He brought courage to decision, and running up he slew him upon the altar. The king's man who was enforcing the sacrifice he also killed at the same opportune time, and pulled down the altar. Thus he showed zeal for the Law, as Phinehas had done toward Zimri, son of Salom. Then Mattathias shouted out in a loud voice in the town saying: "Let everyone who is zealous for the Law, and would maintain the covenant, follow me."
—1 Macc. 2:1–6, 11–28[85]

Siddur

Purely Sacred

Ha-Nerot Hallalu ("These Lights of Praise") is a prayer found in the siddur, a book of daily, Shabbat, and festival prayers. The words are sung during the lighting of the *hanukkiah* to caution us that there is only one reason for this ritual object—a symbolic one. In contrast to Shabbat candles, which are lit to brighten up the room and to increase our joy, Hanukkah candles are lit solely to remind us of God's role in our history and redemption.

These lights that we kindle are for the miracles, for the wonders, for the deliverances, and for the military feats that You carried out for our ancestors in the past and the present, through Your holy *Kohanim*. For each of these eight days of Hanukkah, these lights are sacred and we are not to put them to practical use. Rather we are to simply look upon them as a means of gratitude and praise of Your greatness, recalling Your miracles, Your wonders, and Your deliverance.

Babylonian Talmud
A Martyr's Account

More than one version exists of the heart-wrenching story told below. The original version, found in 2 Maccabees, describes a woman witnessing the murders, in rapid sequence, of her seven sons. Subsequent tellings, such as the one below from the Talmud, omit the gruesome details of the story and connect it to verses in the Hebrew Bible. Another well-known version, one from *Midrash Rabbah* (*Lamentations Rabbah* 1:16:50), has the seventh son pronounce differences between Jewish theology and that of the pagans.

As in the original, the mother in the Talmud is unnamed; although other accountings refer to her as Hannah. Hers is a typical "acts of martyrs" story, a genre that tells of women, children, and the elderly dying for Torah. In ancient times, such stories encouraged others—those who might find themselves being persecuted in the same way—to remain strong. According to Jewish law, a person must do everything possible to save his or her own life except under three circumstances in which death must be chosen instead: if a person is ordered to commit murder; if a person is being forced to participate in a major sexual transgression (adultery or incest); or if a person is being compelled to practice idolatry—thereby denying Torah.

> *It is for Your sake that we are slain all day long, that we are regarded as sheep to be slaughtered* (Ps. 44:23). Rav Yehudah said: "This verse refers to the woman and her seven sons." They brought the first one before the emperor and said to him, "Worship the idol." And he replied, "It is written in the Torah, *I am the Lord your God* … (Ex. 20:2)." So they took him away and killed him. [In this manner they brought each of the seven sons before the emperor, instructing them to worship the idol, and each refusing by quoting a verse from the Torah. Finally the seventh son] was brought before the emperor and they said to him, "Worship the idol." And he replied, "It is written in the Torah, *You have affirmed this day that the Lord is your God … And the Lord has affirmed this day that you are, as He promised you, His treasured people …* (Deut. 26:17–18). We have already

sworn to the Holy One Blessed be He that we will not violate our promise by serving any another god. And so He swore to us that He would not violate His promise by adopting another nation." The emperor replied, "I will throw down my seal to you and you will pick it up, in order that they will say that you have accepted the command of the Caesar." The boy then said, "Woe unto you, Caesar! If your honor is so important, how much more so is the honor of the Holy One Blessed be He." As they led him away to kill him, his mother said, "Let me have him so that I may kiss him." And she said to him "My son, go and tell Abraham your father: you may have bound one altar [for a son to be sacrificed], but I have bound seven altars!" Later [she became mentally unstable] and fell from a roof and was killed. Thereupon a heavenly voice cried out, *A happy mother of children* (Ps. 113:9).
—B. Talmud, *Gittin* 57b

Babylonian Talmud
Gravity of the Miracle

The Rabbinic principle *tadir v'she-aino tadir, tadir kodem* means that frequently occurring rituals take precedence over infrequent rituals. For example, in Jewish tradition, a tallit (prayer shawl) is put on every day and thus with more frequency than tefillin (small black boxes containing passages from the Torah), which are never worn on Shabbat or holidays. On weekdays, when both are worn, we follow the "frequency" principle by putting on the tallit before the tefillin. In another example, on Friday nights, we perform a two-part ritual called making Kiddush (literally, "sanctification"). We say the more frequently spoken benediction first, *borei p'ri ha-gefen* (the prayer of thanks made on wine), followed by the blessing in praise of the Sabbath, *m'kadesh ha-Shabbat.*

Rava was a Babylonian sage, one of the most frequently mentioned in the Talmud, which is the most significant collection of laws, stories, and thought in all Rabbinic literature. Many of Rava's rulings are accepted today as Jewish law; and we might expect that in his discussion on the purchase of a *hanukkiah,* he would be guided by *tadir v'she-aino tadir, tadir kodem.* But instead, the concept of publicizing the miracle is so great that he deems it more important—if one has to make a choice—to obtain a *hanukkiah* (for the infrequent ritual) than wine for *Kiddush* (the frequent ritual).

Rava said: "It is obvious to me that if [on Shabbat a person must choose] between buying lights for one's home and buying a Hanukkah lamp [*hanukkiah*], one should buy lights for one's home because they are necessary for *shalom bayit* ["domestic peace"]. And if a person only has enough money for either lights for the home or wine for *Kiddush*, he should buy lights for the home for the sake of *shalom bayit.*

Rava then asked: "If one only has enough money for a Hanukkah lamp or *Kiddush* wine, what then? Does the wine take precedence because it is a mitzvah that occurs more frequently or perhaps the Hanukkah lamp since it publicizes the miracle?

After asking the question Rava found his own answer: "The Hanukkah lamp is preferable, since it publicizes the miracle."
—B. Talmud, *Shabbat* 23b

Nachmanides
Hanukkah Everlasting

The nine-branched *hanukkiah* has a timeless appeal. For some people, it is the first piece of Judaica they buy for their home. It is also is directly associated with the seven-branched menorah of the Temple in Jerusalem.

Rabbi Moses ben Nachman, known both as Nachmanides and as the Ramban, was a physician and great Torah scholar who lived in 13th-century Spain. In this passage, he cites two places in the Torah with which he uses the rabbinic process of inference and interpretation to learn the origin for the story of the Maccabees. He uses this process even though the story is not explicitly mentioned anywhere in the entire Hebrew Bible, of which the Torah (Five Books of Moses) is the first portion. According to the principle that everything can be found in the Torah, the Ramban interprets references to the menorah and associates them with the *hannukiah*. He is able to help us see God's presence in Judaism, from its origins in the Torah to the Maccabees and beyond.

When you mount the lamps (Num. 8:2) … [The] intention of this text is to create an allusion from this section of the Torah to Hanukkah … I have found in *Megillat Setarim*[86] of Rabbenu Nissim, the following: "I saw in the Midrash:

When each of the twelve tribes brought dedication-offerings and the tribe of Levi did not, the Holy One said to Moses, *Speak to Aaron and say to him, 'When you mount the lamps …'* there is another *hanukkah* ["dedication"] wherein there will be lighting of lamps, when I will perform miracles and salvation for Israel through your children, and a dedication which will be known by their name as 'the Hanukkah of the sons of the Hasmonean.'"

I further saw in *Yelamdeinu* [i.e., *Tanchuma*] and also in *Midrash Rabbah:* "The Holy One said to Moses: Go and tell Aaron—'Fear not! You are designated for a greater purpose than this. The sacrifices are brought only as long as the Temple is in existence, but the *lamps give light at the front of the lampstand* forever; and all the blessings that I have given you with which to bless My children will never cease.'" But the Temple is not in existence and the offerings have not been brought since its destruction [in 70 C.E.], and so the lighting of the lamps also ceased! Therefore the sages of the Midrash must have been alluding to the lights of the Hasmonean Hanukkah, which are lit even after the destruction of the Temple.

—Nachmanides, Commentary on *Be'ha'alotkha,* Num. 8:2

Sefat Emet
Triumph and Wholeness

Special meaning has been found in the name Hanukkah by many rabbis, including Yehudah Aryeh Leib Alter (b. 1847–d. 1905, Poland). A member of the Ger Hasidic dynasty, he is also known by the name of his work *Sefat Emet* (The Language of Truth). He divides Hanukkah into two words and focuses on the value of spiritual rest and wholeness. From this "midrashic move" (an interpretive device by which a rabbi can extract deeper meaning from a word, phrase, or verse), he is able to elucidate how the political, military, and cultural struggles we face as Jews are directly related to our spiritual struggles.

The word Hanukkah can be divided and read as *hanu koh,* meaning: "thus did they camp."

The essential miracle of Hanukkah was the victory in battle over the wicked Hellenistic kingdom. The sages, wanting to show that the true joy and liberation from human bondage is that we are enabled to become servants of God … gave it this name.

We are taught that although there was sufficient oil to burn for only one day, it lasted eight days. This does not have to be seen only in temporal terms. "Eight" represents wholeness. Under the yoke of Hellenistic decrees, the power of holiness in the Jews was weakened, until only a bit of it remained within them. After the terrible struggles and battles against the Greek kingdom, they had no strength left to attain wholeness. Here God helped them, and the tiny point of holiness within them miraculously led them in an instant back to wholeness. They called this Hanukkah, "thus did they camp," because here they attained true rest. Wholeness is the peace and rest of coming back to one's root....

All this shows that were it not for the evil forces and the wicked who cover over the power of holiness, Israel would be ready to ascend to the highest rung, to cleave to the Root above. But *"darkness covers the earth"* (Is. 60:2). As soon as they overpowered the Hellenists, they were blessed in a single moment and enabled to cleave to that Root above.
—Sefat Emet[87]

Sefer Ha-Toda'ah
Earning Eternity

One might think that because Hanukkah—and also the holiday of Purim (see part 4 of this volume)—are not mentioned in the Torah, they are less important than holidays that are indeed mentioned, such as Passover and Shavuot. The Talmud, however, claims that Hanukkah and Purim will outlast the rest. The 20th-century Israeli rabbi Eliyahu Kitov (born Eliyahu Mokotovsky in Poland) offers a compelling reason for this assertion in his most famous work, *Sefer Ha-Toda'ah* (The Book of Our Heritage). He links the meaning found in the Jewish experience of earlier times to the condition of our spiritual existence today, in the Land of Israel and in the Diaspora.

Our sages said: Even if all the other festivals will be abolished, the festivals of Purim and Hanukkah will not be annulled (J. Talmud, *Ta'anit* 2:12). To what can this be compared? To one who was given money to invest in a business. He did so and earned great profit. Even if later they should come and take back that which they give him, what he profited on his own will not be taken from him.

The same is true of the festivals which the Torah ordained. They were given in grace to Israel, who lacked merit to earn them on their own. As for Purim and Hanukkah, however, they earned them through their own deeds—through willingness to sacrifice themselves for their faith … This merit was further enhanced by virtue of the fact that they accomplished all these things despite being in a state of oppression and enslavement … This is the reason that these festivals—as opposed to those ordained by Torah—are not celebrated for an extra day outside the Land of Israel … When we in are in the Diaspora, we lack spiritual strength to absorb the sanctity of the festival in one day alone. In the Land of Israel, the sanctity of the land assists us in absorbing the holiness of the festival. Hanukkah and Purim, however, are festivals which the Jews earned with their own merit. Their sanctity is thus closer to Israel's inner soul … and thus do not require an extra day.

—Rabbi Eliyahu Kitov [88]

Lubavitcher Rebbe

The Flame Within

The Chabad-Lubavitch [89] movement is a branch of Hasidism that began in Russia in the 18th century. The movement is guided by the teachings of its spiritual leaders ("rebbes"). The seventh Lubavitcher rebbe, Rabbi Menachem Mendel Schneersohn (b. 1902–d. 1994) spent his childhood in pogrom-ridden czarist Russia, the 1920s battling the Stalinist attempt to eradicate Jewish life in the Soviet Union, and the 1930s studying secular and religious topics in Berlin and Paris. In 1941 he escaped Nazi-occupied Europe and settled in New York, where for the next half-century he developed a worldwide movement of outreach to Jewish communities. In this teaching from *Sichot Ha-Rebbe*, his collected talks, he uses light as an analogy for the human soul. He finds that Hanukkah captures a hidden meaning for our purpose on earth, inspiring us to increase light in the world through mitzvot and good deeds.

The Hanukkah candles are lit for eight days. This does not mean that the same mitzvah is repeated eight times in succession. Just as in a physical sense new candles are lit each night, so it is in a spiritual sense, every night a new mitzvah is fulfilled with new fire. Also, each night we add another candle, indicating how we must constantly increase our efforts to spread light. The Hanukkah lights reflect the fire within the Jewish soul, as it is written, "The soul of man is the lamp of God" (Prov. 20:27). Each person possesses this light within his body. Hanukkah teaches how this light must be ignited and shine forth and how it must be renewed and increased each day....

The kindling of each person's individual menorah, the fire of his soul, leads also to the kindling of the collective menorah, the Jewish people. The light they produce is not self-contained, but rather shines "outside" and illuminates the world at large, spreading light in the totality of the darkness of exile.

Projecting light to the world at large is the underlying intent of all the mitzvot, as it is written, "A mitzvah is a lamp and the Torah is light" (Prov. 6:23). However, to a greater degree than in other mitzvot, this intent is reflected in the Hanukkah candles, for they produce visible light and they spread that light throughout their surroundings.[90]

—Rabbi Menachem Mendel Schneerson

Theodor H. Gaster

Diversity and Distinction

In America and throughout the rest of the Diaspora, many Jews feel the most different and separate from their non-Jewish neighbors and coworkers during the season when Hanukkah and Christmas festivities overlap. We may even feel this way while simultaneously trying to blend in. It is therefore fitting, but perhaps ironic, that the battle between assimilation and religious identity is at the core of the Hanukkah story. The Maccabees fought for the right to be different, to be Jews in an overwhelmingly non-Jewish culture that was rapidly attracting Jewish followers. This pattern has repeated itself throughout history. On the one hand, Judaism accepts and often welcomes the influence of another nation or culture, whether it be Babylonia, ancient Greece, Spain, Poland, or the United States of America. On the other hand, a line always exists that is risky to cross, beyond which Jews are no longer recognizable as Jews—to themselves or to others. The tension between these two realities is reflected in people who find themselves wanting to accept the existence of multiple paths to the Divine, while needing to maintain their own dignity, value, meaning, and unique religious expression.

Theodor H. Gaster (b.1902–d.1992) was a Romanian-born, American biblical scholar known for his work on mythology and on comparitive religion. In the 1953 book *Festivals of the Jewish Year,* he contextualizes the significance of the Maccabean revolt and, consequently, the holiday of Hanukkah. He does so in a way that relates to our distinctive lives as Jews, whether within a pluralistic or a totalitarian society.

> First, Hanukkah commemorates and celebrates the first serious attempt in history to proclaim and champion the principle of religio-cultural diversity in the nation.... Though inspired by the particular situation of their own people, their struggle was instinct with universal implications. For what was really being defended was the principle that in a diversified society the function of the state is to embrace, not subordinate, the various constituent cultures, and that the complexion and character of the state must be determined by a cultural process of fusion on the one hand and selection on the other, and not by the arbitrary imposition of a single pattern on all elements....
>
> Second, Hanukkah affirms the universal truth that the only effective answer to oppression is the intensified positive assertion of the principles and values which that oppression threatens. What inspired the movement of the Maccabees was not simply an abstract and academic dislike of tyranny but a desire to safeguard and evince an identity and way of life which was in danger of extinction....
>
> The real issue at stake was not the right of the Jews to be like everyone else, but their right to be different; and victory meant not the attainment of civic equality (which, after all, was what Antiochus was offering!) but the renewal, after its forced suspension, of that particular and distinctive way of life which embodied and exemplified the Jewish mission. The mark of that victory, therefore, was not a triumphal parade but an act of dedication— the cleansing of the defiled Temple.[9][1]

Yehezkel Kaufmann

Judaism and Hellenism

We often think that the first conflict between religious ideals and scientific reasoning began during the Enlightenment in 18th-century Europe. In the saga of Hanukkah and the Maccabees, however, we can see that Judaism clashed with a similar enlightenment nearly two millennia earlier, when these ideologies encountered one another on the battlefield.

While ideologies have shifted and evolved since then, some streams of Judaism still contend with certain difficult aspects of scientific reasoning. Yet for the most part, Jews are able to reconcile their faith in Torah and the Jewish tradition with the assertions of science and philosophy to gain benefits and wisdom from both perspectives. Judaism has upheld a timeless, unshakable, and almost universally accepted moral conviction, valiantly defended by the Maccabees.

Yehezkel Kaufmann was a 20th-century philosopher, biblical scholar, sociologist, and teacher who was born in Russia and moved to the Land of Israel in 1927. As an author, he became a major influence on our understanding of the history of the Jewish people and on our approach to the study of Bible.

> During the very period in which the edifice of Judaism was being consolidated, the culture of Greece … was reaching its climax. Both of these cultures have points in common, and yet they are utterly distinct. They were destined to conflict with each other and to influence each other, but they forever remained two worlds. [Judaism's] faith was in a God who gave man Torah and *mitzvot* to show him the path of life and virtue…. Greek culture was distinguished by its idea of scientific reason…. It had faith in the redeeming power of the intellect. It created science and philosophy and believed that reason could show man the path of virtue and life ….
>
> In the course of time, Hellenism also conquered Rome, and with this conquest attained universal dominion. At the same time, Judaism was the heritage of a scattered, exiled, and subject people. The Hasmonean kingdom was a mere episode; Rome put an end to it and vanquished Jewry.
>
> And yet the lesson of history is that the men of that age accepted the Jewish gospel of a redeeming God [as adopted by Christianity and Islam] and rejected the Greek gospel of redeeming reason. The struggle between monotheism and paganism ended with the utter collapse of paganism, and the debris buried Hellenistic enlightenment as well…. It indicates that there was something in Judaism that overbore the great appeal of Hellenism…. [That] moral goodness shall redeem, not supress the power of the intellect! And since man can choose goodness, the keys to the redemption are in his hands ….
> —Yehezkel Kaufman[92]

Interpretations of Sacred Texts

The texts in these pages, each studied on multiple levels, are from three sources: *Midrash Rabbah,* the Babylonian Talmud, and liturgical poetry. *Midrash Rabbah* (Great Midrash) includes homilies on the Bible for Shabbat and festivals. The Babylonian Talmud, a collection of Torah-related writings that explain all aspects of Jewish life,[93] was compiled by Rabbinic scholars whose families had escaped from the Romans' terroristic reign in Israel. Hebrew liturgical poems, first composed in Israel during the talmudic era, were initially used to replace certain fixed portions of prayers. Later, in the Diaspora, they served more as supplements to prayer than as substitutions.

THE THREE LEVELS
Peshat: simple, literal meaning
Derash: historical, rabbinical inquiry
Making It Personal: contemporary analysis and application

The Light of God

Said the Holy One: Do not think that I need the light of the menorah. Rather, you should kindle light before Me as I kindled light before you. For what purpose? To elevate you before the nations who will say, "Israel gives light to The-One-Who-Gives-Light-To-All!"

—*Midrash Rabbah (Exodus Rabbah* 36:2)[94]

Peshat
The nine-branched *hanukkiah,* or Hanukkah lamp, is related to one of the most sacred objects in the Jewish tradition—the seven-branched, golden menorah that was kindled in the Temple in Jerusalem. The Torah tells us that the oil used for the menorah must be "clear oil beaten of olives," which apparently provided the best luminosity (Exod. 27:20). When the Maccabees reclaimed the Temple, they rekindled the menorah. After the Temple was destroyed two centuries later,[95] Jews thereafter memorialized the menorah by lighting the *ner tamid,* an "eternal flame" that is kept burning in every synagogue.

This midrash addresses a question. For what reason were the Israelites commanded to light the menorah? The answer suggests that by lighting the menorah—a ritual performed only by the Jewish people—Israel would demonstrate its unique relationship with God and distinguish itself from all other nations. Jews worshiped the One who gives light to everyone, and just as God bestowed upon the Jews those things that light symbolizes, such as goodness, security, and truth, so would the Jewish people have those qualities available to give back to God and to the world.

Derash

In the Torah, God became manifest in the form of light, particularly fire, in three notable instances: the burning bush (Exod. 3:2), the fire at Mount Sinai (Exod. 19:18), and the fire that consumed sacrifices in the Tabernacle (Lev. 9:24). These are ways that God "kindled light" for Israel. Rabbinic literature expands upon all of the different ways that God "lights up" our world. God supplies the sunlight for us to see in the day and the stars to guide us at night. Metaphorically speaking, God provides the "light of the human mind," which ultimately separates us from all of God's other creatures. God gives us the "light of Torah" and the means with which to explore truth. The hope for future redemption and a messianic era is symbolized by light. Finally, God gives each individual the "light of the soul," and that may be the greatest way God lights up our world.

Rabbi Abraham Isaac Kook wrote about the Hanukkah lights in *Mo'adei Ha-Rayah:*

> Within every single Jew exists an aspect of priesthood, because collectively the Jewish people are a priestly nation and a holy people and are joined by the inner desire for a life of holiness and to know

the secrets of the Torah. This quality remains safely hidden deep within the heart of each and every Jew. This small container, the hidden inner eternal holiness, which is sealed with the seal of the High Priest, this inner holiness could not be contaminated by the Greeks![96]

Making It Personal

The Torah commands that the Jewish people be holy (Lev. 19:2), and God gave Jews rules to live by as a guide. Being holy is not to be taken lightly; furthermore, with the complexities of life, the task can at times seem impossible. The Hanukkah lights serve as symbols of an individual's internal power. The light of the *hanukkiah* is intended to awaken the invisible flame of the soul, the place that possesses the power given by God.

For Judaism, that which is invisible retains great value. God is invisible. Our souls are invisible, but they contain the potential power to illuminate the world through good deeds and kindness. Certain people—the elderly, orphans, widows, and those with special needs— are often described as invisible, because of the way much of society treats them; yet Judaism mandates that we must see, respect, and take care of them. Light itself is not visible, yet it may be the most important part of the world, as it illumines all that would otherwise be unseen.

THE THREE LEVELS
Peshat: simple, literal meaning
Derash: historical, rabbinical inquiry
Making It Personal: contemporary analysis and application

Promote Sanctity— Do Not Diminish It

Our rabbis taught: The mitzvah [the "basic" version] of Hanukkah is for one [light] for him and his household. The *mehadrin* ["zealous" people] light a candle for each member of the household. And the *mehadrin min ha-mehadrin* ["very zealous"] Beit Shammai [scholar Shammai's school of thought] says, "On the first day eight lights are lit and they are gradually reduced [each succeeding day]." But Beit Hillel [scholar Hillel's school of thought] says, "Light one on the first day and continue adding one [each day]."

Ulla* said: "Two *amora'im* [talmudic sages] argued about this in the West [i.e., Land of Israel]: Rabbi Yossi bar Avin and Rabbi Yossi bar Zevida. One said that Beit Shammai's reason was to correspond to the days that had passed. The other maintains that

Beit Shammai's reason was to correspond to the sacrifices offered on Sukkot** [which decreased with each passing day] and Beit Hillel's reason is that we should promote sanctity, not diminish it."
—B. Talmud, *Shabbat* 21b

Peshat

Although lighting the Hanukkah candles is one of the most recognized observances for Jews, there has always been confusion and dispute about the pattern to follow and the reasoning behind the choice. In this teaching from the Talmud, two *amoraim*, Yossi bar Avin and Yossi bar Zevida, debate the reasoning of the schools of Hillel and Shammai, which held differing opinions on whether to decrease the number of candles each night (beginning with eight and ending on the last night with one) or increase the number of candles each night (from one on the first night to eight on the last).

Derash

In trying to understand the Shammai-Hillel dispute about decreasing or increasing the lights, the Tosafot (medieval Ashkenazic commentators on the Talmud) pondered whether Shammai and Hillel thought that the "very zealous" version was an outgrowth of the "basic" mitzvah or an outgrowth of the "zealous" version.[97] They concluded that a dramatic visual and pragmatic distinction exists between the two approaches—basic and zealous—and that Shammai and Hillel must have used the basic version as the underpinning of their argument. The Tosafot reasoned as follows: If one candle is added per night for the family as a whole, a passerby can easily calculate what night it is (the first night of Hanukkah, second, third, and so forth). But if each family member lights his or her own candle, unless the passerby knows how many people are in the family, it would be difficult to calculate which night it is. This confusion would diminish rather than enhance the central mitzvah of candle lighting, *pirsumei nissah* (publicizing the miracle).

The "decrease or increase" debate suggests that Hillel and Shammai understand the values of the "potential" and the "actual" differently. Shammai values the potential state of any matter; he sees the actualization of the maximum potential as occurring immediately, and the passing of time as decreasing wholeness. Hillel understands that the value of an event grows in significance with time. He places more value on the actual state of the matter, wherein the number of candles represents the actual number of days of the holiday; when a light is added with each day of Hanukkah, actualization of wholeness increases.[98]

Making It Personal

Jewish tradition accepts Hillel's value of the "actual." This is explicit in the term

for the eighth day of Hanukkah—*zot hanukkah* ("This was the dedication"). Derived from the Torah reading about the dedication offerings (Num. 7:84), the name acknowledges the final day of Hanukkah as the culmination of the holiday. (Theoretically, we can assume Shammai would understand the first day to be *zot hanukkah*.) We, like Hillel, do not discount any aspect of Hanukkah. Thus increasing the number of candles and the light teaches that each day is a sign of maturation, not degradation.

Applying this lesson to our lives, we see time as moments of hidden potential; each day our individual and collective experiences grow toward actualization of that potential. Unfortunately, we hear too often about the degradation of the Jewish generations, moving away from the "true Torah" and, in turn, our relationship with God. If, however, we value the passing of time and our maturation in each moment, we become aware that the actualization of our existence was not reached in the desert at Mount Sinai with the giving of the Ten Commandments. We have the opportunity in each generation to realize our potential as Jews. With this realization, we can make God a real part of our everyday lives and increase, rather than decrease, sanctity and light.

---

* Ulla was a leading halakhist in Babylonia and Israel, late 3rd to early 4th centuries.

** The biblical holiday of Sukkot is in some ways the model for the post-biblical holiday of Hanukkah.

THE THREE LEVELS
Peshat: simple, literal meaning
Derash: historical, rabbinical inquiry
Making It Personal: contemporary analysis and application

Ma'oz Tzur and Redemption

Ma'oz Tzur yeshu'ati …

O mighty stronghold of my salvation, to praise You is a delight. Restore my House of Prayer and there we will bring a thanksgiving offering. When You will have prepared the slaughter for the blaspheming foe, Then I shall complete with a song of hymn the dedication of the Altar.

Peshat

This is the first stanza of the well-known Ashkenazic liturgical poem, *Ma'oz Tzur* ("Rock of Ages"), traditionally sung after the Hanukkah candles are lit. Written in 13th-century Germany, the lyrics, make up five stanzas, each beginning with a Hebrew letter of the poet's name, *Mordechai (mem, resh, dalet, kaf, yud)*. A sixth stanza was later added, but is rarely printed in prayer books.[99] Many prayer books today include only the first stanza.

The melody for *Ma'oz Tzur* came hundreds of years later and is borrowed from a German folksong that was probably used in military marches. In the 16th century, Martin Luther, the great reformer and founding father of Protestantism, set the melody to Christian lyrics that read: "Now be joyful you dear Christians altogether."

The Hebrew lyrics speak to the rescuing presence of God throughout Jewish history. The first stanza serves as a thematic introduction, poetically referring to God as the "Rock of Ages." Each of the succeeding four stanzas refers to God's presence in a specific historical episode of Israel's deliverance: from Egyptian slavery and from Babylonian captivity; from Haman in the Purim saga and from Antiochus in the Hanukkah story.

Derash

It is not surprising that a 13th-century Jewish poet would be looking for historical images of God as rescuer. He was living in a time when Jewish villages in Germany, France, and the rest of the Ashkenazic world were being overrun and sacked by Crusaders, who brought pogroms, pillaging, financial insecurity, and overall fear. Martyrdom stories about Hanukkah and the Maccabee family (2 Macc., chapters 6–7) found widespread popularity in this era.

The Crusader mission was to spread Christianity throughout the world and maintain control of the Land of Israel under the auspices of successive popes. Under such dire circumstances, the Jews certainly found renewed inspiration to pray for miracles and long for a Messianic Era. This is the theme of the sixth and final stanza, which pleads with God for action:

> Bare Your holy arm and hasten the End for salvation—Avenge the vengeance of Your servant's blood from the wicked nation. For the triumph is too long delayed for us, and there is no end to the days of evil. …"

Superstition, mysticism, and a need for spiritual solace saturated these dark ages. Messianic fervor and the belief in God as an active shaper of history were in full force.

Making It Personal

Today we sing *Ma'oz Tzur* because of its literal reference to the holiday *(hanukkat ha-mizbe'ach)* and its historical references to events of Jewish deliverance, including Hanukkah. We continue to believe in and call upon a God of history who cares for us. We hope and pray for a time when "nation shall not take up sword against nation" (Isa. 2:4); when the Jewish people will not be hated; and when the State of Israel will be universally accepted, and terrorism there will stop.

Our prayers today are grounded as much in reason as they are in faith. The idea of a human Messiah/king who will appear and create world peace has become harder and harder for many people to comprehend. Today, in line with Maimonides' rational approach, we admit that we do not know when the Messiah will come and whether the Messiah will be a person or a symbol of Messianic-like redemption. Maimonides, in his commentary on the Mishnah, clearly speaks of a Messianic Age and places much of the responsibility for it upon us—for we must bring it about and maintain it.[100]

When we sing *Ma'oz Tzur,* we stand with our family and friends in the radiance of candlelight. The experience enhances our faith and summons our courage to overcome the trials of life with the help of God and of each other.

·⟜— Hanukkah —⟞·

Significance of the Holiday: Some Modern Perspectives

Forging a New Partnership between God and Humanity

by Adam J. Raskin

Hanukkah is not typically thought of as a particularly "religious" holiday. Permission to work, the traditional barometer of any holiday's sanctity, is granted on all of its eight days. It is a holiday without a biblical book to tell its story, or a devoted tractate in the Talmud to develop its rituals. With the modern addition of a gift-giving deluge, many adults celebrate this festival more for their children or grandchildren than as a spiritual experience for themselves. Further undercutting the prominence of this holiday is a somewhat schizophrenic understanding of Hanukkah's essential story. There is the well-known tale of one day's worth of oil burning for eight; yet the popular imagination knows of a parallel story out there as well: a story of military campaigns, guerilla warfare, and heroic sacrifice. The avatar of these stories is Judah Maccabee himself, who leads the campaign to expel Hellenistic persecution from the Temple and from Judea. But what can we say about God? Where in these competing tales is God's contribution to the victories enshrined in this story? In truth, Hanukkah is a profoundly religious holiday. Embedded in the history of this festival is a revolutionary Jewish theology, with far reaching implications for how Jews understand God's role in the world today.

The theology of Hanukkah is epitomized in a story recounted in the First Book of the Maccabees (2:29–41). In response to Greek oppression, two unique streams of Jewish resistance emerged. A fiercely pietistic sect called the Hasidim virulently opposed any encroachment of Hellenistic influence in Judea. Nevertheless, the Hasidim refused to actively defend themselves. Their tightly woven theology proclaimed God as the exclusive deliverer of Israel. Humans could not force God's hand; indeed the Hasidim understood the persecution of their day as divine punishment for covenantal disobedience. When God was ready, taught the Hasidim, God would redeem His people. The Maccabean theology turned the tables on this austere fundamentalism. Following the bloody massacre of a band of Hasidim who refused to defend themselves when attacked on Shabbat, the Maccabees "decided that very day" (v. 41) that they had a responsibility to safeguard human life, even when such actions might seem to clash with the letter of Torah law. Resolving this conflict, the Maccabees understood the Jewish people to be in more of a dialogical relationship with Torah than the pietists could ever admit. The Maccabees understood Torah as an organic instrument rather than as a closed cannon. Loyalty to that Torah meant delving deeply into its texture, interpreting mitzvot for new and emerging circumstances. Fighting for their lives on Shabbat did not mean disloyalty to the fourth commandment; it meant preserving life so that, in the end, there would be Jews alive to observe that commandment (not to mention all the others).

A further corollary to the Maccabean theology was the refusal to passively rely on God as the exclusive provider of succor and rescue. In the fundamentalist model, every element of both persecution and salvation was predetermined by God. Human encroachment on that plan was not only useless but heretical. Hanukkah's audacious theology suggests that humans have ultimate responsibility for their destiny. God is the Source that invigorates their perseverance. God is the Power that inspires their commitments. Rather than humans waiting for God's intervention, it is God who awaits human action. The Maccabees were no less faithful or religious than their pietistic counterparts. On the contrary, their valor was in defense of Jewish religious integrity and sacred precincts. Yet they were able to articulate a relationship with God that did not render them powerless in the world. In their formulation, God partners with the Jewish people to make miracles happen. In a departure from the wielding of supernatural power in the Bible, God now acts in concert with His creation. God's outstretched arm was now the *esprit de corps* that animated righteous, brave, indeed miraculous human endeavors. While the liturgical centerpieces of the holiday attribute the victory to God, the human actors in this drama—Mattathias, Judah Maccabee, Judith, and the brave bands of outnumbered Jewish soldiers—are the enduring heroes.

It is no surprise that the observers of the creation of the modern State of Israel harkened back to the Hanukkah story for an inspiring pretext to their experiences. The pilots who valiantly grounded several enemy air forces before takeoff, and the ragtag soldiers who defeated mature armies having more sophisticated weapons were all viewed as modern-day Maccabees. For Yom Ha-Atzmaut, Israel's Independence Day, the body of the *Al Ha-Nissim* prayer, which is recited throughout Hanukkah, was reformulated to retell the events of 1948. However, the framework for both the ancient and modern celebrations of Jewish triumph remains the same.

Hanukkah provided a new paradigm for our experience of God in the world. Human beings are charged with profound responsibility for their fate, while God extends himself as the instigator of noble action. The haftarah (prophetic reading) assigned to the Shabbat of Hanukkah ends with the words: "Not by might, nor by power, but by My spirit" (Zech. 4:6). Raw might or absolute power may, at times, secure temporal victories. But the illuminating spirit of God, symbolized in the prominent and public placement of the menorah, has been the Jewish people's secret of survival for a very long time. By coupling this theology with an interpretive approach to Torah, Hanukkah's radical motifs bequeathed to modern Judaism a faith built on an active, engaging partnership with God.

The Ethical Implications of *Ma'oz Tzur*

by Laurie Hahn Tapper

> *Ma'oz Tzur*
> O mighty stronghold of my salvation, to praise You is a delight. Restore my House of Prayer and there we will bring a thanksgiving offering. When You will have prepared the slaughter for the blaspheming foe, Then I shall complete with a song of hymn the dedication of the Altar.

The warm glow of freshly lit Hanukkah candles fills the room, my family stands arm in arm, and as the wick of the last candle is ignited, we gleefully burst into a rousing rendition of the first stanza of *Ma'oz Tzur*. Somebody laughs as battling versions from my mom's family and my dad's family try to out-sing each other, my brother sticks in some extra jazzy notes and be-bops, and after a couple of rounds of the same stanza, we leave the song behind in eager anticipation of the exchanging of gifts. The memory and the feeling is one of warmth and joy, togetherness and peace. No attention is ever paid to the actual words that we sing, but rather the tune, the song, the joy in the moment.

In college I started taking Hebrew more seriously. I will never forget the first time my Hebrew was good enough to understand the words I was singing to this joyful tune. The warm peacefulness of the moment was shattered by the reality of the words' meaning. There was a sharp dissonance between the feeling of the ritual and the words on the page. Were we really singing that God should prepare the destruction of another people, even if those people were our enemies? And would we really sing such a request in such a joyous manner? Hadn't I been taught at Passover, when we remove wine from our glass in honor of the Egyptians who died, that when our enemies die, we acknowledge their death regretfully and sadly? Why was the tune to these words so joyful?

Why must this evening—one of family togetherness and giving, when we celebrate the survival of our Jewish identity, our liberation from religious oppression, and the miracle of light in moments of darkness—be tinged by a song that beseeches God to carry out violence on our behalf? Where is the line that separates celebrating our freedom and liberation from celebrating the slaughter of those who oppress us? Is it not possible to mark a holiday or to live a life that celebrates our freedom without seeking vengeance on our former oppressors?

Perhaps it could be argued that having such a text actually serves a healthy and cathartic service. The song can be viewed as an opportunity for a redirection of national anger and as an outlet for our vengeful emotions, allowing us the opportunity to sublimate the desire to physically harm those who have oppressed us. However, a text such as this is not an isolated incident in our tradition. Expressions, prayers, and songs that ask God to wreak violence on our behalf appear throughout our liturgy, tradition, and holiday texts. Daily in the traditional *Amidah*, three times a day, we praise a God who "breaks enemies and subdues scoundrels;" and we ask God to "destroy God's enemies." On Passover we open our doors and declare that God should pour out God's wrath on our enemies; and in the prayer for the Israel Defense Forces, we don't just pray for strength for Israel's army, but we go further to say, "May God cause the enemies who rise up against us to be struck down before them." Thus, rather than sublimate a desire for physical aggression, does the repetition of such ideas in our liturgy encourage, affirm, or instigate violence toward those who once oppressed us, even when we are free?

When confronted with such texts in our liturgy—for those of us who find such texts uncomfortable or abhorrent—there are a variety of possible responses. We can rationalize their existence as an outgrowth of the time in which they were created, when physical anti-Semitism was rampant. We can counterbalance them with a textual tradition that is peace-loving and accepting of our enemies, such as, "Who is a hero? One who turns an enemy into a friend" *(Avot d'Rabbi Natan)*.[101] We can reinterpret "the enemy," by psychoanalyzing the external enemy into an internal enemy. Or perhaps we can do nothing. What are the ethical implications if we acknowledge and welcome into our tradition the existence of vengeful, violent, war-loving texts, that pray to a God who slaughters our enemies and who kills on our behalf? How can it be that these prayers have their place alongside the prayers in our liturgy for peace, justice, forgiveness, and compassion or that uttering both kinds of prayers is part of the inner spiritual life of a Jew? It seems that the journey to let both traditions live within us is part of our religious process. Can we allow ourselves to dwell with this discomfort and to accept it into ourselves? Furthermore, how does it affect the way we treat others and live our lives?

To accept a vengeful God alongside a compassionate and forgiving God requires us to accept a more complicated inner life, a spiritual life that is not black and white, but is complex and nuanced. It demands our responsibility, good judgment, and sincere and critical thinking. It exhorts us to think sensitively when we call upon God and reflect thoughtfully when we consider which image of God we turn to. There are ethical implications to believing in a vengeful and violent God alongside a compassionate and peace-creating God, and they obligate us to live a life of tremendous accountability. For how could we ever truly know when it is right to pray for the death of another human being?

Illumining the Chill of December

by Bradley Shavit Artson

December is the most difficult month, not merely because the kids are out of school and not merely because the sun sets so early in the day. For Jews, this month is tough for us because of the prominent Christian holiday that pervades the stores, the radio, the television, and nearly every house on the block.

During the rest of the year, we may encounter the occasional bigotry or ignorance of particular individuals. But our sense of being at home here, of being linked with our neighbors in the endless routine of carpools, sporting events, shopping malls, and sunny days connects us in a deep way to the people living next door.

Not so in December, when all of our neighbors turn their attention to celebrating what they understand to be the birth of Jesus, who they see as the son of God, and which, for Jews, is just the birthday of a Jewish boy who lived a long time ago, who taught, and who was murdered by the Romans.

Once a year, we feel like outsiders in our own country—bombarded by songs announcing the birth of the "king of Israel," watching the seasonal eruption of good cheer and kindness (often dissipated by the time New Year's Eve and its drunken hoopla comes along), and returning home to dim, undecorated houses amid the stirring colors, smells, and lights of Christmas.

December can be a depressing time to be Jewish.

Yet December also provides evidence for the uncanny sense of the Jewish people to institute whatever it takes to survive as a people, whatever it takes to keep our faith and our heritage strong. December, you see, witnesses the American-Jewish invention of the mega-Hanukkah.

In the talmudic period, Hanukkah was a minor festival, celebrating the liberation of Israel from foreign domination, the restoration of sacred worship in a place of pagan desecration, and the ensuing political autonomy of the Maccabees and the Jewish people.

From the time of the Maccabees (around 160 B.C.E.) until the 20th century, Hanukkah was celebrated simply—one *hannukiah,* a few coins for the kids, and some oily foods (like latkes) to remember the miracle of the oil that burned for seven extra days. Lighting the candles was a talmudically instituted mitzvah that defined the celebration: the Rabbis instructed each household to *pirsum ha-nes,* to proclaim the miracle by placing a *hanukkiah* in the window so its light would shine out to the world.

But our century provided a unique challenge to American Jews. Surrounded by a welcoming, yet imperial, culture—one that accepted anyone who would take on its ways—Christmas became a major threat to Jewish unity, purpose, and continuity.

How did the Jews respond? Some reacted by melting in—by putting up "Hanukkah bushes" (can you imagine how offensive that must seem to pious Christians?). Many Jews, however, reacted by feeling altogether uncomfortable with the season and with their Jewishness.

Others reacted assertively by putting up outrageous blue and white lights on their roofs, their windows, and around their homes. They purchased electric *hannukiot* to shine through their windows; some even built Maccabee statues for their front lawns. Rather than passing a few small coins to their kids, they began giving significant gifts—not just once, but on each day of the holiday.

While we may not all go for this decorative response or upwardly mobile giftgiving, there is something wonderful about the zest and brazenness—demonstrating a refusal to be an outcast, to be invisible in one's own country. There is something stirring about seeing a Jewish family respond to feeling threatened not by diminishing the family's Jewish celebration, not by blurring it, but by augmenting it.

The Rabbis of the Talmud established the lighting of the *hanukkiah* as a way to proclaim the miracle for all to see. They used the flames of burning oil—the brightest lights of their age. Who knows? If they lived in our time, they might have mandated big, blue light bulbs on the roof, and a giant *hanukkiyah* in every window!

There is nothing wrong with using the building blocks of our Jewish tradition to strengthen Jewish resolve and to inspire Jewish affirmation. Our people have always expressed a determination to thrive by utilizing whatever rituals or customs were at hand. We are witness to that same dynamic unfolding in our midst.

As we let our lights shine, creating a public affirmation that we are distinct, we then need to come to terms with being different.

I would like to propose that we understand different as "special," rather than as "strange." Each person is different from each other person; that's what makes each individual unique and special. The ancient Rabbis saw that individuality as evidence of God's greatness. They noted that when a human being makes a coin using the same dye, each coin turns out exactly alike. But when *Ha-Kadosh Barukh Hu*—the Holy Blessing One—created all humanity through Adam and Eve, no two people turned out the same. How great is God, who is able to make each one of us distinctive!

As a natural consequence, no two families can be identical. While we all use some constellation of the same terms—mother, father, son, daughter, grandmother, grandfather—to describe our relationships, no two mothers are the same and no two relationships are the same. Instead, each connection bears the unmaskable stamp of the two people who are connected through the distinctive contours of their love.

Just as each individual and each relationship is unique and special, so too is each culture and each religious tradition. Being Jewish is special and distinct—not in a bad way but in the unique way it contributes to what it means to be human. Every culture enriches the sum total of human accomplishment, story, and insight when it remains true to its own perspective and genius.

We Jews must do the same, remaining faithful to our unique contribution to humanity in general and to the good Jews who have come before us.

And what makes Jewish life distinctive?

We are chosen by God to live lives of Torah, which we do by:

- Participating in regular study of Jewish sacred writings through which we make room in our hearts and minds for the continuing and millennial conversation between God and the Jewish people

- Practicing the mitzvot (commandments) through which each of us can continue to grow in the service of God. Both deeds of lovingkindness and of ritual profundity constitute the mitzvot

- Saying *tefillot,* the beautiful prayers and supplications of Jewish tradition, which can create a Jewish rhythm and open a space for the soul to find a haven and a home

December is less chilly when we are warmed by our love of God and our sense of belonging to the Jewish people, walking the path of mitzvot.

The Messages behind the Music: Israeli Songs*

by Gail Diamond

In the Torah commentary of the *Sefat Emet* ("Language of Truth"), Rabbi Yehudah Leib Alter of Ger describes Hanukkah and Purim as holidays that the Jewish people "merited by their own deeds" rather than received through the commandments of the written Torah.[102] They each represent a celebration of Jewish peoplehood; and as such, they are particularly open to interpretation and reinterpretation from both secular and religious viewpoints. Early Zionists such as Theodor Herzl (b. 1860–d. 1904) adopted Hanukkah in particular as a celebration of Jewish national strength. In the succeeding years, Hanukkah has received unique Israeli interpretations as a national holiday, with symbols and themes given new meanings. These popular Israeli Hanukkah songs show some of the nation's perspectives on the holiday.

MIRACLE?

According to Rabbinic tradition, Hanukkah celebrates a miracle brought about by God. Traditional texts speak about both the miracle of the oil that lasted eight days and the miracle of the victory of the few over the many. But in the Hebrew song "The Days of Hanukkah" *("Yemei Ha-Hanukkah"),* the lyrics speak of miracles brought about by the Maccabees. Although religious Israelis use a more traditional interpretation, saying that God caused the miracles, the majority of Israelis are secular and sing about the miracles as wrought by humans.

* All English translations by Gail Diamond.

The Days of Hanukkah

Words: Avronin
Melody: Folk tune

This song was originally written in Yiddish and titled "Oy Hanukkah." Here are the translated lyrics of the Hebrew version. (There is also a familiar version with lyrics written directly in English; it begins, "O Hanukkah, O Hanukkah, come light the menorah …")

The days of Hanukkah, the dedication of our Temple
With joy and gladness fill our hearts
Day and night we will spin our dreidels
We'll eat lots of doughnuts.

Chorus:
Light! Kindle! Many Hanukkah lights
For the miracles and the wonders
That the Maccabees performed.

The victory of the Maccabees we will tell and sing about
Against the enemies their hands overcame
Jerusalem returned to life [many versions have "Jerusalem our capital"]
The people of Israel made it happen.

Let Us Raise

Words: Zeira
Melody: From the oratorio Judah Maccabee *by George Frideric Handel*

Another song reinterprets the word *nes*—"miracle." An additional meaning of the word *nes* is "flag" or "standard." The song "Let Us Raise" (*"Hava Narima Nes Va'avuka"*), describes lifting a flag and a torch to celebrate Hanukkah. The *nes* of miracle has been transformed to the *nes* of the victory flag.

Let us raise the flag and torch
And sing together here the song of Hanukkah.

We are Maccabees
Our flag is raised rightly

We fought the Greeks and
Victory is ours.

Flower to flower
We bind a large wreath
On the head of the victor,
The hero Maccabee.

Let us raise the flag and torch
And sing together here the song of Hanukkah.

We Carry Torches
A. Zeev, M. Zeira[103]

The song "We Carry Torches" *(Anu Nosim Lapidim)* questions the existence of miracles, at least in modern times, and focuses instead on the human actions of the Zionist pioneers. In the lyrics, the language of religion is appropriated to serve the purposes of a new ideology. For example, midrash *Va-yikra Rabbah* describes how the light that was made on the first day of Creation was hidden away by God.[104] According to the midrash, this is the meaning of the biblical phrase, "Light sown for the righteous" (Ps. 97:11), which will be revealed only in the Messianic future. But in the song, the Zionist pioneers are described as bringing about their own redemption through their connection with the Land of Israel, where they discover this hidden light. The last Hebrew phrase of the song is *vayehi,* which literally means "let it be"; and in the English translation, the last phrase is "And there was light." They hearken back to the two halves of the well-known description of Creation in the Bible, when God said, "'Let there be light'; and there was light"—*yehi or vayehi or.*[105] The creation of The modern State of Israel by the pioneers becomes a quasi-divine act; they are re-creating, as it were, the world.

We carry torches in the foggy nights
The paths shine under our feet
And anyone whose heart thirsts for light
Will lift up his eyes and come to us to the light
He will come!

A miracle did not happen for us
We found no container of oil
We walked to the valley and climbed the mountain

We discovered the springs of hidden light
A miracle did not happen for us
We found no container of oil
We quarried in the rock until we bled
And there was light.

VICTORY

The military victory and subsequent autonomous reign of the Hasmoneans provided an important example for the early Zionists, and these historical highlights continue to be important to the modern state. Jews regard the Hasmonean dynasty as a reference point of pride—the most recent period of autonomous Jewish rule in the Land of Israel until the founding of the State of Israel.

Early in the 20th century, the song "Who Can Retell?" ("*Mi Yemalel?*") was written to celebrate the deeds of humans in bringing about both the victory of the Maccabees and the hoped-for victory of people in modern times. This song references Psalms 106:2, which celebrates God's mighty acts. The biblical verse was transformed into lyrics that extol the mighty acts of Israel. The Maccabees are described in the song as bringing redemption and salvation, two acts usually associated with God.

Such a bold celebration of a human-centered, military victory can challenge both Rabbinic and Diaspora sensibilities. The talmudic Rabbis downplayed the role of military might and lifted up the role of God in their celebration of Hanukkah. In the contemporary Diaspora, celebrations of might are sometimes similarly viewed as lacking in proper humility or spirituality. Many people do not want to appear jingoistic or to look as though they were celebrating a version of "might is right"; and they are uncomfortable with taking pride in military strength or victories. Yet many Jews, remembering centuries of oppression, take pride in the prowess of the State of Israel. The ability of Jews to defend, protect, and rule themselves is one of the country's values; and the Hanukkah celebrations in Israel highlight this theme.

Who Can Retell?

Words: Ravina
Music: Folk tune

Who can retell the mighty deeds of Israel, who can count them?
In every generation a hero will arise, a redeemer for the people.
Listen!

In those days in this time
The Maccabee saves and redeems
And in our day the whole people of Israel
Will join together and arise and be redeemed.

LIGHT

Light is a major theme of Hanukkah, as one of the descriptive names of the holiday, *Hag Ha-Urim* ("Festival of Lights"), makes clear. In most of Israel, in regard to Hanukkah, the *halakhah* (Jewish law) is strictly followed. It says that Hanukkah lights must be kindled very close to nightfall and the *hanukkiah* must be placed where the light can be seen.

In the book *A Different Light: The Big Book of Hanukkah*, Noam Zion describes how the Rabbis of the talmudic era made the lighting of Hanukkah candles a family event rather than a national event.[106] In modern day Israel, that situation has in some ways been reversed. A torchlight parade from Modi'in, where the Maccabees lived, to Jerusalem marks the beginning of Hanukkah celebrations; and large *hanukkiot* appear on public buildings to emphasize the national character of the holiday.

We Have Come to Cast Out Darkness

Words: Sarah Levy-Tanai
Melody: Emanuel Amiran

The well-known song "We Have Come to Cast Out Darkness" (*"banu Hoshech Legaresh"*) equates light with the individual and the community. Each of us, says the song, is a small light; and together we are one powerful light. This song may hearken back to the prophecy of Isaiah 49:6 that Israel will be "a light of nations." It also emphasizes the power and importance of community for the State of Israel. Only by banding together were the Maccabees able to succeed; only by having citizens who support one another will the modern country survive.

We have come to cast out darkness
In our hands are light and fire
Each one is a small light
All of us are a powerful light
Turn back darkness
Turn back dark
Turn back from before the light.

OIL

The famous miracle of Hanukkah happened through a cruse of oil, and olive oil is important to the celebration of Hanukkah in Israel. Many people perform the mitzvah of lighting the *hanukkiah* by doing so with oil. The staple food of the holiday is a never ending supply of doughnuts called *sufganiyot*, deep-fried in oil. In the song "The Days of Hanukkah," children often parody the line that mentions how we will eat lots of doughnuts; they sing, "We will throw them in the street." This rephrasing recognizes the tendency of *sufganiyot* to become like hockey pucks when left out for a day or two!

The cruse of oil itself is personified in the song "A Small Cruse" (*"Kad Katan"*). For eight days, according to the song, this small jug gave its oil to light the Temple. In the lyrics, the jug becomes the center of the miracle—its small size representing the ability of the few to conquer the many.

A Small Cruse

Words: Aharon Ashman
Melody: Yoel Valba

> A small cruse, a small cruse
> Eight days gave its oil
> All the people wondered
> From where it was being refilled
> All the people gathered
> And proclaimed it a miracle
> If this cruse had not remained
> Our Temple would not have been lit.

Several Hebrew Hanukkah songs, besides "A Small Cruse," also mention the rededicated Temple in Jerusalem and also refer to it as "Our Temple" (*Mikdashenu*). Later this Temple was destroyed (70 C.E.); and despite the centuries that have elapsed since then, the songs have no difficulty proclaiming our present-day connection with the place. These lyrics contrast to those of numerous Hanukkah songs written in English that do not even mention the site. Perhaps Israelis who are singing about the Temple are not connecting with the Temple as a center of worship but rather as a national symbol. The Temple in Jerusalem, in its time, represented the unity of the Jewish people and their geographic center. For modern Israel, Hanukkah reaffirms the connection of the Jewish people to their ancient holy site and their ancient home.

The various secular interpretations of traditional Hanukkah symbols strengthen communal ties, nourish hopes for victory and success, and remind us of the eternal connection of our people and our history to the sacred land. In Israel, Hanukkah celebrates real political aspirations and achievements, alongside spiritual goals and ideals.

·✦— Hanukkah —✦·
Alternative Meditations

The Menorah[106]

*by Theodor Herzl**

Once there was a man who deep in his soul felt the need to be a Jew. His material circumstances were satisfactory enough. He was making an adequate living and was fortunate enough to have a vocation in which he could create according to the impulses of his heart. You see, he was an artist. He had long ceased to trouble his head about his Jewish origin or about the faith of his fathers, when the age-old hatred reasserted itself under a fashionable slogan. Like many others, our man, too, believed that this movement would soon subside. But instead of getting better, it got worse. Although he was not personally affected by them, the attacks pained him anew each time. Gradually his soul became one bleeding wound.

This secret psychic torment had the effect of steering him to its source, namely, his Jewishness, with the result that he experienced a change that he might never have in better days because he had become so alienated: he began to love Judaism with great fervor. At first he did not fully acknowledge this mysterious affection, but finally it grew so powerful that his vague feelings crystallized into a clear idea to which he gave voice: the thought that there was only one way out of this Jewish suffering— namely, to return to Judaism.

When his best friends, whose situation was similar to his, found out about this, they shook their heads and thought that he had gone out of his mind. How could something that only meant an intensification and deepening of the malady be a remedy? He, on the other hand, thought that the moral distress of modern Jews was so acute because they had lost the spiritual counterpoise which our strong forefathers had possessed. People ridiculed him behind his back, some even

*Translated by Henry Zohn.

laughed right in his face, but he did not let the silly remarks of people whose judgment he had never before had occasion to value throw him off his course, and he bore their malicious or good-natured jests with equanimity. And since his behavior otherwise was not irrational, people in time left him to his whim, although some used a stronger term, *idée fixe,* to describe it.

In his patient way our man over and over again displayed the courage of his convictions. There were a number of changes which he himself found hard to accept, although he was stubborn enough not to let on. As a man and an artist of modern sensibilities he was deeply rooted in many non-Jewish customs, and he had absorbed ineradicable elements from the cultures of the nations among which his intellectual pursuits had taken him. How was this to be reconciled with his return to Judaism? This gave rise to many doubts in his own mind about the soundness of his guiding idea, his *idée maitresse,* as a French thinker has called it. Perhaps the generation that had grown up under the influence of other cultures was no longer capable of that return which he had discovered as the solution. But the next generation, provided it were given the right guidance early enough, would be able to do so. He therefore tried to make sure that his own children, at least, would be shown the right way; he was going to give them a Jewish education from the very beginning.

In previous years he had let the festival which for centuries had illuminated the marvel of the Maccabees with the glow of candles pass by unobserved. Now, however, he used it as an occasion to provide his children with a beautiful memory for the future. An attachment to the ancient nation was to be instilled early in these young souls. A menorah was acquired, and when he held this nine-branched candelabrum in his hands for the first time, a strange mood came over him. In his remote youth, in his father's house, such little lights had burned and there was something intimate and homelike about the holiday. This tradition did not seem chill or dead. The custom of kindling one light with another had been passed on though the ages.

The ancient form of the menorah also gave him food for thought. When had the primitive structure of this candelabrum first been devised? Obviously, its form had originally been derived from that of a tree: the sturdy stem in the center; four branches to the right and four to the left, each below the other, each pair on the same level, yet all reaching the same height. A later symbolism added a ninth, shorter branch which jutted out in front and was called the *shammash* or servant. With what mystery had this simple artistic form, taken from nature, been endowed by successive generations? And our friend, who was, after all, an artist, wondered whether it would not be possible to infuse new life into the rigid form of the menorah, to water its roots like those of a tree. The very sound of the name, which he now pronounced in front of his children every evening, gave him pleasure. Its sound was especially lovely when it came from the mouth of a child.

The first candle was lit and the origin of the holiday was retold: the miracle of the little lamp which had burned so much longer than expected, as well as the story of the return from the Babylonian exile, of the Second Temple, of the Maccabees. Our friend told his children all he knew. It was not much but for them it was enough. When the second candle was lit, they repeated what he had told them, and although they had learned it all from him, it seemed to him quite new and beautiful. In the days that followed he could hardly wait for the evenings, which became ever brighter.

Candle after candle was lit in the menorah, and together with his children the father mused upon the little lights. At length his reveries became more than he could or would tell them, for his dreams would have been beyond their understanding. When he had resolved to return to the ancient fold and openly acknowledge his return, he had only intended to do what he considered honorable and sensible. But he had never dreamed that on his way back home he would also find gratification for his longing for beauty. Yet what befell him was nothing less. The menorah with its growing brilliance was indeed a thing of beauty, and inspired lofty thoughts. So he set to work and with an expert hand sketched a design for a menorah which he wanted to present to his children the following year. He made a free adaptation of the motif of the eight arms of equal height which projected from the central stem to the right and to the left, each pair on the same level. He did not consider himself bound by the rigid traditional form, but created again directly from nature, unconcerned with other interpretations which, of course, continued to be no less valid on that account. What he was aiming for was vibrant beauty. But even as he brought new motion into the rigid forms, he still observed their tradition, the refined old style of their arrangement. It was a tree with slender branches; its ends opened up like calyxes, and it was these calyxes that were to hold the candles.

With such thoughtful occupation the week passed. There came the eighth day, on which the entire row of lights is kindled, including the faithful ninth candle, the *shammash,* which otherwise serves only to light the others. A great radiance shone forth from the menorah. The eyes of the children sparkled. For our friend, the occasion became a parable for the enkindling of a whole nation. First one candle; it is still dark and the solitary light looks gloomy. Then it finds a companion, then another, and yet another. The darkness must retreat. The young and the poor are the first to see the light; then the others join in, all those who love justice, truth, liberty, progress, humanity and beauty. When all the candles are ablaze everyone must stop in amazement and rejoice at what has been wrought. And no office is more blessed than that of a servant of light.

Lights by Night[108]

by Jonathan Wittenberg

> Here do I take pen
> in this cave of light,
> this cage of heaven and hell,
> in here unreel my life. I know
> what is inside this jail; this chapel my song is dawnlight;
> I must sing.
> —Nick Naydler[109]

Our parents gave my brother and me the lasting gift of many wonderful holidays. One of my most exciting memories is traveling by train through the night. Nothing in the whole holiday could ever quite equal the excitement of lying rocked by the rhythm of the wheels while pushing back the curtains to watch the lights fly by. There were the individual lights of farmhouses, rows of street lamps drawing nearer or slanting off at the edge of some field; there were the rushing, rocking lights of other trains, the bright lights of stations where I could see the men walking along the train and banging the wheels with their hammers, making them ring out. Watching, I felt uniquely alive, privileged to see the life of things at night.

This is a joy my wife and I have successfully communicated to our children—not that it was an especially difficult undertaking. Now they regularly play going to bed on the train, though unfortunately the highlight of the game concerns the little bags with toiletries and toothbrushes which the railways present to even the youngest passengers. For me, however, and I hope (or fear) they will follow suit, the excitement lay not in sleeping but in steadfastly refusing to do so. I could never comprehend why my parents insisted that I should "lie down properly" and close my eyes, but at that age it went well beyond my powers to explain to them that even for a little child there were moments of such wonder that it was inwardly essential to dispense with the banalities like sleep. For already then, I believe, the contact with those lights had a spiritual value. There is nothing greater I would like to communicate to my own children.

To see through the darkness into the life of things is part of the special wonder of Hanukkah. The Talmud teaches that we kindle the lights for the sake of *pirsumei nisa*—the proclamation of the miracle. Officially, the miracle referred to is, of course, that of the single jar of oil which lasted eight times as long as it should. But in our actual experience of Jewish life through the generations, the miracle means much more. For there are many shades of darkness, requiring many kinds of light.

The depth of night is real enough in winter, when the sun sets early and dusk seals off the houses. Safe from the suffering that the chill and gloom impose on so many, I have always loved the long evenings that draw people together round the fire and light within. But the long nights symbolize other kinds of darkness as well, for with the death of nature comes the intimation of our own. Many elderly people hate the arrival of November, with its dark days bringing loneliness, anxiety, and cold. Night, too, is a spiritual state: the absence of hope, vision, inspiration. Night can mean the nemesis of good. Elie Wiesel chose *Night* as the title of the short and terrifying account of his family's descent into Auschwitz.

There is all the more reason, therefore, to be grateful for light. For light expresses companionship, creativity, hope, and inspiration. Put on a candle in a dark room, and all at once the space has a center; everyone looks toward the flame as if the small, dancing fire had the power to unite our spirits and harmonize our thoughts. Even a small candle illumines a large area, even the littlest flame creates a community around it. Its radiance spreads out beyond the immediate circle. I love to watch the reflection of candles in a window. If the angles are right, one can sometimes see reflections within reflections in a diminishing perspective, as if one were traveling through time, backward down the generations. Lights shine to each other across the distances. Kindle a flame, and life speaks to life across the lands and years that cease to intervene and interfere. The one little candle by the windowsill relates to others, down the same street across the same history, all the way back to the first dawn, when God said, "Let there be light!" This connectedness is also part of the miracle of Hanukkah. It is the radiance to which even a small candle, even an amount of oil sufficient only for one day, can allude and which it can provoke, enabling it to illumine an entire history.

It is said that everyone is ultimately alone. In the end, no one else can absolutely know the contours of our consciousness or share the pain where we are cut by the blades of experience. In the intimacy of mental suffering, no one but the person alone can put up the fight for each breath. Only our internal companions can sustain us, the small population of family and close friends which has over a lifetime come to inhabit our mind. Closed within that darkness we struggle for our most intimate and absolute quality, the sweetness or bitterness of our own consciousness.

Sometimes the physical world imposes on us in outward reality those same conditions that create internal loneliness—pain, isolation, cruelty, the absence of hope or relief. Sometimes the world is configured in a formulation of absolute night—hunger, torture, death camps, hell.

Yet perhaps, for all that, darkness and loneliness are not the final reality. Perhaps it would be truer to think of the materiality of our existence in general, and of evil and pain in particular, as if they were a vast tarpaulin dividing us from the warmth and brilliance of an infinite supply of light. That light is capable of piercing the fabric of the dark. Even within our restricted world of matter it glows in candles of courage and hope and creates about itself a radiance that transcends the limitations of space and time.

Those are the lights one sees as one travels through the swaying, rocking dark. Those are the lights, which once perceived, burn for longer than one day.

An Entirely Different Gift List[110]

by Wayne Dosick

On the first night of Chanukah, take your children with you when you volunteer to serve meals at the local homeless shelter. Light one candle to illuminate their darkness.

On the second night of Chanukah, take your children to the local hospital, and show them how to give a teddy bear or a doll to one of the young patients. Light one candle to illuminate the darkness.

On the third night of Chanukah, you and your children take an old coat or an old blanket downtown and give it to a homeless person who is cold. Light one candle to illuminate the darkness.

On the fourth night of Chanukah, you and your children take a pair of socks downtown and give it to the same homeless person you met last night. If he needs a coat, he probably also needs a pair of socks, but no one ever thinks to give away a pair of socks. Light one candle to illuminate the darkness.

On the fifth night of Chanukah, take your children to visit some of the folks living at the local retirement home. Sing a few songs, tell a few stories, hold a few hands, and listen to the loneliness—and to the wisdom. Light one candle to illuminate the darkness.

On the sixth night of Chanukah, take your children with you to the local blood bank, and let them watch as you donate a pint of blood, as you give the gift of life. Light one candle to illuminate the darkness.

On the seventh night of Chanukah, take your children to play with the young ones at the local women's shelter. Light one candle to illuminate the darkness.

On the eighth night of Chanukah, take your children to an elderly neighbor's house and cook, straighten up, vacuum, scrub the bathtub and the toilets, clean the oven. Light one candle to illuminate the darkness.

On every night of Chanukah, invite friends and neighbors, teachers and classmates, relatives and business associates into your house. Make your home a place of learning and light, of high purpose and deep spirit. Hold your children, hug them tight, tell them how much you love them. Give your children the gift that will last a lifetime—the gift of compassion, of sweetness, of humanity, of soul. Light one candle to illuminate the darkness.

PART 3

Tu b'Shevat

*When you enter the land and plant any tree for food, you shall regard
its fruit as forbidden. Three years it shall be forbidden for you, not to be
eaten. In the fourth year all its fruit shall be set aside for jubilation before
the LORD; and only in the fifth year may you use its fruit—that its
yield to you may be increased: I the LORD am your God.*

—Lev. 19:23–5

▲ ▲ ▲ ▲ ▲ ▲ ▲ ▲ ▲ ▲ ▲ ▲ ▲ ▲

Awakening to Nature

TU B'SHEVAT HAS HISTORICALLY BEEN a minor holy day of the Jewish year with few references in our written tradition. Yet, with our modern ability to integrate science and mysticism, it has come to remind us of the relationship between humankind and nature. We have been given a vast and magnificent intelligence, which we use today, for example, to erect gigantic towers of concrete and steel within urban wildernesses. We then live together in these metropolises, where we surround ourselves with distractions and wander about drunk with power over our environment. And yet, underneath it all, we are merely the dust of the cosmos infused with the breath of God. Just as we are brothers and sisters within all of humanity, so too are we kin to animals, plants, and the earth itself, because we are all made of the same fundamental molecules and atoms. Through the shared rhythms and seasons of life, we rely upon the natural world and all its variety of inhabitants for the functioning of our very lives.

The name of this holiday, in its simplicity, tends to belie the deeper meaning. In *gematria*, the letters that spell "Tu" (*tet* and *vav*) equal 15; Tu b'Shevat literally means "The 15th of [the Hebrew month of] Shevat." On the Gregorian calendar, it usually falls between the end of January and the middle of February, when the rainy season in Israel is ending and the trees begin to sprout flowers and fruits. It is the recognized date of *Rosh Hashanah La-Ilanot,* "New Year for the Trees." Some say that it is the Arbor Day of Judaism. This statement is clearly incomplete, because the American Arbor Day[1] was founded solely to foster the planting of trees and lacks the larger significance and breadth of spirit that characterizes Tu b'Shevat. Although Tu b'Shevat does speak to the welfare of trees, it is rooted in an age-old legal tradition based on a particular manifestation of theology, a view of morality, and a conception of agriculture. Tu b'Shevat is just as much about the relationship between humanity and God as it is about the relationship between humanity and nature. The holiday heightens our awareness of spirit and season in the Jewish year, by helping us see the interconnectedness that binds us into the entire universe.

Ancient and Biblical Seeds

Sometime between 9000 and 7000 B.C.E. (during the Mesolithic and Neolithic periods) in the ancient Near East, humans began to master domestication of both plants and animals.[2] Perhaps this happened because of an expanding, hungry population or because of climate changes leading to the extinction of game species or because of the layered increase in security that accrued to a less nomadic life.[3] Whatever the reason, human control of food production was undeniably one of the most significant developments to affect our world. What's more, the advent of agriculture presented much more than evidence of human ingenuity. As Rabbi Arthur Waskow has said, "This was not merely a sociological event: Through it, one of God's powers became more manifest in human hands."[4] In fact, farming is one of the best examples of human and divine partnership, in the continuing relationship between humankind and God.

Such a profound link between human beings, the earth, and the Creator is reflected in several passages of the Torah. The most obvious one is the story of Creation itself in chapter two of Genesis. God creates the first human, Adam, "from the dust of the earth" (*adamah* is the Hebrew word for earth).[5] This wordplay expresses far more than the earthly origin of humankind; rather, it teaches that there is an inherent and eternal union between human life and the rest of the world. Furthermore, the chapter explains quite clearly that the reason for the creation of humans is to "till the soil";[6] and as it says in verse 15, "the LORD God took the man and placed him in the Garden of Eden, to till it and tend it." In chapter three, after Adam is expelled from Eden, his purpose continues to be to work the land, but God says that doing so will now be difficult—requiring sweat and toil.[7] Therefore, according to the paradigm for all of human life as set in the Torah, our purpose is bound to the earth and specifically to agriculture.

The Book of Leviticus (19:23–25) provides the next striking expression of the connection between human beings, the earth, and the Creator. The Israelites are specifically instructed that once they enter the Land of Israel, they are to maintain discipline indicative of their gratefulness and responsibility to God for the crops. They may plant fruit-bearing trees, but they are forbidden to do anything with the crop for three years. The tree at this stage is described as an *orlah*, which literally means "hindered" or "restricted" and, in this context, conveys the figurative definition "uncircumcised" (an *arelah* is an uncircumcised penis).[8] This term and the anthropomorphic parallel suggests that the sapling has the status of being underdeveloped and not yet ready for treatment as a full-fledged tree. In the fourth year, the fruits of are to be gathered and taken to Jerusalem to be eaten. In the fifth year the fruit may be used anywhere in any conventional manner. These laws establish an inherent relationship between God and us that is defined by our gratitude for the God-given ability to grow food; the Torah demands our respect both for the tree and for God who causes it to grow. According to the Rabbis, the verses in Leviticus represent the first stage in the process of tithing—the setting aside of one-tenth of one's crop for sacred purposes, a process that actually begins earlier, at the moment when the tree begins to grow. We must watch the tree for years; once the fruit is born, we will dedicate a portion back to God.

The process of tithing had a practical purpose as well. The tithes described in Leviticus (chapter 27) and in Deuteronomy (chapters 14 and 26) were to be taken to the local priests and used to pay for the upkeep of the sanctuary and support of the priesthood. Later, when the Israelites were centralized in Jerusalem under King David, tithes served as a national tax, which not only was used for physical upkeep of the Temple and support of the Levites who maintained this holy site but also provided funds for the kingdom itself. The portion that supported the kingdom was scrutinized at times by fiery prophets such as Isaiah, particularly when Solomon and other kings used this income to erect idols and indulge in unnecessary luxuries.

Date of Birth

To determine the age of a tree, how do we know which moment is the start of a new year? Although rabbis throughout the ages have argued whether Tu b'Shevat occurs at the beginning of budding or at the beginning of ripening, the sages designated the 15th of Shevat as the boundary between one year and another. By that date most of the winter rains in the Land of Israel have already fallen, and a certain percentage of the fruit has reached the stage referred to as "begun to ripen." This stage spans the period from the time of blossoming until the fruit has reached one-third of its full growth. Fruit that has reached this stage is attributed to the previous year; any new blossoming of fruit belongs to the new year.

Despite the human tendency to abuse the system, it is important to remember that the concept of tithing is ultimately about our partnership with God:

> *All tithes from the land, whether seed from the ground or fruit from the tree, are the* LORD's; *they are holy to the* LORD.
> —Lev. 27:30

Of this powerful statement, we must ask, Why? Why are tithes given such sacred status? To understand, we must consider the world during the biblical period. Most people were pagans who believed that separate, free entities controlled each aspect of the world, with different gods for the sun, the trees, the wind, the sea, the fertility of the land, and so on. These deities were understood and interpreted as being subject to human emotions. Furthermore, the gods needed to be appeased, for their actions could be guided by anger, lust, or even a whim. The God of the ancient Israelites, however, was the ruler of the entire desert and all the universe—the one and only God who brings the sunrise each morning, the desert breeze, and the rains; who enriches the soil; and who oversees the welfare of the bud and the sapling. In this light, we can understand the holiness of the agricultural and food-making processes. Consider, for example, the chain of events that must occur for a seed to become wheat, the wheat to become flour, the flour to become bread, and how many links in this chain are utterly beyond our control. In recognition of the gifts from God, on every holiday and Shabbat, we say blessings over wine and bread. These foods are the classic and traditional representations of our partnership with God—God gives us grapes and we make wine; God gives us wheat and we make bread.[9]

Rabbinic Roots

After the Romans destroyed the Second Temple in 70 c.e., they expelled the Jews from the Land of Israel. Tithing as then practiced ended, because the concept applied only to produce grown in Israel, not in the Diaspora. Even the very small number of Jews who managed to remain in the country no longer tithed; the central Jewish administration, to whom tithes had been conveyed, was gone.

Tu b'Shevat began to grew in significance. The sages of the Mishnah were responsible for transmitting Jewish law and tradition in a post-exilic world. They tried to better understand and clarify tithing for those who might never see the original practice with their own eyes. One way was to identify a question drawn from the following verse in the Torah: "You shall set aside every year a tenth part of all the yield of your sowing that is brought from the field" (Deut. 14:22). The question was this: How do we mark the beginning of each year to establish the span of time for tithing? The Mishnah, the foundational Rabbinic text, explains:

The first of Shevat is Rosh Hashanah La-Ilan *[the New Year for the Tree] according to the School of Shammai [Beit Shammai]. The School of Hillel [Beit Hillel] says that it is on the fifteenth of [Shevat].*
—Mishnah, *Rosh Hashanah* 1:1

Maimonides (the highly influential medieval rabbi and philosopher) in his commentary on this Mishnah explains that this date is the beginning of the agricultural fiscal year for tithing. In other words, this date is the cutoff for taxing produce. The Jerusalem Talmud helps elucidate this concept:

Until this day, they [the trees] live off the water from the past year and from this day forward, they live off the water of this [new] year.
—Mishnah, *Rosh Hashanah* 1:2

Consequently, the tradition observes that fruit trees lie dormant during the cold winter months from December through February in Israel. The almond trees blossom around the middle of the Hebrew month of Shevat, toward the end of that three-month period. Since fruits were taxed in ancient Israel and Shevat was the obvious seasonal turning point, it became the choice time for these taxes to be levied. Any fruits that blossomed before this date were understood to grow from the rainwater of the outgoing year and were taxed for that year; any fruits blossoming after that date were taxed as part of the incoming year.

The Talmud and tradition side with Beit Hillel in the Mishnah quoted above, designating the 15th as the official date. There are different authoritative opinions about why the tradition sided with Hillel as opposed to Shammai on this particular matter. The most commonly heard, rational approach claims that the 15th, in the middle of the month, is climatically more accurate. In other words, the 15th of Shevat is closer to the exact time when sunlight is the strongest, increasing the trees' absorption of the ground waters.[10]

Medieval Budding

The observance of Tu b'Shevat was dormant during most of the Februaries in medieval Europe. This dormancy was possible because no halakhic obligations are associated with Tu b'Shevat—for example, no additions to the liturgy (no *Hallel* to recite) and no special Torah reading. Over time, Jews began to develop some very minor customs associated with the calendar date of the 15th of Shevat, even if it was not directly marked as the holiday of Tu b'Shevat. One was to say the 15 Psalms of Ascent (120–34) that had been recited by the Levites upon ascending into the inner court of the Temple. Another custom was to eat 15 types of fruit, with particular emphasis on the Seven Species of the Land of Israel mentioned in the Torah.[11] For Jews in the Diaspora, the resurgent interest in the day may have been prompted by new anti-Semitic decrees and the ever-worsening conditions of serfdom. Tu b'Shevat, a holiday tied directly to the land, encouraged a nostalgic longing for Israel.[12]

Two developments grew from these circumstances that altered the nature of the holiday. First, during the medieval period (by the 10th century), rabbis were increasingly referring to Tu b'Shevat as the New Year for the Trees and comparing it to Rosh Hashanah, the fall Jewish New Year known frequently as the Day of Judgment.[13] The medieval rabbis made this parallel despite the Mishnah saying (eight centuries earlier) that the summer holiday of Shavuot is the day of judgment for trees, the day when God decides how bountiful the fruit crop will be. Such a perspective is logical because the first spring crops are harvested in summer. The medieval rabbis chose nonetheless to transform Tu b'Shevat from a date of minor importance to that of a festival and, furthermore, likened it to the major holy day of Rosh Hashanah.

Second, the hope of the Diaspora Jews for a speedy return to the Land of Israel may have directly resulted in the joy that Tu b'Shevat came to express. Such hope and anticipation are embodied in the *Shemoneh Esrei for the New Year of the Trees*,[14] a special prayer written by the 10th-century poet Yehudah ben Hillel, a rabbi living in the Land of Israel, who based it on the central Jewish prayer—the *Amidah*. The pain and longing associated with the Jews' physical separation from the Land of Israel evolved into a messianic-like hope for return, which is celebrated in the increasing significance of Tu b'Shevat observances during the medieval period.

Trunk and Branches from Kabbalah

Tu b'Shevat plays a distinct role in the Jewish mystical tradition of Kabbalah. In 1492, when Spain expelled its Jewish population, some of the refugees migrated to Israel. They took with them the extremely popular Zohar (literally,

"Illumination"), the classic text of Kabbalah, which had been compiled, most likely, by the Spanish mystic Moses de Leon 200 years earlier. In the 16th century, Rabbi Isaac Luria and his followers, who were studying and teaching in the community of Tzfat, captured the hearts and minds of the Jewish world with a newly conceived understanding of the order of the universe. This particular kabbalistic system, known as Lurianic Kabbalah, likely grew out of the attempt to understand the seemingly inexplicable Spanish expulsion. It told of a new model for the concept of Creation and formulated a newly understood relationship with God.[15]

Before the advent of Lurianic Kabbalah, when a loss or tragedy occurred, the Jews believed it must have happened solely because they deserved it. This philosophy is expressed in a passage from the Book of Deuteronomy that is recited in the daily liturgy as part of the *Shema:*

> *If, then, you obey the commandments that I enjoin upon you this day, loving the LORD your God and serving Him with all your heart and soul, I will grant the rain for your land in season, the early rain and the late. You shall gather in your new grain and wine and oil—I will also provide grass in the fields for your cattle—and thus you shall eat your fill. Take care not to be lured away to serve other gods and bow to them. For the LORD's anger will flare up against you, and He will shut up the skies so that there will be no rain and the ground will not yield its produce; and you will soon perish from the good land that the LORD is assigning to you.*
> —Deut. 11:13–7

According to this text, when people follow God, God rewards them; and when people stray from God, God punishes and exiles them. When the Romans destroyed the Second Temple and the Jews were driven from the Land of Israel, the Jews believed they must have had transgressed in some serious way to deserve this treatment. When they were exiled again—this time from Spain—many turned to that same understanding.

Isaac Luria provided a novel idea about the reason for suffering. His kabbalistic theology asserted that when God, Who Is Everything, decided to create the universe,

God had to withdraw (*tsimtsum*) God's Self to make space for that universe. This divine creation of space and time became the "vessels" of our world. God then began pouring divine energy into the vessels in the form of the 10 *sefirot* or "divine emanations," which were meant to fuse with the vessels. But before the process was completed, the very large amount of divine energy caused the vessels to shatter in an event called "The Breaking of the Vessels" (*Shevirat Ha-Keilim*). Creation was neither completed nor perfected. Our world, very simply described, is broken, because the emanations incompletely connected to the vessels and to each other. We are left, literally, picking up the pieces. God has given us the responsibility and the ability to repair the world, which we can accomplish through our rituals and our ethical behavior.[16]

Lurianic Kabbalah maintains, therefore, that suffering, such as the expulsion from Spain and general hostility experienced by Jews throughout history, occurs because the world is not whole and needs healing. Hope comes from the concept of *tikun olam*, which literally means "repairing the world." People have the power to fix the shattered vessels, a correction that allows the positive aspects of God's light to be released from that which is evil and to reunify with God's Self. We have the ability to draw upon the appropriate aspects of God and to act as agents of world harmony, a role we fill through self-reflection, good deeds, and observance of Jewish law.

This school of thought teaches that the best symbol for the 10 *sefirot* is a great tree, which explains the meaning hidden in the phrase "Tree of Life." Because Tu b'Shevat commemorates the tithing of trees for the welfare of the poor, the holiday connects with ease to the metaphor of God as the abundant Tree of Life. What's more, Lurianic Kabbalah teaches—using the notion of *tikun olam*—that every single thing we do has the potential for improving the world, because we embody the *sefirot* and Tree of Life within ourselves. Our potential to affect the world even extends to eating.[17] By ingesting certain fruits and drinking certain wines, which are categorized by their traits and imbued with symbolism and divine potential, we have the means to advance the world toward wholeness and cause the holy sparks to ascend to heaven. These ideas led to the creation and practice of a seder (literally, "order"), a ceremonial dinner specially devised for the evening of Tu b'Shevat. This seder includes an order of eating fruits and nuts, making blessings, and, like Passover (the spring holiday with the age-old traditional seder), the drinking of four cups of wine.

Tree of Life: The 10 Sefirot

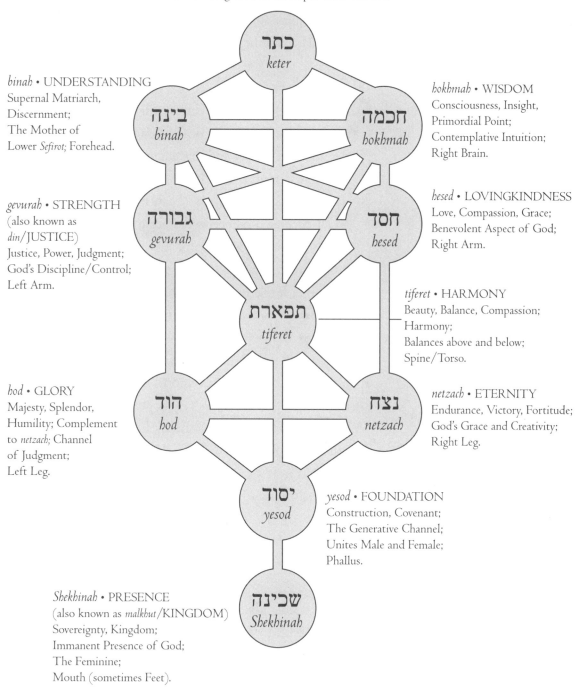

keter • CROWN
Nothingness, Will; Supreme Omnipresence;
Overarching Aura of the Super-consciousness.

binah • UNDERSTANDING
Supernal Matriarch,
Discernment;
The Mother of
Lower *Sefirot;* Forehead.

hokhmah • WISDOM
Consciousness, Insight,
Primordial Point;
Contemplative Intuition;
Right Brain.

gevurah • STRENGTH
(also known as
din/JUSTICE)
Justice, Power, Judgment;
God's Discipline/Control;
Left Arm.

hesed • LOVINGKINDNESS
Love, Compassion, Grace;
Benevolent Aspect of God;
Right Arm.

tiferet • HARMONY
Beauty, Balance, Compassion;
Harmony;
Balances above and below;
Spine/Torso.

hod • GLORY
Majesty, Splendor,
Humility; Complement
to *netzach;* Channel
of Judgment;
Left Leg.

netzach • ETERNITY
Endurance, Victory, Fortitude;
God's Grace and Creativity;
Right Leg.

yesod • FOUNDATION
Construction, Covenant;
The Generative Channel;
Unites Male and Female;
Phallus.

Shekhinah • PRESENCE
(also known as *malkhut*/KINGDOM)
Sovereignty, Kingdom;
Immanent Presence of God;
The Feminine;
Mouth (sometimes Feet).

The Blooming of Zionism

Zionism is a worldwide political movement founded to support the establishment and success of a modern Jewish homeland. In the late 19th and early 20th centuries, as waves of Jewish immigrants reached the Land of Israel, tree planting became an intense religious and national activity. For many Zionists and for the early pioneers, their Jewish identity and spirituality were expressed best in a direct relationship with the very soil of Israel. Planting trees and working the earth was, in fact, a primary rite of Zionism.

Everything from Fruit to Nuts

It is no surprise that the most common customs practiced on Tu b'Shevat relate to food. One is the eating of fruits and nuts, for example, almonds to celebrate the trees in bloom. Another is making Israeli-style dishes, particularly those associated with the "seven species," a series of fruits and grains representative of the Land of Israel: olives, figs, dates, pomegranates, grapes, barley, and wheat.[19] Many people have a custom of eating bokser (carob), which was once the only fruit grown in Israel that could withstand the long journey to Jewish communities in Europe and North Africa. Etrog (citron) is served, too, as preserves or sugared slices made of the fruit saved from the fall holiday of Sukkot.

Underlying the symbolism of planting saplings was a highly practical purpose. Israel had long been denuded of trees and by planting them the Jews restored fertility to the soil, helped ecosystems become reestablished, and beautified the land. After Israel became a recognized state in 1948, the Jewish National Fund undertook the role of collecting money for planting trees in Israel. Tu b'Shevat became a hook for this endeavor, as it continues to be today. What's more, the Tu b'Shevat tree-planting custom has expanded to include tree-planting outside of Israel, as children often recognize this holiday by a special ceremony and the planting of trees right at their own synagogues and Jewish day schools.[18] The effect of Tu b'Shevat has spread in other ways as well, some of them beyond the actual day. It is now a custom to sponsor the planting of a tree in Israel to honor a birth or a religious rite of passage in the Diaspora; and on group tours to Israel, a common activity is that of physically planting trees.

On a broader scale, the renewed interest in Tu b'Shevat has coincided with both a surge of concern for the environment and the rejuvenated popularity of Kabbalah. These factors have brought about the cross-pollination of mystical, scientific, religious, and nationalistic currents.

Reform and Conservative Jews, in particular, have embraced the principle of *bal tash'hit* (literally, "do not destroy"), a biblical prohibition against wanton waste and destruction, linked it to Tu b'Shevat, and fostered Jews' awareness of environmental concerns.

SEASONAL CUSTOMS

Beyond tree planting and seders, Tu b'Shevat has inspired a variety of practices that grew out of its relationship to nature and the flow of the year. People stay up very late studying two tractates of Mishnah. One is *Berachot* (Benedictions) because of its association with blessings, for example, those said before consuming various types of food. The other tractate is *Rosh Hashanah* because of its association with the calendar and the new year. Singing songs is popular, especially songs related to trees or the Land of Israel: *Atzei Zeitim Omdim* (The Olive Trees Are Standing); *Ha-Shekeidiyah* (The Almond Tree); *Etz Ha-Rimon* (The Pomegranate Tree); and *Eretz Zavat Chalav* (Land of Milk and Honey). Storytelling involves tales that include elements of nature and, of course, trees in particular. In one from the Talmud, Honi Ha-Ma'agal (Honi the Circle Maker) is walking down a road and sees a man planting a carob tree. Honi asks him how long it will be before the tree bears fruit, and the man says, "Seventy years." When Honi asks whether he expects to be alive then to reap the reward, the man says "Just as I found the world with carob trees planted by my ancestors, so will I plant them for my children."[20]

Often, the Psalms of Ascent (120–134) are recited. All 15 of them begin with the same header: *Shir Ha-Ma'alot* (literally, "Song of Ascent"). Many scholars believe that the psalms were given this heading because they were intended to be sung while traveling on the road to Jerusalem (perhaps on a pilgrimage) or while ascending the steps of the Temple to make an offering. Today Ashkenazim customarily recite these psalms not only on Tu b'Shevat, but on Shabbat afternoons during the time between Sukkot and Passover. On an even more regular basis, Psalm 126 is sung on Shabbat and festivals as the introduction to *Birkat Ha-Mazon,* the grace said after meals. This practice originated with a kabbalistic interpretation from within the Zohar.

The citrus fruit called *etrog* is one of the *arba minim* (literally, "four species"), a group of plant products used in rituals during Sukkot, a fall holiday. The Four Species symbolize joy for life and dedication to God. During Tu b'Shevat, prayers are said that the *etrog* tree may develop beautiful fruit for the following Sukkot.[21] And so the cycle continues.

▲　　▲　　▲　　▲　　▲　　▲　　❧　　▲　　▲　　▲　　▲　　▲　　▲

The Color of Wine

Tu b'Shevat sits on the threshold of winter into spring, and the wine drunk at the seder symbolizes that transition: white wine represents the growth cycle when it appears dormant; red wine represents nature in bloom. At the seder, the first cup is white; the second and third cups are red with white mixed in; and the fourth cup is red wine with a drop or two of white. In between the ceremonial consumption of each cup, the guests partake of one of the three groupings of fruits and nuts.

The Divine Meal

Kabbalists believed that eating fruit on Tu b'Shevat was a way of expiating the original sin committed by Adam and Eve, who ate the forbidden fruit of the Tree of Knowledge of Good and Evil. From the desire to perform *tikun olam*, to repair this spiritual damage, came the practice of holding a special seder, as a kind rebirth on Tu b'Shevat, the New Year of the Trees.[22]

In 1753, the idea for a Tu b'Shevat seder was published, along with instructions, as part of a compendium of holiday practices called Chemdat Yamim (Treasure of Days). The passage specific to Tu b'Shevat, *Pri Etz Hadar* (Fruit of the Lovely Tree), was later also published as a separate work. The seder includes a number of rituals: making blessings; eating three groupings of fruits and nuts in a specific order; and, like the Passover seder, drinking four cups of wine. Every aspect of the seder is infused with profound mystical symbolism. For example, within each of the three groupings, the fruits and nuts must be from 10 different varieties to represent the 10 different emanations, or *sefirot*, through which God radiates into the world.

According to Kabbalah, there are four worlds or spheres of creation through which the *sefirot* flow. These are *atzilut* ("emanation"), *beriyah* ("creation"), *yetzirah* ("formation"), and *assiyah* ("action"). Each world corresponds to one of the four letters of the ineffable name of God, the Tetragrammaton—formed of the Hebrew letters *yud, heh, vav, and heh*. All together, the worlds show the unity of the universe; and as we elevate spiritually from one world to the next, we are better able to understand the unity of God. Each of the fruits and nuts consumed during the seder is associated with one of the four spheres, as is each of the four cups of wine. Accompanying the portions of food are reflective meditations (*kavanot*) from the Bible, the Talmud, and the Zohar. The purpose of the ceremonial meal is to delve deeper into the hidden meaning of the universe, to elevate each of our souls and to aid in *tikun olam*.

Although the physical world masks the realm of the divine, kabbalists believe that the two are so intricately linked that human beings have the capacity to affect the divine.

Furthermore, the world continuously models itself on the divine realm. So if we interpret our world correctly, we can know the true essence of the divine realm and understand how we can affect it through our actions. At the Tu b' Shevat seder, the fruits—each a spiritual conduit—combined with our meditations affect the spiritual makeup of both our world and that of the divine realm. As we ingest the foods, we internalize them and connect to God.

Four Worlds of Creation and the Tu b'Shevat Seder

WORLD	EXPLANATION	PRINCIPAL *SEFIROT*	FRUIT GROUP	LETTER
atzilut ("emanation")	That which is infinite and immeasurable, associated with the initial inspiration.	*hokhmah* ("wisdom")	None	*yud*
beriyah ("creation")	Independent existence, being generated and expanded; moving from the intangible and nothingness *(ayn)* to somethingness *(yesh).*	*binah* ("understanding")	Totally Edible 10 examples: grapes, figs, apples, *etrogim,* lemons, strawberries, blueberries, carobs, quinces, pears	*heh*
yetzirah ("formation")	Emotion and prayerfulness. The world of thought and language, the place where actual connection between the divine and the earth is made.	*hesed* ("lovingkindness") through *yesod* ("foundation")	Inedible Pit, Edible Skin 10 examples: olives, dates, cherries, jujubes, persimmons, apricots, peaches, loquats, plums, hackberries	*vav*
assiyah ("action")	Implemented reality: mineral, vegetable, animal, and human; an independent reality with a Ruler; the realm of doing and performing mitzvot.	*malkhut* ("kingdom")	Edible Kernel, Inedible Skin or Shell 10 Examples: pomegranates, walnuts, almonds, pine nuts, chestnuts, hazelnuts, coconuts, pecans, pistachios, peanuts	*heh*

·✦— Tu b'Shevat —✦·
Pathways Through the Sources

Tosefta
A Blessing upon Beauty

Judaism established global consciousness of the concept that there is a single Creator of all life. This belief elevates the significance and sacred status of every aspect of the world, because it means everything has roots in the Soul of All Souls. The following blessing from the Tosefta, a collection of teachings by Rabbinic sages (circa 300 C.E.), acknowledges human kinship with the natural world and praises the wonder of beauty, wherever it is found.

> When one sees beautiful people or beautiful trees, one should say the blessing, Blessed be the One who has created beautiful creatures.
> —Tosefta, *Berachot* 6:7

Babylonian Talmud
Trees and Taxes

Living in our modern world with cities of colossal proportions and millions of people, it is easy to forget that the rhythms of nature and the rhythms of humankind coincide. This close association exists in both the practical and the spiritual sense—on one hand, for example, the way climate, season, agriculture, and economy are intertwined; and, on the other, for example, the way the liturgy of Judaism changes by season and raises our awareness of conditions in nature. Tu b'Shevat exemplifies the appreciation we have for the value found in the interconnected rhythms shared by human beings and the world in which they live.

The Babylonian Talmud, the most commonly studied version of the accumulated knowledge of the Jewish people, was completed in the 6th century C.E.. Its compilers were descendants of rabbis who had escaped to Babylon four centuries earlier, when the Romans had killed or enslaved the majority of the Jewish population in Israel.

> *Mishnah:* On the first of [the month of] Shevat is the New Year for the tree according to Beit Shammai. Beit Hillel said that it is on the fifteenth [of Shevat].

Gemara: The rabbis taught: A tree that blossoms before the fifteenth of Shevat is tithed for the year that has just passed; if after the fifteenth of Shevat, it is tithed for the year to come.

—B. Talmud, *Rosh Hashanah* 1a;15b

Babylonian Talmud
The Earth Waits for Mankind

Ours is a time that is tarnished by deforestation, pollution, endangered species, a depleting ozone layer, and global warming, all caused by human activities. We must remember the teaching in Judaism that humankind's original vocation was agriculture. Human caring and maintenance of the earth were (and continue to be) necessary elements for the fulfillment of Creation.

> Rabbi Assi pointed out a contradiction between two verses [in the Torah]. One verse, referring to the third day [of Creation], says, "The earth brought forth vegetation:…" (Gen. 1:12), whereas the other verse, when speaking of the sixth day, says, "… no shrub of the field was yet on earth …" (Gen 2:5). However, the verses, seemingly contradictory, teach us that plants commenced to grow [on the third day] but stopped just as they were about to break through the soil, until Adam came [who was created on the sixth day] and implored for mercy [i.e., rain] upon them; and when rain fell, they sprouted forth.
> —B. Talmud, *Chullin* 60b[23]

Sefer Ha-Bahir
The Tree of Souls

As one of their primary methods of study, kabbalists identify words in sacred texts that have—according to the tradition of mysticism—multiple connotations and symbolic meanings. From these words, the students of Kabbalah extract multiple interpretive meanings; and it's from such interpretations and insights that Tu b'Shevat emerges as a significant holiday. As expressed in the 12th-century *Sefer Ha-Bahir* (The Book of Illumination), which is the earliest source of kabbalistic literature, the tree is one of the most important images in Kabbalah. It is the metaphor used for the Torah and for the *sefirot* ("divine emanations"). Thus Tu b'Shevat, as the holiday "for the tree," becomes a most holy day for celebrating of all Creation.

I [God] am the one that planted this tree, for all the world to delight in; and I hammered out all with him, and I called his name "all *(hakol)*," for all depends on him, and all comes out from him. And all are needing him, and to him they look forward and on him they wait. And from there blossom the souls in joy. Even in the time that I hammered out my earth ... I planted and rooted this tree in her, and I rejoiced in them.

—*Sefer Ha-Bahir,* 22[24]

Sefer Ha-Hinukh

Do Not Destroy

Judaism demonstrates utmost concern for how we treat our environment. God expects us to contribute to the natural harmony of the world and to partake of its bounty. But wanton destruction is absolutely unacceptable. As stewards of the earth, there are times when we have the right and authority to destroy for controlled purposes, such as cutting down trees to create space for younger trees to grow or to obtain lumber for building a shelter or a boat. Judaism defines and limits such purposes and occurrences.

Sefer Ha-Hinukh (literally, "The Book of Education") is an anonymous work from the 13th century. It was written as a simple guide to Jewish belief and practice.

The root reason for the precept [of *bal tash'hit*—"do not destroy"] is known: for it is in order to train our spirits to love what is good and beneficial and to cling to it; and as a result, good fortune will cling to us, and we will move well away from every evil thing and from every matter of destructiveness. This is the way of the kindly men of piety and the conscientiously observant; they love peace and are happy at the good fortune of people, and bring them near the Torah. They will not destroy even a mustard seed in the world, and they are distressed at every ruination and spoilage they see; and if they are able to do any rescuing, they will save anything from destruction, with all their power.

... Among the laws of the precept, there is what the Sages of blessed memory said: that the Torah did not forbid chopping down fruit trees if any useful benefit will be found in the matter: for instance, if the monetary value of a certain tree is high, and this person wanted to sell it, or to

remove a detriment by chopping them down—for instance, if this was harming other trees that were better than it, or because it was causing damage in the fields of others. In all these circumstances, or anything similar, it is permissible.
—*Sefer Ha-Hinnukh* 529[25]

The Zohar
The True Tree of Life

For kabbalists, Tu b'Shevat and its inherent symbolism are clear reminders of how the world was created and what our purpose on earth has become. When Adam and Eve ate fruit from the Tree of Knowledge of Good and Evil, their sin caused the vessels of divine light to shatter. It was this light that had led to the creation of our universe. Now we are to turn to another tree for nourishment—the Tree of Life, which is both the Torah and the divine emanations of God, called the *sefirot*. By faithfully clinging to this tree, we will be given the strength and guidance for healing the world (*tikun olam*)—fixing the vessels and reunifying the divine light. Abraham, who opened the gates of Torah and faith, was the first to explicitly show this path.

The Zohar comprises mystical commentaries on the Bible that mix together theology, psychology, myth, ancient Gnosticism, and superstitions. This classic work of Kabbalah is meant to uncover the deepest mysteries of world—namely, why God created the universe, how God is manifest in the world, and what the forces of life are.

Come and see: Wherever Abraham resided, he planted a tree; but nowhere did it sprout fittingly until he resided in the land of Canaan. Through that tree, he discovered who embraced the blessed Holy One and who embraced idolatry. Whoever embraced the blessed Holy One—the tree would spread its branches, covering his head, shading him nicely. Whoever embraced the aspect of idolatry—that tree would withdraw, its branches rising above. Then Abraham knew and warned him—not departing until he embraced faith. Whoever was pure the tree would welcome; whoever was impure it would not, so Abraham knew and purified them with water. Underneath the tree was a spring of water: if someone needed immediate immersion, water gushed toward him and the tree's branches withdrew ….

Come and see: Even when he invited the angels, he said to them *Recline under the tree* [Gen. 18:4], in order to see and test them; for with that tree, he tested all inhabitants of the world. He enacted a mystery corresponding to the blessed Holy One, who is the Tree of Life for all; so *recline under the tree*—not under idolatry.

Come and see: When Adam sinned, he sinned with the Tree of Knowledge of Good and Evil, inflicting death upon inhabitants of the world. When Abraham appeared, he mended the world with another tree, the Tree of Life, proclaiming faith to all inhabitants of the world.
—Zohar 1:102b[26]

Ben Ish Chai
Soul Blossoms

Do plants and trees have souls? For kabbalists, who believe in reincarnation, not only do these elements of nature have souls, they may even embody souls who were once human. During Tu b'Shevat and at the start of springtime, when we make a special acknowledgment of the natural world, it is good to remember to bless the trees.

Yosef Chaim ben Eliyahu Al-Hacham (1833–1909) had the nickname Ben Ish Chai, which was also the title of his volume of sermons. He was a prolific writer, influential teacher, and the Chief Rabbi of Baghdad.

Blessed are You *Yah,*[27] our God, Majesty of Earth.
You made the world so that nothing lacks in her
And You created good creatures and good trees for people to enjoy!
This blessing is to be recited in the month of Nisan when the trees are budding. Kabbalists felt that that was a special time to participate in the rescue of wandering spirits, incarnated in lower life forms [such as flowers and plants]. Looking at the buds and blossoms, one can become aware of their presence, like Rabbi Yitzchak [Isaac] Luria, who took his students out into nature to teach them there.... When a person passing by offers a blessing of delight in the blossoming of nature [these souls] are reclaimed to holiness.
—Ben Ish Chai[28]

Tanchuma Buber

Natural Consquences

The spirit of Judaism embodies the idea that everything we do has an effect on everything else, even in seemingly unrelated matters. Tu b'Shevat, by focusing its attention on the natural world, highlights this concept. All of the elements of Creation exist in concentric ecosystems, and eventually they will meet and engage one other. We must learn from past sins to anticipate how natural events will unfold in their inevitable, relentless manner.

Tanchuma is well-known collection of midrashic literature on the Torah. Different editions of *Tanchuma* were published over time, and the material within varies. One of the most common versions, *Tanchuma Buber,* was organized and published in 1875 by Solomon Buber, a scholar and independent researcher who lived in Ukraine.

> There is an old legend that tells us that God originally created each tree so that it could yield many different kinds of fruit. In that way they produced hundreds more different kinds of fruit than we now have. Then a terrible thing happened. Cain killed his brother Abel and the trees went into mourning. They refused to yield their fruit on account of the grief over Abel. Did not God say that the voice of Abel's blood cries out from the ground and that the earth will no longer yield its full strength? From then on each tree would yield just one kind of fruit. Only in the World to Come will they return to their full fruitfulness.
>
> —*Tanchuma Buber,* Introduction 158 [29]

Martin Buber

I Contemplate a Tree [30]

In this life on earth, we are forced to confront, contemplate, and accept God's Creation. This world is not one we initiated or conceived; yet we were born into it with our Creator's intention that we deal with it and learn from it.

Martin Buber was a Jewish religious philosopher of the 19th and 20th centuries. This meditation from his greatest discourse, the book *I and Thou,* puts our relationship with nature into perspective.

I contemplate a tree.

I can accept it as a picture: a rigid pillar in a flood of light, or splashes of green traversed by the gentleness of the blue silver ground.

I can feel it as movement: the flowing veins around the sturdy, striving core, the sucking of the roots, the breathing of the leaves, the infinite commerce with earth and air—and the growing itself in its darkness.

I can assign it to a species and observe it as an instance, with an eye to construction and its way of life....

I can dissolve it into a number, into a pure relation between numbers, and eternalize it.

Throughout all of this the tree remains my object and has its place and its time span, its kind and condition.

But it can also happen, if will and grace are joined, that as I contemplate the tree I am drawn into a relation, and the tree ceases to be an It. The power of exclusiveness has seized me....

Whatever belongs to the tree is included: its form and its mechanics, its colors and its chemistry, its conversation with the elements and its conversation with the stars—all this in its entirety.

The tree is no impression, no play of my imagination, no aspect of a mood; it confronts me bodily and has to deal with me as I must deal with it—only differently.

—Martin Buber

Ismar Schorsch

Creation and Crisis

Torah and Judaism are meant to serve us in every generation and in our daily lives. As the Ramban (the great scholar of 13th-century Spain) said in his *Iggeret Ha-Mussar* (literally, "The Ethical Letter") to his son, "When you rise from study, ponder carefully what you have learned and see what it is you can put into practice."

Ismar Schorsch, a modern scholar and chancellor emeritus of the Jewish Theological Seminary, shows how we may apply our Jewish values and our learning to challenges in the rapidly changing world of today. The very worrisome state of the environment is certainly a topic that merits employing the ideas that Shorsch conveys.

As trees fall at the end of the twentieth century at an ever-quickening pace, victims of the need and greed of humankind, they give incontrovertible evidence of the dismal fact that for us God is dead …

A planet overrun by Homo sapiens will have less and less space for trees, other species, or even the presence of God. The kabbalists of Safed [Tzfat] long ago enriched the mystical thought of Judaism with the stunning concept of *tsimtsum*—an act of divine contraction prior to Creation. If God were omnipresent, they reasoned, then how could the universe ever come into being? What kind of space would there be for it to fill? To address this conundrum, they came up with the idea of *tsimtsum:* the emptying of space for the existence of something other than God. The universe fills the void left by God's self-imposed exile. Creation begins with withdrawal.

No concept in Judaism's theological repertoire could be more relevant to our crisis of overpopulation. God again stands forth as the model for human behavior. … If we were everywhere, our presence would herald the end of the teeming diversity of nature. Our fragile and unique habitat needs a reprieve from human assault. We, its most sentient creatures, must gain the self-mastery to rein in our personal wants, to reverse the growth of cities evermore uninhabitable, and to contain the explosion of our numbers. For us to heed the biblical injunction of planting trees, there must be soil in which to plant them.
—Ismar Schorsch[31]

· ◆— Tu b'Shevat —◆·
Interpretations of Sacred Texts

The texts studied in these pages are from *Midrash Rabbah,* Deuteronomy, and the *Mishneh Torah.* An extensive collection of aggadic midshrashim, *Midrash Rabbah* (Great Midrash) explains verse by verse each book of the Torah and the five *megillot* of the Bible. Deuteronomy,[32] the final book of the Torah, records Moses' last words to the Israelites as they prepare to enter the Promised Land without him. Among the things it contains are commandments concerning agriculture, family life, rituals, ethics, and civil government. The *Mishneh*[33] *Torah* is the philosopher Maimonides' great treatise in which he meticulously and systematically summarizes and arranges the entirety of Jewish law and teachings.

THE THREE LEVELS
Peshat: simple, literal meaning
Derash: historical, rabbinical inquiry
Making It Personal: contemporary analysis and application

The Blessings of Fruit and Life

Just as a vine produces wine and vinegar, each requiring a different blessing, so too must a Jew make a blessing over good and over bad—over good: "Blessed is God who is good and does good"; over bad: "Blessed is the just Judge."

—*Midrash Rabbah* (*Leviticus Rabbah* 36:2)[34]

Peshat
The origin of most blessings is found in the Torah, one of the best known being *Birkat Ha-Kohanim* ("The Priestly Blessings") in Numbers 6:24–6, which is the basis for the "Blessing of the Children" that parents say each Friday night. Many of the formulaic benedictions in Judaism begin with the word *baruch* ("blessed"); its use is derived from a prayer by King David (I Sam. 25:32).[35]

Blessings are a pervasive aspect of Jewish life; there is one for nearly every human experience. In fact, the Talmud claims that we should say at least 100 blessings every day,[36] which is accomplished, for example, when we recite 19 blessings— three times daily in the *Amidah* prayer— and dozens more blessings before and after consuming any food.[37]

This teaching from the Midrash highlights that there are blessings for all sorts of experiences, both good and bad; and by saying them, we identify God as the proprietor of all we encounter.

Derash
We praise our one God for both the good and the bad. We glorify God upon good news and for the joy of life, symbolized by wine, as well as upon

bad news and for the bitterness of life, symbolized by vinegar. Each seemingly opposite kind of event has a different blessing, but a blessing nonetheless.

At the time of our Rabbinic sages, Zoroastrianism (the Persian religion founded in the 6th century B.C.E.) was at its height. It maintained belief in two distinct, creative powers, one for good (Ahura Mazda) and one for evil (Angra Mainyu/Ahriman). In contrast to the dominant religion of the region, our sages took Isaiah 45:7, which refers to God as the source of both good and evil, and developed it into a more encompassing statement, part of a blessing recited every morning. The blessing calls upon "God Who Creates Everything" (Borei et Ha-Kol).

Making It Personal

Jewish spirituality relies upon blessings. They are the units that form our bond with God. Through these acknowledgments, affirmations, and prayers of thanks, we stop to frame the moments of life. Along with the stillness they create, we are given a picture that enables us to perceive the world from the broadest perspective—from as close as we can get to God's perspective. Similar to the way we gain appreciation for other people by opening our hearts to them, we lead ourselves to care about God's concerns by saying a heartfelt multitude of blessings. Gratefulness and empathy are a large part of the Jewish way of building relationships—with God,

the world, and our immediate community and within ourselves.

Blessings also help us to affirm the gifts of life. We are often very quick to stack up weights on the negative side of the universal balance scale. We note all of life's injustices and evils, yet we are apathetic about recognizing daily miracles. How often do we note the beauty of nature or the gifts of the human body and mind or the ordinary securities and luxuries many of us continuously enjoy and take for granted?

In the book *God in Search of Man*, Abraham Joshua Heschel, one of the most influential religious leaders of the 20th century, makes the point this way:

> They [mitzvot and blessings] are indications of our awareness of God's eternal presence, celebrating His presence in action. The benedictions are in the present tense. We say, "Blessed be Thou Who *creates* … Who *brings forth.*" To say a benediction is to be aware of His continuous creation.[38]

Tu b'Shevat is a celebration of God's blessings and the daily miracles of nature and season. For our kabbalistic ancestors, Tu b'Shevat represented the expression of God's continuous *shefa* ("divine flow") into our world—a world that has not only miracles but also injustices and imperfections. It is the season to bless the Tree of Life.

THE THREE LEVELS
Peshat: simple, literal meaning
Derash: historical, rabbinical inquiry
Making It Personal: contemporary analysis and application

Bal Tash'hit: Custodians, Not Owners

When in your war against a city you have to besiege it a long time in order to capture it, you must not destroy its trees, wielding the axe against them. You may eat of them, but you must not cut them down. Are trees of the field human to withdraw before you into the besieged city? Only trees that you know do not yield food may be destroyed; you may cut them down for constructing siegeworks against the city that is waging war on you, until it has been reduced.

—Deut. 20:19–20

This is not only for one who cuts down trees, but anyone who destroys containers, tears clothes, destroys a building, stops up a spring, or deliberately wastes food, violates the prohibition of "do not destroy."

—*Mishneh Torah,* Laws of Kings 6:10

Peshat
Chapter 20 of Deuteronomy is one of the oldest collections of rules of warfare. It ends with the two verses quoted here. Apparently, destroying the groves and trees of an enemy's city was common practice in the ancient world, a means of threatening the city's long-term economy. The Torah understands this tactic to be immoral and unfair; it therefore sets limits on an army's activities during a siege.

Maimonides infers an underlying moral principle *(bal tash'hit)* from these regulations and applies it to other circumstances. Simply put, if we are not permitted to wantonly destroy in the extreme case of warfare, we are not allowed to wantonly destroy in any lesser circumstances.

Derash
In the book *Etz Hayim: Torah and Commentary,*[39] the explanation accompanying these verses points out that American law permits the destruction of one's own property. This law underscores American individualism and its intense focus on the rights of private ownership. Judaism, on the other hand, understands that our property ultimately belongs to God: "… the heavens to their uttermost reaches belong to the LORD your God, the earth and all that is on it!" (Deut. 10:14). The *Etz Hayim* commentary concludes, there-

fore, "… we are only the custodians, not the true owners, of our property."

In the classical source *Ecclesiastes Rabbah,* a midrash tells of God's conversation with Adam about the world, and it emphasizes this most essential point, "Behold My works and how beautiful and splendid they are. Everything I have created, I did for your benefit. Be careful not to become corrupt and destroy My world. For if you become corrupt [and destroy it], there will be no one to restore it after you" (7:13).

Making It Personal

Our duty as custodians extends to how we treat each other and ourselves. The most outstanding lesson of Tu b'Shevat, with its kabbalistic overtones and allusions, is that we are on earth to develop ourselves and mend the world. Recognizing God's Oneness in Creation (and that God is beyond space and time) helps motivate us in our collective and individual responsibility as custodians.[40]

Hinting at this idea, the Maharal of Prague (the post-medieval, seminal thinker Rabbi Yehudah Loew) weaves an inspired teaching around an imaginative translation he provides for the last two sentences of Deuteronomy 20:19, in which he interprets the first sentence as a statement rather than a question.

For man is a tree of the field, and his branches are in heaven, for the head, which is the root of a man, faces upwards, and this is why man is called a "tree of the field" planted in heaven, and through his intellect, he is planted in his place, which, if all of the winds were to come and blow, they would not move him from his place.
—*Gur Aryeh,* Gen. 9:21

The Maharal's teaching affirms that because of our intellect, we have the ability to consider God's will and act constructively. Furthermore, like the trees, our lives are transitory, blowing in the wind; and we can be cut down if we do not take care to remember who and what we are and to guard what we have.

THE THREE LEVELS
Peshat: simple, literal meaning
Derash: historical, rabbinical inquiry
Making It Personal: contemporary analysis and application

Tithes as a Way to Presence and Reverence

You shall set aside every year a tenth part of all the yield of your sowing that is brought from the field. You shall consume the tithes of your new grain and wine and oil, and the firstlings of your herd and flocks, in the presence of the LORD your God … so that you may learn to revere the LORD your God forever.

—Deut. 14:22–3

Peshat

This is the biblical instruction for the annual tithe. The farmer and his household are to take the tithe to Jerusalem and eat it in the sanctuary of the Temple. This particular law refers to the second tithe, which was given in years one, two, four, and five of the seven-year cycle.[41] In years three and six, the second tithe is given to the poor in the town; in year seven, which is the *shemitah*—the sabbatical year for the land—no harvesting is done whatsoever.[42]

This injunction is the foundational source for Tu b'Shevat, because we learn from it that we should not tax "the new for the old" (*Sifrei* 105; B. Talmud, *Bechorot* 53b). Tu b'Shevat marks the season for taxing and tithing of food-producing trees.

Derash

These verses demand that the farmer consume the tithe in Jerusalem. The succeeding verses (Deut. 14:24–6) teach that if the tithe is too large to carry, one may exchange the tithe for its monetary equivalent and bring the money to Jerusalem. Once there, the farmer is to spend that money on whatever he desires and to have a feast "in the presence of the LORD."

Why must each farmer consume his tithe in Jerusalem instead of in his town and with the local Levites? In his commentary on verse 23, Rashbam, the medieval commentator and talmudist, suggests that being in Jerusalem was central to the tithing experience, since a person was to act as an "eyewitness to the priests performing their service in the Temple at the site where God's presence in manifest." The 15th-century Italian commentator Rabbi Ovadiah S'forno adds that it is also important to personally observe the Sanhedrin, the Jewish supreme court, from which knowledge and understanding is dispensed.

The medieval commentators identify a

link between tithes and service of God. It would not be enough to merely separate tithes and give them to the Levites; one must bear witness and be physically present for the most intimate of divine services, such as the priestly conduct in the sanctuary and the dispensation of Torah law and knowledge by the court.

Making It Personal

Sociologists have identified three factors that are most likely to cause American Jews to identify with their religion: education in Jewish day school; attending a Jewish summer camp (such as the legendary Camp Ramah); and visiting Israel.[43] The first two reasons are similar and fairly clear: Jewish schools and camps integrate Jewish life with academic and social benefits. Why, however, would visiting Israel (and, it can be argued, specifically Jerusalem) be a major factor?

For Jews who live away from the center of Jewish life and are surrounded by non-Jews, a suppressed anxiety exists in the form of denying Jewish self-expression. When these Jews arrive in Israel, their eyes look out over the ancient City of David and the Judean Hills. At the western and southern walls of the Temple Mount, they see other Jews, both religious and secular, place their hands upon those walls in prayer. In one organic moment everything makes sense. The sparks of Jewish self-

affirmation and the motivation to be a better Jew seem to ignite simultaneously.

These verses refer to reverence for God, a reverence expressed in the motivation to be a better Jew. In *Tomer Devorah* (Palm Tree of Deborah) the renowned, 16th-century kabbalist Moses ben Jacob Cordovero explains that reverence for God means understanding three things:

• God is the sole Creator of all existence.
• God's providence is always at work, watching and involved with each of us.
• God is the root of all souls desiring good and compassion, while repelling evil.[44]

Like the ancient Torah-directed process of tithing produce at the Temple, our presence in Jerusalem today teaches us to revere God by acknowledging God's omnipresence and affirming our unique Jewish spirituality.

·+——— Tu b'Shevat ———+·
Significance of the Holiday: Some Modern Perspectives

The Heart of Jewish Ecology

by Daniel S. Isaacson

Today, Tu b'Shevat does much more than mark the stages in a tree's development. It reinforces on an annual basis the importance and priority of ecology in Jewish values. Though other holidays such as Sukkot, Passover, and Shavuot relate significantly to the natural world, Tu b'Shevat has become, since biblical times, unrivaled in its concern for preserving the earth and its resources.

IDEOLOGICAL GROUNDS

The Torah is filled with laws and references to the Jewish ideal of harmony between human beings and the environment. Indeed, the name of the first human being, *Adam,* is connected to the word *adamah,* meaning "earth" or "land." Thus from its initial concept of humanity, the Torah establishes an unequivocal and profound relationship between humankind and the earth. Furthermore, the laws of the Torah explicitly emphasize that although we may use and benefit from the land, we must preserve it and never abuse it.[45] Similarly, we are to treat the creatures of the earth respectfully and without abuse.[46] The Torah portrays a picture of people living in thoughtful relationship to the seasons and agricultural cycles of the year, aware of their responsibility as a community, to each other, and to the animals and the land.

It was not until the emergence of Lurianic Kabbalah in 16th-century Tzfat that Tu b'Shevat figured prominently in Jewish cosmology. Kabbalah—and especially Hasidism, a later movement deeply rooted in the mysticism of Kabbalah—painted the natural world in dramatic theological terms. Kabbalists and Hasidic masters preached and wrote about the awe of the Divine that is found in natural settings, as they perceived God to be manifest in nature itself. Many of their poems, prayers, and blessings express the conviction that human beings can come to know God through contemplation of nature's inherent divinity. In fact, the kabbalists expressed God's divine emanations, called *sefirot,* by representing them in the symbolic configuration called the "Tree of Life." In light of this expanded cosmology, Jewish mystics endowed Tu b'Shevat, the New Year of the Trees, with entirely new meaning and generated new customs for the holiday.

WORKING THE LAND

Tu b'Shevat enjoyed a second surge of interest and vitality with the rise of Zionism in Europe and the settling of Palestine in the 19th and 20th centuries. The Zionist movement embraced a theme of redemption that was associated with earlier medieval conceptions of Tu b'Shevat. But in contrast, Zionism viewed salvation as part of a distinctly secular, nationalist framework. The return of Jews to the Land of Israel, the cultivation of ancient soil, and the planting of trees were in themselves redemptive acts. Jews in Europe had become accustomed to eating fruits from Israel on Tu b'Shevat, and the pioneers found great meaning in celebrating the day by planting actual biblical species. The tree became one of the more prominent visual and literary metaphors for national revival and endurance. Of the many rituals, customs, songs, and poems that were spawned to celebrate Tu b'Shevat, perhaps the most well known is the tree-planting campaign of the Jewish National Fund. Oddly enough, because of fluctuations in groundwater temperature during Israel's winter, Tu b'Shevat falls at a poor time in the seasonal cycle for planting deciduous fruit trees. Nevertheless, the day's symbolic significance compelled both Israeli and Diaspora Jewry to firmly establish tree planting as a central custom of the holiday.[47]

ENVIRONMENTALISM

In recent decades, Tu b'Shevat has gained added significance as a banner holiday for Jewish environmentalists. Responding to deforestation in critical ecological areas around the world, American Jews began to create seders and other rituals that incorporated Tu b'Shevat's kabbalistic traditions with a growing sense of responsibility over the natural world and its resources. The first Jewish organization devoted to environmental awareness, *Shomrei Adamah* ("Guardians of the Earth"), was born out of these experiences on Tu b'Shevat. By the mid-1990s, various mainstream Jewish organizations had established the Coalition on the Environment and Jewish Life (COEJL), which treated Tu b'Shevat as a kind of Jewish Earth Day and used it as a platform for promoting environmental education and activism among Jews worldwide.

This new development in Tu b'Shevat's meaning has created a unique opportunity for Jews to address global environmental concerns as a community. No doubt, cause for concern over the sustainability of the planet has become abundantly clear: global warming, deforestation, toxic pollution, and shrinking wildlife habitat are among the many pressing ecological issues that we must face for the sake of humanity's future. Tu b'Shevat challenges us to become sensitive to the impact that our daily actions have on the environment, and to find ways of being responsible stewards of natural resources.

Though the threats to global sustainability have become particularly grave over the last century of industrial proliferation, the principles that inform a modern Jewish response and environmental ethic have their basis in the long history of rabbinic tradition. One of the fundamental prohibitions underlying such an ethic is *bal tash'hit*, "you must not destroy," learned from Deuteronomy 20:19: "When in your war against a city you have to besiege it a long time in order to capture it, you must not destroy its trees, wielding the ax against them." The Rabbis interpreted this prohibition against wanton destruction during wartime to apply to the whole material world, in peacetime as well as in war.[48] The principle was also understood to apply to the inefficient use of resources. Thus the Babylonian Talmud teaches, "Rabbi Zutra said, 'One who covers an oil lamp or uncovers a naptha lamp [thereby causing unnecessary fuel consumption] breaks the rule against needless waste.' "[49]

In the 19th century, Rabbi Samson Raphael Hirsch, gave *bal tash'hit* a most poignant and far-reaching expression. He wrote this, no doubt, in response to the rampant consumption of resources during the burgeoning industrial revolution:

> "Do not destroy!" is the first and most general call of God which comes to you … when you realize yourself as master of the earth …." I lent [the things around you] for wise use only; never forget that I lent them to you. As soon as you use them unwisely, be it the greatest or smallest, you commit treachery against My world, you commit murder and robbery against my property, you sin against Me!" This is what God calls unto you ….[50]

A second principle with direct consequences for an emerging Jewish environmental ethic is the prohibition against *tsar baalei chayyim*, or "inhumane conduct toward animals." The main source for the prohibition is found in Deuteronomy 22:6–7, which forbids the killing of a mother bird with her young. By the medieval period, rabbinic commentators understood these verses to ensure the perpetuation of animal and plant species. For example, Nachmanides wrote in the 13th century, "The Torah does not allow the total destruction of a species, even though it allows us to slaughter some of its kind."

Another Spanish commentator, Don Yitzchak Abarbanel, wrote more broadly about this verse: "The Torah's intention is to prevent the possibility of untimely destruction and to rather encourage Creation to exist as fully as possible …; when Creation is perpetuated, one will be able to partake of it again in the future."[51]

At the heart of Judaism's environmental ethic is the simple yet profound awareness that, in the words of the Psalmist, "The earth is the LORD's and all that it holds, …"[52] This fundamental tenet underlies the biblical and Rabbinic notion that private ownership is fleeting and that, as the Talmud teaches, "God acquired possession of the world and apportioned it to humankind, but God always remains the master of the world."[53] Jewish law has therefore limited the extent to which humanity may exploit nature and assume a sense of mastery over it. The Torah required that the land lie fallow every sabbatical year so it could return, as it were, to its owner; the Rabbis instituted an array of blessings to be said before and after eating food so Jews would continually remember that all food is given as a gift. The Sabbath observance itself is a reminder that human intervention in the workings of nature has its fundamental limits.

This sense that nature is essentially a gift from God, on loan to humanity for safekeeping, has provided Judaism with a distinctly spiritual foundation for its emerging environmental ethic. By designating Tu b'Shevat as a day on the religious calendar for exploring environmental issues, we have broadened the scope of environmentalism by placing it within its spiritual context. Indeed, sensitivity to nature and the impulse to protect it are born out of the awareness that humanity and the natural world are intimately connected, bound together through their infinite source in God. To see the divinity within one's self is to recognize the divinity within all things. Furthermore, concern for the welfare of the planet, and the desire to act on this concern, arise naturally and invariably within a person who has realized this inherent divinity. A Hasidic tale illustrates this impulse:

> Rabbi Nachman of Bratzlav was once traveling with some disciples, and they stopped at an inn. He slept outside because of the nice weather. In the middle of the night he woke up screaming. When his disciples ran to him, he told them that the inn had been rebuilt with young trees that had not been allowed to reach maturity. "And when you cut down a young tree before its time," he said, "it is as if you have killed a person."[54]

Rabbi Nachman could not help but care; he awoke in a state of fervor in the middle of the night. His quote echoes a teaching in the midrashic work *Sifrei*, which understands the phrase *ki ha-adam etz ha-sadeh* in Deuteronomy 20:19

to mean, "For a person is like a tree of the field." In typical midrashic fashion, this reading is taken out of context; it is actually the opposite of the verse's plain meaning about the vulnerability and limitations of trees, in which Moses asks rhetorically, "Are trees of the field human to withdraw before you into the besieged city?" The implied answer in the Torah is no; the answer in the midrash, as well as the Hasidic tale of Rabbi Nachman, is yes.

Tu b'Shevat invites us to explore this idea that "a person is like a tree," that all of Creation is an expression of God. Such an understanding compels us to feel the impact of the earth's degradation within our souls and to respond accordingly. To respond thus is a present-day *tikun;* in terms used by the kabbalists, this response helps restore the flow of divinity that was damaged by Adam's primordial sin. Before this sin, God had placed Adam in the Garden of Eden "to till it and tend it," *l'ovdah ul'shomrah* (Gen. 2:15). According to the midrash, God then warned Adam, "If you destroy this world, there will be no one to come and set it right after you."[55] Tu b'Shevat gives us pause to heed this warning, to take up the original charge to work the garden and to watch over it.

The Tu b'Shevat Seder

by David Seidenberg

The Tu b'Shevat seder is a kabbalistic ritual meal in honor of the mishnaic New Year for the Tree. We travel through the four worlds of Kabbalah from the beginning to the end of the Tu b'Shevat seder in order to strengthen "the Tree"— the kabbalistic Tree of Life.

On the simplest level, the four worlds can be thought of as levels of intimacy with God. At the lowest level *(assiyah),* we see and create divine patterns in the physical world; while at the highest level *(atzilut),* we stand alongside God's sustaining power and merge our will into the divine.

The goal of the seder is to draw all these levels close together and to unite their *ko'ach* (power) and *shefa* (overflowing energy) with the fertility of the earth and the trees themselves, so that both physical and spiritual abundance will express themselves in this world.

THE BLESSING FROM *PRI ETZ HADAR*

The original instructions for the Tu b'Shevat seder in the 18th-century *Pri Etz Hadar* (Fruit of the Lovely Tree) describes the divine image as being embedded in the heavens and mirrored in the earth, creating symmetry between the highest realms and the lowest. God gave this symmetry to the universe "to join the tent together to become one."

We have the task of seeing and deepening this unity in our intentions, prayers, and senses, as we taste the fruit and drink the wine of the seder. Just as it is our unique power, according to Kabbalah, to drive the sparks of divine energy into exile, it is also our unique power and privilege to draw these sparks back together, and, as the original Tu b'Shevat seder states, to restore them to the Tree of Life.

Through our intentionality, we engage ourselves with the image of God that can be found in the created world. When we do this in order to bring blessing to all of Creation, we also bring blessing to ourselves, and ultimately back to God. Our consciousness then becomes a vessel that provides for all and receives blessing for all.

THE ONE-PAGE "SAVE-THE-TREES" HAGGADAH

The chart on page 111 shows each step of the seder, flowing from the bottom to the top, as a circle with varying attributes. At each level, which corresponds to one of the four worlds, we mix a certain color of wine and encounter (by consuming or by smelling) a certain category of fruit or plant, as a representation of that world.

Traditionally, the kabbalistic seder consists of eating 10 varieties of fruit within each category (inedible shell, pit inside, and totally edible) for each of the first three levels, along with reading a paragraph from the Zohar about that fruit. This Tu b'Shevat haggadah differs from that ritual and from the haggadah for the traditional Passover seder in its focus on having leaders and participants bring texts and teachings of their own choosing.

The schematic of the chart is designed to be open to many interpretations and interpreters. Each level can be interpreted psychologically, historically, politically, kabbalistically, and so on. A few concrete interpretations, according to the seasons and elements, are suggested on the chart. The important thing is to experience the flow of the seder as a process with a purpose and direction.

Conducting the Seder

The seder starts with white wine (or juice) and fruit with a hard shell (for example, a walnut) at the first level, where material reality and separateness are strongest. Traveling to ever-deeper spiritual levels (from the branches into the roots of the Tree of Life), we next taste white wine with a drop of red, along with fruit with a pit and an edible exterior (for example, a peach), at the level of creativity; then half white wine and half red, along with a wholly consumable fruit[56] (for example, a grape), at the level of conceptualization; and finally red wine with a drop of white, without any fruit at all. At this final level, the absence of fruit and inclusion instead of sweet smells and special tastes is representative of the world of pure spirit.

As we move symbolically from one world to the next, each level is an opportunity for a new blessing over fruit, and especially a chance to say an additional blessing of *Shehecheyanu* over a fruit not tasted since Rosh Hashanah. However, unlike the traditional Passover seder, where a blessing is said over each cup of wine, a blessing is said only over the first cup. The form of different blessings for tasting and smelling is shown in boxes on the chart.

In between each step of tasting and sensing, there are opportunities for sharing, interpretation, singing, and discussion. A seder leader can come prepared with texts, poetry, songs, even pictures or objects appropriate for each level, according to his or her interpretation.[57] But participants can also be assigned to bring material for specific levels. For a more challenging method, invite people to bring anything related to trees or the earth and then decide together at the start of the seder where each of their offerings should be shared.

My own custom has been to share teachings and texts after drinking the wine and then sing songs and recite meditations after each fruit. But the best way to use this haggadah is to decide for yourself how the rhythm of movement though the levels should unfold.

Last, the concluding prayer from the *Pri Etz Hadar* can be used in a few ways: it can be read at the beginning of the seder as a map or *kavanah* ("intention") for what is to come; it can be used as a study text; or, in a way that seems to work best with people who have not studied Kabbalah, the prayer can be read at the end of the seder, as a vision of what the seder journey has meant.

פרי Fruit   יין Wine

אצילות *atzilut* | Emanation, Birthing, Being Next to God.
Fire—*hokhmah* חכמה

Spring

8. Level beyond physical fruit. Enjoy sweet smells, such as cinnamon or bay leaf, or special tastes, such as scotch.

7. Red with a drop of white. Secret, Transcendent Mysticism, Kabbalah

סוד
sod

בריה *beriyah* | World of Creation, Creating Something from Nothing.
Air—*binah* בינה

6. Fruit completely edible, no shells. Open on all levels. Eat apples, pears, oranges, grapes.

5. Half red, half white. Mythic, Midrashic Poetry, Anagoge

דרש
derash

יצירה *yetzirah* | World of Formation, Crafting One Thing from Another Thing.
Water—*tiferet* תפארת

4. Fruit with a pit: shell on the inside, inner defenses. Eat olives, dates, avocados, cherries.

3. White with a drop of red. Moral, Ethical Parable, Allegory

רמז
remez

עשיה *assiyah* | World of Doing and Making.
Earth—*malkhut* מלכות

2. Fruit with hard outside shell, outer defenses. Eat walnuts, almonds, coconuts, pomegranates.

1. All white, make the blessing here for all four cups. Simple, Literal

פשט
peshat

Winter

Start at the bottom of the column with level one. Drink wine with each level.

Each of the four elements of medieval science (fire, air, water, earth) is paired here with a divine emanation (*hokhmah, binah, tiferet, malkhut*), bridging the natural world and the divine realm.

Some people begin or end the seder with grains that grow in Israel, such as barley and wheat.

How to Do the Seder
For each level:
1. Drink the wine
2. Learn a Torah text
3. Eat the fruit
4. Share songs, poems, and meditations

Blessings for Smelling
FRUIT:
borei re'ach tov ba-peirot
TREES:
borei atzei b'samim
PLANTS:
borei isvai b'samim
PREPARED SPICES:
borei minei b'samim

Blessings for Eating
WINE:
borei p'ri ha-gefen
DRINKS:
she-ha-kol niheyeh bi-devaro
TREE FRUIT:
borei p'ri ha-etz
GRAINS:
borei minei mezonot
VEGTABLES AND FRUIT OF PERENNIALS:
borei p'ri ha-adamah

A Special Blessing
can be made when we move from one kind of wine to a higher quality wine or liquor:
ha-tov v'ha-metiv
Who is good and does good.

Sweetest All-purpose Blessing after Eating:
Blessed be You God, our God, ruler of the world who created many souls and what they lack, for everything you created, to give life through them to the soul of all life. Blessed be the Life of the Worlds.

Chart by Rabbi David Seidenberg

•┼── Tu b'Shevat ──┼•
Alternative Meditations

Re/Membering Nature

by Rami Shapiro[58]

A story is told about a rabbi and a gardener.

The rabbi was working with his gardener friend as the latter set out to plant several trees about his property. In the midst of their planting they heard a great tumult arising from the city, about a mile to the east.

Outside the city gates a massive cloud of dust arose as hundreds of people made their way out to the surrounding fields and farms. The rabbi and the gardener stopped their work to watch the approaching throng. Men, women and children were dancing joyously; their faces lifted skyward; their voices ringing with praise.

As the crowd drew near, its leaders called out to the rabbi and his friend: "Come quickly! The Messiah has arrived and we go out to greet him!"

The gardener tossed his hoe aside and made to join the crowd, but the rabbi laid a heavy hand upon the other's shoulder and bade him wait. In time the throng passed, and the two men were alone.

"How dare you keep me from the Messiah," the gardener cried out, his voice cracking with anger and despair.

The rabbi picked up the fallen hoe and handed it to his friend. "Messiahs come and go," he said softly, "but the task of planting never ceases."

Thus Rabbi Nathan reminds us: If you are planting a tree and they come to you saying: "Come and greet the Messiah," first plant the tree and then go meet him. Redemption is in the very act of planting.

Rabbi Nathan's pithy comment is the basis for this little tale. I imagine Rabbi Nathan half listening to a group of sages argue over when it is proper to greet the Messiah. One after the other, the masters of Torah offer objections to each other's positions.

Their delight is in the quickness of their responses, the sharpness with which they deflate what on the surface seems a reasonable proposition.

Two things the sages take for granted: the first is that the Messiah will probably never show up; the second is that we must go out to greet him when he does.

This is the wonderful paradox at the heart of Jewish teaching. The world is not a case of *either/or*: either sin or redemption, either right or wrong, either good or evil. The world is not *either/or* but *and*: sin and redemption, right and wrong, good and evil. The God of the Jews is the imageless "And" that is infinite possibility.

When we forget the "And," however, we seek to impose the *either/or* idolatry of limited human reasoning. When the *either/or* takes hold, we take ourselves far too seriously, and inflict much unnecessary suffering on the world. When we insist that the world is *either/or,* we divide person and planet; we invent scarcity and the national boundaries needed to enforce it; we see the stranger as enemy and the other as stranger. When we fall into the trap of *either/or,* we replace virtue with law, symbol with sacrament, *aggadah* with *halacha.*

When our sages get caught up in the minutiae of their own *either/or* reasoning, their words become more important than the reality to which they once referred. It is then that the law becomes God and God is reduced to law. It is then that the simple reality of everyday living is lost beneath the pseudo facts of legal fiction.

So I imagine Rabbi Nathan, a sage of "And," half listening to the *either/or* wranglings of his friends. Do we greet him first, or second? What if we are reciting the *Shema?* Or what if we are in the privy? Or what if we are planting a tree—

"Enough!" Nathan shouts, no longer able to ignore their foolishness. "First plant the tree," he yells at them. "Just plant the tree!" For a moment his friends stare at him, open mouthed, their attention pulled away from themselves and their cleverness.

"What are you saying, Nathan?"

"Listen: if you are planting a tree and the people come and tell you the Messiah has arrived, finish planting before you go to see him. That's all. Finish the planting."

"So, Mister Big Shot Sage, that's all? Just finish the planting? And where is this written?"

Rabbi Nathan smiles. He enjoys rattling his friends. He knows that they are just playing with this kind of *either/or* talk, though he fears that what is fun for them now will one day become deadly serious for their heirs. "People will remember our words," he would often caution his colleagues, "but who will pass on the laughter that accompanied them?"

"Messiah comes in response to one of two situations," Rabbi Nathan says to his friends. "If we fulfill our nature, Messiah will arrive. And if we totally degrade our nature Messiah will arrive. Now the question is: What is our nature, and what does it mean to fulfill or degrade it?

"What is our nature? Our nature is to plant. Is this not what *Torah* tells us? *Adam,* the human, from *adamah,* the earth. Adam the earthling raised up out of the dust to plant, till, and tend the Garden. When we cease to tend we cease to be *adam.* When we cease to be *adam,* we pervert our true nature.

"We fulfill our nature when we plant. We degrade it when we uproot. We plant when we live in a manner that reveals the connection between all things. We uproot when we live in a manner that separates and divides. We fulfill our nature when we make plain the interdependence of all things. We degrade our nature when we pretend to independence.

"We plant when we take our place in the world, recognizing that we are *adam* from *adamah,* earthlings at one with earth. We degrade ourselves when we insist upon being homeless, without place, aliens and strangers rather than gardeners and tenders. This is why we call God *haMakom,* the Place. Do we call God *that* Place, as if there was some place devoid of God? No! God is *the* Place, *this* Place, *every* place we happen to awaken to the interdependence of each and all."

Rabbi Nathan looked from one face to the other. His friends were listening, but were they hearing? For a moment he felt a terrible urge to make it all a joke, and let them get back to their discussion. He could tell himself that humor is the greater teacher. True enough, but Nathan was no humorist. He frowned instead of smiling, and plunged ahead.

"Messiah will come when we have totally lost our Place, for then we will have completely degraded nature, ours and everything else's. But even if Messiah did come then, we would be unable to go out to greet him. Why? We would no longer be able to recognize him. So long would we have devoted ourselves to rooting out the stranger that we would no longer recognize the face of the Friend. So busy would we be carving the earth into parcels upon which to build fences and house armies, that we would have no time to build a gate and welcome the other. The Messiah would arrive and none would care.

"But if we maintain the planting, if we attend to tending, we will attend to ourselves, to our true nature, and to the true nature of all things. When we attend to ourselves we see that we are *adam,* earthlings. When we see we are *adam* we suddenly see we are also *adamah,* earth. We will see that we are not alien to this world, but an expression of it. Just as the fig tree figs, so *adamah adams,* God peoples.

"When we see that *adam is adamah,* we cease to be separate from our Place. Ceasing to be separate, we cease to war within ourselves. Ceasing to war within ourselves we cease to war among ourselves. Taking our Place, or better discovering that *the* Place is *every* Place, we are no longer blinded by the false scarcity we invent to maintain the illusion of us and them, ours and theirs. No longer driven by the fear of having less, we can help all to have more.

"Coming to Place is coming to our senses. Coming to our senses is awakening to the wonder of being *adam/adamah.* Our whole being is alive as an expression of God. We suddenly know that God is all and all is God.

"And then we would have no need to stop our planting to greet the Messiah. For then we would greet the Messiah in each seedling we plant, in each sapling we water, in each tree we prune and harvest, in each face we meet. If you need to stop the planting to greet the Messiah, you are already lost, for you have already mistaken the Messiah for someone else. For the planting is Messiah. So too the planter and the planted. Finish the planting and then greet him, if indeed you still feel the need."

Rabbi Nathan turned back to the task at hand: bundling wood for kindling. His friends, stood quietly looking—first at Nathan, then at each other, then again at Nathan, and then again at each other. At last one of them spoke:

"But, what if you're planting and the High Priest comes to you and says,…"

Tu B'Shvat[59] is not Jewish Earth Day. Tu B'Shvat is not a call to go back to Nature. Nature is not nostalgic. Nature doesn't long to go back to anything. To what would Nature return? Nature is acutely present. Nature tends to what is.

Tu B'Shvat is a call to return to our nature. Tu B'Shvat is an opportunity to recognize that we are *adamah;* to remember (literally to re-member, to put back together) the supposedly shattered self that pretends to be other than Nature. Tu B'Shvat is an opportunity to plant ourselves firmly in the Place that is every place, and to awaken to the fundamental unity of God, woman, man and Nature.

You and I are Nature! We are Nature's way of looking at herself, of thinking about herself, of recreating herself. We are Nature's way of tending; Nature's way of doing what must be done. If we are to fulfill our nature, we must reclaim the ability to attend. To attend means to be at the task of tending, to be at the work of doing what needs to be done.

How do we reclaim the ability to attend?

We must learn to take root. Socially, politically, and economically this means to take responsibility for the place in which we live: to hold fast the soil of community. Spiritually, it means to quiet the mind and be still.

We quiet the mind when we do what needs doing without self-conscious hesitation. When we act without hesitation we act without ego, without pride, without prejudice, without error. When we act without hesitation we act from the Whole for the Whole. When we act without hesitation we act as Messiah.

When we act this way we have no need to stop the planting to greet the Messiah. We know that Messiah neither leaves nor arrives. With Rabbi Nathan we know that redemption—awakening to the unity of each and All—is in the very act of planting.

Gleaning the Harvest: A Torah Meditation[60]

by Paul Steinberg

> When you reap the harvest in your field and overlook a sheaf in the field, do not turn back to get it; it shall go to the stranger, the fatherless, and the widow—in order that the LORD your God may bless you in all your undertakings.

The earth is the LORD's and all that it holds.

When you beat down the fruit of your olive trees, do not go over them again; that shall go to the stranger, the fatherless, and the widow.
The earth is the LORD's and all that it holds.

When you gather the grapes of your vineyard, do not pick it over again; that shall go to the stranger, the fatherless, and the widow.
The earth is the LORD's and all that it holds.

Always remember that you were a slave in the land of Egypt; therefore do I enjoin you to observe this commandment.
The land is Mine; you are but strangers resident with Me.... you must provide for the redemption of the land.

Melody of the Grasses[61]

by Nachman of Bratzlav

Know that every shepherd has a special melody, depending on the grasses and the place where he herds, for each grass has a song, and the melody of the shepherd is composed of the singing of the grasses.

Oh that I would merit to hear the sound of the songs and paeans of the grasses, how each grass recites a song to the LORD, may He be blessed, without any questions and without any foreign thoughts, without expecting any recompense! How beautiful and fine it must be to hear their singing! And it must be very good among them to serve the Lord with awe.

As soon as a person awakens and desires the Land of Israel, then, in accordance with his awakening and his desire, illumination from the sanctity of the Land of Israel is drawn to him.

Opening Our Eyes to Miracles:
A Modern Midrash on the Burning Bush[62]

by Matt Biers-Ariel, Deborah Newbrun, and Michal Fox Smart

Jews have struggled throughout history to interpret this miracle. Here is one interpretation: The shepherd Moses was a keen observer of his environment—

he had to be in order to spot dangerous animals and find pastures for grazing and water sources. One day he was gazing at an ordinary bush. The longer he looked, the more intrigued he became with this plant. After watching for a long time, Moses began to see the bush's life force, its divine spark. It appeared to Moses as if the bush was on fire, but actually Moses was observing the divine spark of life that is present in all things. This indeed was a miracle. Through this ordinary plant Moses had reached toward heaven, and God reached out to him.

The Baal Shem Tov about Joy on Tu BeShvat

by Yitzhak Buxbaum[63]

Once, on Tu BeShvat,[64] the New Year of the Trees, the Baal Shem Tov was sitting with his closest disciples in Medzibuz. They were eating fruits in honor of the day, drinking *"L'hayim!"* (To life!) and discussing the importance of joy. During this conversation, the Baal Shem Tov said:

"Joy is so great, because by joy a person can reach an exalted spiritual level where he sees the *Shechinah*. After the verse, 'you shall be only joyful' (Deut. 16:15), the Torah continues (v.16), 'Three times a year every man of you shall be seen [appear in the Temple] before the presence of the Lord your God.' When a Jew is happy, he reveals that he is satisfied with the world of the Holy One, blessed be He, and also with the behavior of all the Children of Israel, the people close to Him. He has no complaints against Heaven and no demands or grievances against any other Jew. Everything is good, upright, acceptable, fitting, and sweet, and this kind of joy, which brings a person to have a good eye, to look on the Creator and His creatures lovingly, can cause a revelation of the *Shechinah*. That is the secret of the teaching of our Sages, who said about the person who goes to the Temple to 'be seen' by God, that 'Just as he came to be seen, so does he come to see'—that is, to see the Divine Presence."

After this conversation about joy, the Baal Shem Tov suggested to his Hasidim that they all go out for a sleigh ride in the snow-covered countryside and take with them some wine, honeycake, whiskey, and fruits for Tu BeShvat.

As they careened along in the sleigh, the snow was falling and they were so joyful that they felt they were lifted up on a cloud of light. Remembering that it was Tu BeShvat, they sang songs from the mystic Book of Song *(Perek Shira)* that tells how all creatures, even plants, sing to praise their Creator. They sang: "The fig tree says, 'The one who tends the fig tree shall eat its fruit.' The pomegranate says, 'Your cheeks are like the halves of a pomegranate.' The palm tree says, 'A righteous person shall flourish like a palm tree.'"

The road entered the forest, and the horses galloped in pleasure, kicking up snow all over. On the two sides of the road an ancient forest stretched out, dense, with trees whose branches leaned out, arching over the road, almost touching in the middle and almost blocking out the light of the sun. But here and there the sun peeked through the branches, lighting the travelers' path as they careened along in the sleigh. And as they went, they sang another song from the Book of Song, "Then shall the trees of the forest sing for joy before the Lord …!"

Their singing grew stronger and stronger and flocks of birds flying above them began chirping so loudly that it seemed that they were singing along with the joyful travelers in the sleigh.[65]

The Baal Shem Tov and his disciples knew the secret—that God is within the world. How could they not sing? When we know that secret, we too will sing and will hear the songs of the trees and the birds praising God.

PART 4

Purim

*In the time to come all the other parts of the Prophets
and the Writings will lose their worth and only the Torah of Moses
and the Scroll of Esther will retain their value.*

—J. Talmud, *Megillah* 1:5

Celebrating the Truth in Fantasy

A HASIDIC TEACHING SAYS THAT we can learn three things from small children: how to keep busy, how to cry for what we need, and how to laugh and be cheerful.[1] What do these three things have in common? They tell us that children are able to become completely absorbed in what they do. The mind of the child is free; it is not constrained by the responsibilities, expectations, or complexities of life. Engrossed in each moment, children busy themselves with anything of interest; they cry out with the wholeness of their hearts and laugh with every fiber of their being. This same freedom and exuberance inform the spirit of Purim. It is the one day of the year that we are not just given permission, but mandated, to let go of restraint. We express this gay abandon by putting on masks to hide our true faces, but ironically—and Purim is all about ironies—hiding behind masks enables us to exhibit normally concealed countenances.

Purim is also characterized by the reading of *Megillat Esther* (*megillat* means "scroll of"), which recounts a fantastic story. In it, the normal state of affairs—Jewish second-class citizenship, hateful and reckless governmental officials, and powerless women—is turned inside out. When the Jewish nation is rescued by its own wise and faithful Mordecai and his patient, courageous niece Esther, such a happy ending contradicts the painful reality of the conventional Jewish experience.

Because the historical accuracy of the Purim story cannot be confirmed, it rings in our ears as a fable—one with a deep spiritual truth. That truth lies within the very fantasy of the Scroll of Esther and the customs of frivolity, gregariousness, and drunkenness (if responsibly limited) that it encourages. We mock ourselves and laugh away the grief caused by our own imperfections. As the wispy, illusory curtains that divide reality and fantasy are pulled back, we find ourselves in the place where the controls of the mind are unbound. Here is where a portion of the soul dwells and where we tap into the piece of our spirit that Purim represents.

The Whole Megillah

Megillah (plural *megillot*) is Hebrew for "scroll." In everyday conversation, the word megillah has come to mean a long, involved story told in great detail. This usage, which began with Yiddish speakers, was taken from the idea of listening on Purim to the "whole Megillah," the entire story about Esther with nothing omitted.

Purim occurs in the month of Adar (on the 14th day), during the season when we relinquish some of our rigidity and allow fantasy and amusement to bring out their hidden truths. It is a time when the fool is king, when it is acceptable to play like children, letting our imaginations sweep us away. We turn the presumed reality of the world on its head. We see justice exacted from those who are evil, and we see attention and gifts being used to enrich the day for people who are traditionally poor. And even though God's name is absent from the telling of this fantasy, set in the ironic world of the city of Shushan, we gain an understanding from the story that the there can be a truth beyond "the truth." This realization broadens our concept of God.

Storytelling

On Purim during a communal gathering, the full story of Esther is read aloud from a parchment scroll. A participant can fulfill the commandment "to read" the story by listening closely to every word.[2] The atmosphere is often loud and silly with friends and family members playing off each other's enthusiasm. The relatively brief, nine-chapter story is read twice—once during the evening service after the *Amidah* prayer is said and once during the morning service after the Torah is read.[3]

Purim in the Bible

The biblical account of Purim, called *Megillat Esther*, is found in Kethuvim (The Writings), the third section of the Bible. It holds our attention with plot twists, suspense, and intrigue. The opening chapter sets the tale in Shushan, the capital city of the Persian empire, described as "a hundred and twenty-seven provinces from India to Ethiopia" (Esther 1:1). We are soon thrust into an extravagant royal banquet given by King Ahasuerus not only for all his officials, courtiers, noblemen, and governors but also for all the people "high and low alike" (1:5). Royal wine is served from golden beakers, and "the rule for drinking is 'No restrictions!'" (1:8). On the seventh day of this pageant of inebriation, Ahasuerus orders his queen, Vashti, to appear at the party to "display her beauty" (1:11).[4]

Vashti flatly refuses, which sends the king's counselors into an uproar over the concern that Vashti's behavior "will make all wives despise their husbands" (1:17). They decree that Vashti is forever banished from entering the presence of the king. Now a citywide search begins for the greatest beauty of all, someone to replace her. Esther (known in Hebrew as Hadassah) is chosen to be the queen. At the direction of her adoptive father Mordecai (biologically her cousin), Esther does not disclose her Jewish identity.

Mordecai learns of a plot to do away with Ahasuerus, and Esther reports it to the king in the name of Mordecai, though without revealing that he is her relative. The schemers are put to death, and Ahasuerus gives Mordecai recognition "in the book of annals" (2:23). Meanwhile, Haman, a noted descendant of Agag, king of the evil tribe of Amalek, is promoted as the king's chief official. With such an honor comes the king's order that all should kneel or bow low before Haman. Mordecai refuses do so; and when asked for a reason why, he reveals that he is a Jew.[5] Enraged by this insubordination, Haman convinces Ahasuerus that Jews do not obey the king's laws and need to be exterminated. Ahasuerus accepts Haman's opinion and grants him the power to carry out a plan for total annihilation.

When they hear of the terrible decree, Jews everywhere weep and fast. Mordecai appeals to Esther that she must do something: "Perhaps you have attained to royal position for just such a crisis" (4:14). To appear before the king without being summoned is a death sentence, but Esther succeeds in approaching him. When he asks what is troubling her, she requests, "Let Your Majesty and Haman come today to the feast that I have prepared …"(5:4). This is the first in a series of three feasts that she holds for them.

Haman continues to be furious with Mordecai, who sits in sackcloth at the palace gate, to mourn the decree, and still will not bow down to him. Haman's wife and his friends encourage the minister to put up a very high stake for Mordecai's impalement once the decree is enacted. That very night, however, a sleepless Ahasuerus decides to have the book of records brought to him for review. The annals remind him that a man name Mordecai saved his life and nothing has been done to honor him. He appoints someone in his court to arrange for a festive parade through the city for Mordecai. That someone happens to be Haman!

Haman's Game

The word *pur* is from *puru,* a word in the ancient Semitic language of Akkadian (spoken in Mesopotamia). *Puru* means "lot," an object used as a counter to decide a question by chance. In the biblical telling of the story of Purim, we read that "*pur* … was cast before Haman … [until it fell on] the twelfth month, that is the month of Adar" (Esther 3:7), which he then determined would be the time for destroying the Jews. Because Haman cast a lot on more than one day and also because the Megillat Esther refers to "observ[ing] these two days" (9:26), the name of the holiday is pluralized as "Purim."

At the third banquet, Esther humbly reveals her Jewish identity to the king and tells him that she and her people are about to be destroyed by Haman. A furious Ahasuerus rushes out to the garden, and when he returns, finds Haman, who is pleading with Queen Esther for mercy, lying on a couch with her. "Does he mean," cries the king, "to ravish the queen in my own palace?" (7:8). The executioner's hood immediately is placed over Haman's head.

The story in Megillat Esther concludes with layers of unexpected reversals, as Haman is impaled on the stake that he constructed for Mordecai, Esther receives Haman's property, and Mordecai becomes a powerful figure in the royal court. Furthermore, Ahasuerus countermands the decree to exterminate the Jews, and instead, Haman's sons and thousands of other foes of the Jews are killed. The Jews undertake to recall these days "in every generation: by every family, every province, and every city. And these days of Purim shall never cease among the Jews, and the memory of them shall never perish among their descendants" (9:28).

The Fast of Esther

The spirit of a holiday is set in the days that lead up to it, a time when we make preparations and establish the proper mood. The Fast of Esther (Ta'anit Esther) takes place on the 13th of Adar, the day before Purim, which is the most joyful day on the Jewish calendar, a celebration of the salvation of the Jewish people in a time of terrible despair. On Purim, we will dance, sing, and play, to mark our redemption from the clutches of evil and acknowledge our gratitude to God. During the Fast of Esther we raise our spiritual readiness and make ready to find the exalted meaning of Purim.

Not So Fast

When Purim falls on Sunday, the Fast of Esther is held on Thursday, because we try to refrain from fasting on Friday, the day on which we prepare for Shabbat or on Shabbat itself.[6]

Purim is a relatively minor holiday on the scale of the Jewish tradition, yet the only one with a communal fast as its spiritual preparation—in advance of the day, rather than part of the day itself. It is not a major, 25-hour fast, as are those that occur directly on Yom Kippur (the Day of Atonement) and Tisha b'Av (the day we mourn the fall of both the First and Second Temples) when the fasts begin before sunset and end after nightfall the following day. The Fast of Esther begins at dawn and ends at sunset the same day, and the only requirement is abstention from food and drink (working and bathing are permitted).[7] Fasting is not mandatory if a person is in ill health, pregnant, or nursing.[8]

The great 16th-century authority Moses Isserles of Poland points out that the Fast of Esther is not an obligation to the same extent as other public fasts; however, it would still be best to fast and maintain oneness with our community.[9] He follows the reasoning that leniencies exist for the Fast of Esther because the fast is not mentioned anywhere in the Talmud. It became part of the literature of *halakhah* ("Jewish law") and *minhagim* ("customs") only by way of medieval inferences drawn from a particular talmudic discussion, one that describes gathering to read the Scroll of Esther on the 13th of Adar.[10]

The renowned legal authority Asher ben Yechiel (known as "the Rosh") may be the best elucidator of the intrinsic value and spirituality in the fasting on the day before Purim. He writes in his medieval *Sefer Ha-Halakhot* (The Book of Laws):

> *Everyone gathers for the Fast of Esther and the villagers come to the town to say penitentiary prayers* (selichot) *since on that day they [the Jews] gathered to defend their lives, and they were in need of Heaven's mercy. And similarly we find that Moses, Our Great Teacher, fasted when he waged war against Amalek [Haman's ancestor] ....*[11] *Thus the Gemara can be interpreted as a source for the Fast of Esther—that we now have to fast as the Jews did in the time of Mordecai and Esther to defend their lives—and we have no talmudic source for the fast other than this.*[12]

Fasting serves three primary purposes in Judaism. The first is exemplified by Yom Kippur, when it is a means to reach atonement. The Yom Kippur haftarah (a reading from the biblical Book of Prophets) reminds us that fasting is not the actual source of atonement; rather, it helps to induce our genuine regret and care.[13] Furthermore, according to the Bible and the Talmud, a fast for the sake of atonement can also preempt or minimize divine punishment, as was the case with the people of Nineveh in the Book of Jonah.[14] Much of an entire volume of the Talmud—tractate *Ta'anit*—is dedicated to discussing fasting for this purpose.[15]

The second purpose of fasting is to commemorate a sorrowful moment in history, as on Tisha b'Av and on the other three statutory fasts (the 10th of Tevet, the 17th of Tammuz, and the Fast of Gedaliah), which are memorials to calamities that befell the Jewish people and Jerusalem.[16] During this sort of fast, we remember the hardships our ancestors endured, and we continue to bear that pain at a spiritual level by engaging in rituals that generate a mood of suffering. While the objective is to make this connection everlasting, we also focus energy on the hope that such tragedies will not occur again.

The final purpose for fasting is to realize our utter dependence on God and to demonstrate, in a communal setting, gratitude for all that humanity has received. By refraining from satisfying our physical needs and focusing instead on our spiritual state, we come to better appreciate the sustenance that God provides This observation elevates our sense of joy and thankfulness.[17]

All three of these purposes underpin the reason for the Fast of Esther, which is also supported by two particular events in the story of Purim. The first one occurs after Esther has learned of Haman's despicable extermination plot. She sends word to Mordecai that he should assemble all the Jews and instruct them to join her in a three-day fast. Esther is preparing herself spiritually for a dangerous and desperate plan to save the Jews; the first step will be taken on the third day when she will make an illegal, self-initiated request to appear before the king.[18]

The second event takes place on the 13th of Adar, the day when Haman's annihilation had been scheduled to take place. Instead, the Jews take to arms and strike all of their enemies; they kill 75,000 of them.[19] Many sources, including the Rosh, associate the Fast of Esther with this war.[20] It commemorates a sorrowful day, not only because it recalls Haman's evil decree, but also because of the deadly battles.[21] The Purim celebration itself is joyous, like the moment of victory; but the fast reminds us that the battles—all the moments that precede victory—are ones of great pain.

Megillah for All

The Scroll of Esther is commonly referred to simply as "the Megillah," even in Rabbinic literature. Reading or hearing the Megillah is the central observance of Purim; and the commandment to do so is of such importance that there is only one halakhically accepted reason for not obeying it—the need to bury the dead.[22] Being present at the Megillah reading is still one of the most-observed Jewish practices, although today's high attendance may be attributable to the fun involved, rather than to the weight of the obligation.

The observance of the commandment is exceptional in three ways. First, on no day of the Jewish year, except Purim, are we under mandate to give an identical reading of a sacred text at night and on the following morning (a "day" on the Hebrew calendar).[23] This dictum is based on a statement in the Talmud that we are to read the Megillah at night and then repeat it in the morning.[24] Second, women are obligated to hear the Megillah, even though it is a positive, time-bound commandment,[25] the kind from which women are mostly exempt according to traditional sources.[26] Authorities maintain that women are obligated because "the miracle happened to them, too."[27] Third, reading the Megillah takes the place of chanting *Hallel* (special prayers of thanks and praise), which occurs on most Jewish holidays and on Rosh Hodesh (the celebration of the new moon).[28] The Talmud states that the Megillah is itself *Hallel.*[29] No other biblical reading acts as a direct form of prayer in this manner.

WHERE MEANS WHEN

Among all the Jewish holidays, Purim has the singular distinction of having its date determined by whether or not a person lives in a city surrounded by a wall. The distinction is derived from a passage in the Megillah:

> *(But the Jews in Shushan mustered on both the thirteenth and fourteenth days, and so rested on the fifteenth, and made it a day of feasting and merrymaking.) That is why village Jews, who live in unwalled towns, observe the fourteenth day of the month of Adar and make it a day of merrymaking and feasting, and as a holiday and an occasion for sending gifts to one another.*
> —Esther 9:18–9

The story differentiates between Jews who lived and fought their enemies for two days within the walled, capital city of Shushan and those who lived in unwalled towns, where only one day was needed to subdue the enemy. The Rabbis determined we should make that same distinction when memorializing the event. Accordingly, if a person lives in a city that has been walled since the days of Joshua (circa 1250 B.C.E.), as Shushan was, Purim is celebrated on the 15th of the month of Adar, a day referred to as "Shushan Purim." Those who live in unwalled cities celebrate on the 14th, the day referred to as just "Purim."[30] The sages considered making Shushan Purim conditional on whether a city was walled from the time of Ahasuerus; but they did not wish to honor a Persian city over one in the Land of Israel, given that Israel was in ruins at the time of the Purim miracle. Joshua was chosen because, in the Book of Exodus, he is the general who begins the effort to annihilate the descendants of Haman's ancestor, Amalek.[31] In addition, the time of Joshua is related to the Israelite conquest of the Land of Israel, the memory of which reinforces Purim's theme of Jewish victory.[32] For Jews who have been living in the Diaspora, the observance of Shushan Purim is not even a consideration, because we know of no cities in these countries that were walled 3,000 years ago.[33] Anyone visiting Jersualem, though, should be prepared to celebrate a joyous Shushan Purim.[34]

LEAP FOR THE SEASONS

Besides knowing whether or not we are celebrating Purim in a walled city, we need to know whether or not we are experiencing a leap year according to the Hebrew calendar. The Jewish calendar, unlike the secular (Gregorian) calendar, follows the lunar cycle rather than the solar. In a 12-month year, the solar calendar has 365 and one-half days, while the lunar calendar has 354 and one-third days (more than 11 days shorter). The particular dilemma about this discrepancy is that the holidays are bound to their respective seasons. According to biblical statute,[35] Passover must occur in spring, Shavuot in summer, and Sukkot in fall. The 11-day difference, if not accounted for, would cause these holidays to fall 11 days earlier each succeeding year. Eventually, they would occur in the opposite season.

To ensure that the holidays remain in their mandated seasons, the Jewish calendar was ingeniously adjusted to accommodate the 11-day difference between the lunar and solar years. In the 4th century C.E., Hillel II[36] scheduled an extra month at the end of the biblical year, as necessary. The biblical year begins in spring with Nissan (Exod. 12:1–2) and ends with Adar. Hillel II, in conjunction with the Sanhedrin (Jewish supreme court) chose to repeat Adar (Adar I and Adar II) every 3rd, 6th, 8th, 11th, 14th, 17th, and 19th year over a 19-year period. This method accomodates the 207-day discrepancy that adds up between the lunar and solar calendar every 19 years. In seven out of every 19 years, a "leap month" of Adar II is included in the Jewish calendar.

When a leap year occurs, Purim is celebrated in Adar II. Because both Purim and Passover recount a deliverance of the Jewish people, the Talmud sees the seasonal bond between the two holidays and notes that it must be preserved.[37] Consequently, the tradition concludes that Adar II is the "main" Adar, wherein we observe yahrzeits (anniversaries of deaths) and celebrate bar and bat mitzvahs (commandments related to birthdays).[38] Yet many of the observances associated with the traditional joy of Adar are practiced in Adar I as well, to uphold the Rabbinic principle that forbids "postponing fulfillment of precepts."[39] There is even a Purim *katan* ("little Purim") observed on the 14th and 15th of Adar I, making these days on which things denoted as mournful, such as fasting and eulogizing, are prohibited.[40]

Making Merry

The same days on which the Jews had enjoyed relief from their foes and the same month which had been transformed for them from one of grief and mourning to one of festive joy. They were to observe them as days of feasting and merrymaking, and as an occasion for sending gifts to one another and presents to the poor.
—Esther 9:22

THE JEWISH WAY OF GIVING

From the biblical description of the celebration in Shushan, we learn how to preserve a proper memorial to the story of Esther. A principal way is by giving charity, *matanot l'evyonim*, to supply the poor with the financial means to celebrate Purim, in particular, to have a feast. In the biblical text, the word for "poor" is plural—*evyonim*—from which we are taught to make a gift of charity also in the plural, to at least two individuals.[41] And the donation should be made without the needy person having to request it.

In recent years, in light of the numerous charitable organizations available to receive donations and make distributions, most of us tend not to give face-to-face to people in want. Yet giving directly to another human being adds emotionally and spiritually to the experience and establishes a unique sense of relationship. It can mean giving to someone destitute on the street or it can mean giving to those in need whom we know personally or through the introduction of friends or family. Surely there are many people who might not be begging on the streets, yet due to unforeseen circumstances are unable to afford medical care; the cost of Jewish education; and general living expenses such as rent, utilities, transportation, or child care. Although this sort of giving may seem awkward in our contemporary society, it is certainly necessary; and it establishes a mutual affirmation of spirit, when giver and receiver become acquainted as witnesses to each other's act.

Giving charity on Purim is a law, not a custom; it is a commandment built into the structure of the holiday. In the context of the biblical story, the giving was an expression of gratitude for being saved and of love for other people, and it was voluntary. With the advent of Rabbinic Judaism—which became normative 2,000 years ago—the act of giving charity on Purim assumed the status of obligation.

For those of us living in Christian-dominated societies, an important point can be made about the nature and practice of Jewish giving. In Christian thought, giving charity is more a way to emulate the self-sacrificing love of Jesus[42] than it is a duty. In fact, the English word "charity" is derived form the Latin *caritas*, meaning "love." The Apostle Paul (1st century C.E.), Christianity's greatest missionary and author of many parts of the Christian Bible, perpetuated Jesus' message that the spirit of "cheerful" charity is more important than how often and how much one gives.[43] For Christianity, giving charity is certainly a commendable thing to do, as "there is more happiness in giving than receiving,"[44] but the religion has no commandment obligating a person to do so.

Judaism, on the other hand, recognizes that the world in which we live is uneven and fraught with injustices. The Torah devotes considerable attention to issues of poverty and prepares us for the sobering news that "there will never cease to be needy ones in your land" (Deut. 15:11). The word for charity in Judaism is *tzedakah* (etymologically associated with the word *tzedek*, meaning "justice"). *Tzedakah* represents what is minimally required and expected of everyone, even the poor themselves. The Talmud tells us, "Even a poor person who lives entirely on charity must also give charity to another poor person."[45]

The Torah, which bases its laws upon an agrarian society, delineates several laws to ensure that those who have will give and those who need will take. Among them are these: a tenth of one's produce must be set aside for the poor (Deut. 26:12); crops from the corners of one's field should be left uncollected for the poor to come and take (Lev. 19:10, 23:22 and Deut. 24:19); and special donations must be made at festive seasons so that the needy can join in the celebration (Deut. 16:9–14). For Jews, giving charity defines the way we are supposed to understand our relationship to other human beings. In everything we say and do, we should consider the poor and needy. Our liturgy, our social obligations, and our habits are tied into the essence of Judaism and Jewish existence. An anonymous medieval source on ethics explains the Jewish ideal of generosity and charity in this way:

The quality of generosity depends on habit, for a person cannot be considered generous unless that person gives of his or her own free will at all times, at all hours, according to his or her ability. A person who gives a thousand gold pieces to a worthy person is not as generous as one who gives a thousand gold pieces ... [over the course of] a thousand different occasions, each to a worthy cause. For the person who gave a thousand gold pieces at one time had a sudden impulse to be generous, but after that the desire left him.[46]

The source is not implying, of course, that giving out of obligation is the ideal. Consistency of habit and giving the required minimum amount are undeniably important factors in giving, but complete generosity is defined differently in Judaism. When we serve God by aiding others, the greatest form of this endeavor is giving to the needy with a blend of *tzedakah* and *gemilut chasadim* (intentional acts of righteousness). In other words, not only giving because we are obligated but also because we sincerely care about the person or cause.

In Judaism we recognize that there is a relationship and often a tension between the intention of giving and the act of giving. In Rabbinic literature, volumes have been written on this topic over the centuries. The magnitude of this discussion is a testament to Judaism's perspective on both the value of giving and the complexity of the spiritual conduct that accompanies it. In just one example of the hundreds of teachings on this subject in the Talmud, this 2nd-century sage offers one of the most cogent insights into that tension and Judaism's priorities within the act of giving.

Rabbi Elazar said: "Giving charity is greater than offering sacrifices, as it is written To do what is right and just is more desired by the LORD than sacrifice [Prov. 21:3]." Rabbi Elazar also said: "The reward for giving charity depends upon the lovingkindness therein, as it is written, Sow righteousness for yourselves; reap the fruits of goodness [Hosea 10:12]." Our rabbis taught: "There are three ways that intentional acts of lovingkindness [gemilut chasadim] are greater than charity [tzedakah]. Tzedakah is done through money, whereas gemilut chasadim *are done with personal involvement and money;* tzedakah *is done for the poor, whereas* gemilut chasadim *are done for both rich and poor;* tzedakah *is done for the living, whereas* gemilut chasadim *are done for both the living and the dead."*[47]

Triangular Delights

Hamantashen—small pastries, traditionally filled with poppy seeds or prunes—are certainly the most popular Purim food. The name comes from a Yiddish phrase that means "Haman's pockets." In Hebrew, they are called *oznei Haman,* which means "Haman's ears."[50] These names are both a bit odd. After all, why would anyone want to eat, or even memorialize, Haman's pockets or his ears? True, their triangular shape slightly resembles pockets or ears; and one tradition goes even further, claiming that hamentaschen represent the hats worn by members of the Persian court, including Haman. Whatever the symbolism may be, hamantashen originated relatively late in Jewish history; their first known mention is in an 11th-century poem. Historians believe they evolved from the German pastry *mohntaschen,* meaning "poppy-seed pocket."[51]

DAYS OF FEASTING AND JOY

The Seudah

The special Purim meal, which usually takes place in mid to late afternoon,[48] is designated as a *se'udah,* meaning feast. Such a feast is actually a Purim obligation, hearkening back to the Book of Esther's triumphant decree: "They were to observe them as days of feasting and merrymaking …"(9:22). Besides being a commemoration, the Purim *se'udah* ensures that the entirety of Purim is spent in merriment and joy, from the first reading of the Megillah in the evening all the way through the next day, when we feast on food and wine in the company of friends and family.

The eating and drinking associated with the Purim *se'udah* are seen as ways to elevate the soul. As opposed to the ascetic elements of Yom Kippur, which elevate the soul through denial of physical pleasure, the experience of Purim is just the opposite. Accordingly, the physical pleasure we gain by feasting on Purim is a way for us to praise God and affirm our victory over the forces of Haman and his ancestor Amalek—representatives of evil incarnate.[49]

The Special Deliveries

In our customs, we want to reexperience the joy felt by the Jews of Shushan as described in the Bible. Among the ways they celebrated the defeat of Haman was by sending gifts of food to one another.[52] The Hebrew phrasing in the Book of Esther tells us exactly what to do: *mishloach manot ish le-re'aihu*. The first word, *mishloach*, means delivery. The second word, *manot*, refers to food portions. Because that word is plural, the Rabbis interpreted the directive as mandating at least two different food items in each gift.[53] Although two is the minimum, many people today include at least three different items to enhance the tradition and the experience by doing more than the minimum. "Different" can mean different kinds of drink or different kinds of cake, not necessarily completely different categories. The food should be of the "ready-to-eat" category, not anything that needs cooking or preparation, so it can be eaten soon thereafter at the Purim feast. For those who cannot afford sufficient food for the feast, the contents of *mishloach manot* serve as a special enhancement to their celebration.

The final words of the phrase are *ish le-re'aihu*, which, using the singular, describe one person giving to one friend.[54] Thus the minimum requirement of the *mishloach manot* tradition is to send the gift of two food portions to one person (although giving to more than one person is considered praiseworthy).[55]

Basic Guidelines for Delivery

- Send the gifts on Purim day, not before or after. Doing so on the day itself demonstrates an effort to reenact the Jews' experience as described in the Purim story.

- Have the gifts delivered by a third person. The word *misloach* is related to the word for messenger, *shaliach*. The gifts may be shipped, but having a familiar person make the delivery can often be an extremely rewarding experience for giver and receiver. Many families have a child be the "third person" who takes the gifts directly to the door.

- Identify the giver on a card. The purpose of the gifts is to boost friendship; they should not be sent anonymously.

Despite the established simple standards and customs, the sending of *mishloach manot* has evolved into a substantial practice, especially in the United States. Some people will send dozens of baskets—one to each of their friends and family, teachers and co workers—and filled with not just two food portions, but with a bounty of sugar-coated and fatty delights or even a bottle of aged Scotch whiskey. Other people, however, are determined

What Good Are the Goodies?

In the Megillah, Haman approaches King Ahasuerus to request permission to exterminate all the Jews. He says, "There is a certain people scattered and dispersed among the other peoples in all the provinces of your realm …" (Esther 3:8). According to the Talmud, Haman was implying that the Jews suffered from internal strife and dissension and that this lack of unity would render them vulnerable both physically and spiritually. To prove Haman wrong, we demonstrate the fullness of our unity by sending gifts to all our Jewish acquaintances. What's more, *mishloach manot* can go one step further, providing an opportunity to help repair broken relationships.

to include something among the goodies made by their own hand (home-baked hamantashen, for example), which is a commendable and meaningful practice that fulfills the intention of the observance. It is also meritorious for children to prepare *mishloach manot* to give in their own names. In doing so, they learn to focus on something other than "receiving."

BLOTTING OUT AMALEK

Therefore when the LORD your God grants you safety from all your enemies around you in the land that the LORD your God is giving you as a hereditary portion, you shall blot out the memory of Amalek from under heaven. Do not forget!
—Deut. 25:19

In 1947, David Ben Gurion, who would become the first prime minister of the State of Israel, appeared before the United Nations Special Commission on Palestine. He described the Jews as a people whose nature it is to remember.[56] We are constantly drawing upon and reliving events from the past—whether it is the Exodus from Egypt or the miracle of the Hanukkah oil—to understand what is happening in the present. On Purim, listening closely to every word of the Megillah, we are especially attuned to the name of Haman, who was a descendant of the tribe of Amalek. Each time Haman is mentioned, we stamp our feet, bang on the table, and whirl our noisemakers to blot out his name along with that of his ancestors. Amalek represents the most intense, unwavering human evil found in every generation. What do we know of this mysterious being?

In the Book of Exodus,[57] we learn only that after the splitting of the sea and before the giving of the Torah on Mount Sinai, the Israelites battled with the unidentified "Amalek." The Torah explains that "whenever Moses held up his hand, Israel prevailed; but whenever he let down his hand, Amalek prevailed." When Moses grew tired, two important people (Aaron and Hur[58]) supported his hands, while Joshua led the troops to full victory. Afterwards, God proclaimed, "I will utterly blot out the memory of Amalek from under heaven." In a curious contrast, two verses later, Moses adds that God will "be at war with Amalek throughout the ages."

The Book of Deuteronomy[59] recounts the same battle with Amalek and provides a few more details about the divine instruction through Moses to the Jews: "You shall blot out the memory of Amalek from under heaven." This passage explains that the Amalekites, "undeterred by fear of God," attacked the famished and weary Israelites and cut down the weakest and most defenseless, "all the stragglers" at the rear. The descendants of this tribe, who were themselves descendants of Esau ("troublesome twin brother of the patriarch Jacob"), have come to figuratively represent the ever-present evil on earth. The Torah identifies Amalek's evil nature, and God commands the Israelites to blot out the memory of Amalek and yet never to forget him.

Perhaps because of the paradoxical nature of this commandment—to both remember and forget—rabbinic literature, from early times to this day, expounds upon the significance of Amalek. The Zohar, the quintessential book of Jewish mysticism, goes so far as to say that Amalek is the embodiment of the *yetzer ha-ra* ("the inner impulse toward evil").[60] Many commentators expanded upon that belief by identifying Amalek as the biblical symbol for both spiritual and physical corruption.[61] The modern *Etz Hayim* commentary elucidates this point:

> *Amalek is the Torah's symbol of pure malice, attacking without cause. Some people commit crimes for profit or revenge, but Amalek acts that way for the sheer joy of hurting people. God's "war from generation to generation" is not only with the tribe of Amalek (which disappears early in the biblical period) but with those people in every generation who revel in cruelty and hatred.*[62]

The biblical account of Amalek resurfaces in the dramatic story in I Samuel, chapter 15, which depicts the theological reason for King Saul's demise. This passage is the prescribed haftarah (prophetic reading) for the Shabbat preceding Purim (*Shabbat Zakhor*—"Sabbath of Remembrance"). The prophet Samuel tells Saul that God commands him to take his army and destroy the Amalekites for their transgression against the Israelites when they fled from Egypt. Samuel includes God's instruction to "Spare no one..." and to destroy everyone and everything—including all livestock and items of value. Saul fails to follow God's command. He defeats Amalek, but gives over the best booty to his troops; and he spares the life of Agag, the king of the city of Amalek, whom he merely imprisons. Saul's act of defiance leads to his downfall and David's rise to the throne. In the end, Samuel fulfills the will of God and executes Agag himself.

Now we can see the direct genealogical and moral connection between Amalek and Purim. At the beginning of the third chapter of the Scroll of Esther, Haman is introduced as the son of Hamedatha the Agagite, who is the very same Agag spared by Saul and killed by Samuel. A midrash claims that while Agag was held in captivity, he somehow managed to impregnate a maidservant who conceived the ancestor of Haman.[63] So during the Megillah reading, when we drown out Haman's name with ringing, rattling, stomping, banging, and whistling, we are not merely booing the bad guy. We are hearkening back to the commandment given in Deuteronomy that we should blot out the memory of Amalek, here in the guise of Haman. The custom is unique to the boisterous spirit of Purim, as we do not attempt to drown out the name Amalek when we read from the Torah at various times during the year or the name Agag during the haftarah that precedes Purim.

SHAKE, RATTLE, AND RUB

The popular and traditional Purim noisemaker for blotting out Haman's name is called a *grager* (pronounced and sometimes spelled "grogger"). The name is Yiddish and comes from the Polish word for rattle. In Hebrew, the noisemaker is called a *ra'ashan*. Most *gragers* today are simple metal cases that spin on a ratchet mounted to a handle, although some are elaborately made pieces of Judaica. Children sometimes make their own *gragers* by putting beans or rice in a can. *Gragers* are usually decorated with designs of other Purim symbols, such as masks or hamantashen, and sometimes with the quote "cursed be Haman."

The custom of using noisemakers during the Megillah reading originated as an Ashkenazic practice and developed gradually. *Gragers* were first used by children in France and Germany, as early as the 9th century, who banged rocks together when Haman's name was mentioned.[64] Children also inscribed Haman's name on the soles of their shoes and stomped every time they heard his name. Communities in Holland and Germany erected stones with Haman's name on them and invited children and congregants to hammer the name off of the stone with rocks, thus literally blotting out his name.[65] Since those times, *gragers* have become one of the central symbols of Purim, especially because they promote the frivolity of the holiday and the involvement of children.

A Carnival of Illusions

As Jews, we spend our lives learning what it is to be holy, separating ourselves from what we consider to be base and uncivilized; yet as human beings, we undeniably continue to possess the more primitive tendencies. On one day each year—Purim— we are given the freedom to deliberately break down the barriers of our socially trained selves and are encouraged to reveal aspects of our being that are normally meant to be hidden. We do so by entering the Purim farce and constructing a world of illusion that rejects certain inhibitions.[66] Directing our energies toward artistry, song, dance, and fraternization, we are permitted to blow off steam. This open expression of self is a part of the overflowing Jewish spirituality that brings us full circle in the cycle of spiritual seasons. Perhaps this spirituality is what inspired the Rabbis to claim that although the Torah was given to the Israelites in the desert, it was not until Purim that it was officially reaccepted and confirmed by the Jewish people.[67]

Party Time

At some point during Purim, as part of the feast or in a separate celebration, the holiday takes on the nature of a carnival. Costumes, role-playing, and drunkenness are not merely permitted, but in fact encouraged. Even though they are unique and late-blooming in the repertoire of Jewish customs, these practices have long been part of the general human experience.

Wearing masks and acting out roles is one of the most ancient human rituals. We have evidence from cave paintings that prehistoric shamans wrapped themselves in animal skins and wore horned masks. It was believed that wearing a mask and, for example, acting as an animal, enabled one to commune with the spirit world, particularly the dead. In fact, the word mask or, alternatively "masque," is derived from the Latin word *masca*, meaning "dead person" or "ghost."

Costumes Only

Purim is often compared to Halloween because of the masquerading, yet any similarity stops there. Halloween developed from the ancient Celtic New Year (a time to thank the sun god for the harvest), November 1. It was believed that on the night before, October 31, the curtain between the material and spirit worlds collapsed, allowing evil demons to come in. Celts lit bonfires and offered sacrifices to honor Samhain, the lord of death, and to appease the evil spirits. In the 9th century, the Roman Catholic Church, presumably to usurp a pagan date and attract converts,[68] moved All Saints' Day from May 13 to November 1. The night before became hallowed (or holy) evening— "Hallowe'en." Transported to the United States by 19th-century immigrants, with the paganism and religion both diluted, Halloween has become an increasingly popular, totally secular holiday that is focused on masquerade. The Jewish religious celebration of Purim, with its story of redemption and joy, is clearly cut from a different cloth.

When a pagan wears a mask of an animal or legendary figure, the people participating in the rite believe that the mask has magical powers from the spirit world. These powers strip off the veil that covers the material world and reveal the supernatural, thus concealing one reality only to reveal another. The reasons for performing these rituals include the desire to chase away evil spirits, to aid hunters, to promote fertility, and to heal illness. Places where such ceremonies have been performed span the globe, including New Guinea, Africa, South America, and Ireland.

During the Greco-Roman period, theater became very popular. Actors commonly wore masks portraying the gods, especially the Greek Dionysus and the Roman Bacchus, the respective gods of wine, who also presided over communication between the living and dead. Masks and costumes enabled actors to better portray comic roles such as jesters or outrageous and ridiculous representations of the opposite sex. Also during this period, masquerading became a prominent part of carnivals and parades. Such processions had been conducted as far back as the times of ancient Egypt and originated as a way to mark the changing of seasons. They eventually were used to express the upending of earthly order, especially social order, and became a setting in which people mocked society. The rich dressed as the poor, the poor as the rich, and the wise as fools. Although a sense of the supernatural remained, a comical atmosphere emerged and grew throughout the Middle Ages and the European Renaissance.

Drunkenness was a key element in this release of inhibitions. In Greek theater, for example, not only the actors who portrayed Dionysus became intoxicated but also the audience, including the women. At medieval carnivals, raucousness was standard behavior, highlighted by blatant immodesty, sexual abandon, unbridled gluttony, and a general howling at the wind. In later centuries, carnivals such as the New Orleans Mardi Gras and the Brazilian Carnival have served as more than a toppling of social order and release of inhibition. They express intense artistic creativity and, despite the varying social strata of the participants, a communal oneness.

On some level, Purim shares many of the attributes of theater and of carnival. Embedded in the story of Esther and Mordecai are irony, comedy, and the overturning of social order. The story begins by masking the attributes of each character. As the scroll and the plot unfurls, the total accumulation of one ironic event after another results in an unexpected final outcome. The reversal of the fate of the characters is such that what could have been a tragedy becomes a comedy. The lowly Jews become powerful, the king and his senior minister are made to be fools, and near devastation turns to triumph.

It was not until the end of the 15th century that masquerading appeared as part of the Purim celebration. The cultural influence was the Catholic holiday season known as Carnival,[69] which occurs during the two weeks before Lent, around the time of Purim. At Carnival time people wore masks and took to the streets for a public celebration. One of the common costumes was clothing of the opposite gender— typically controversial for Jews since the Torah forbids a woman dressing as a man and vice versa.[70] Even so, many rabbis allowed cross-dressing on Purim as a way to add joyousness to the festival, and, according to Moses Isserles, the Ashkenazic authority whose rulings are included in the Shulchan Arukh, this position became an acceptable one.[71] Medieval rabbis also found talmudic justification for masquerading based on the name of the heroine of the Purim story—Esther—which

Safety First

Drunkenness has long been a part of Purim frivolity. The Talmud offers the authoritative opinion that one should become intoxicated on Purim until he or she is no longer able to distinguish (ad delo yada) between "cursed be Haman" and "blessed be Mordecai."[74] Yet as Rabbi Alexander Ziskind of Grodnow wrote in the 18th century, the Talmud does not explicitly use the word lehishtaker (to become drunk), an observation that teaches us we should drink just enough to lighten the heart. Rabbi Ziskind says that because the Jewish people have so often been burdened with sadness, just a little bit of wine is appropriate to help achieve the spiritual mood of thanksgiving and joy required on Purim.[75] In modern times, especially with our concerns about driving while intoxicated and the serving of alcohol to minors, such moderation— and even abstinence—can be very appropriate on Purim.

shares the same etymological root as the Hebrew word for "conceal" (*hester*).[72] Then as now, Jewish costuming primarily involved dressing as the one of the characters in the story of Purim.

As a further example of turning social order upside down, Purim became a time to play pranks and perform plays called *Purim-spiels.* It is difficult to know exactly when the latter began, but there is record of such *spiels* (Yiddish for "plays") in 16th-century Germany. *Purim-spiels* generally included a satire of the rabbi or other esteemed communal figures;[73] and sometimes there were interludes with jesters, acrobats, and ventriloquists. Many of the great Yiddish playwrights and actors who lived in Holland and Germany began as Purim players.

Echoing Themes in the Book of Esther

LIVING AMONG NON-JEWS

Many historians have noted that the survival of the Jewish people is undeniably remarkable, given the millennia of hatred and violence against Jews (who constantly remind themselves of this situation in prayer and ritual). The legacy of Jewish history and identity at this point is largely that of living as the "other," a small minority, away from the homeland of Israel amid foreign customs and in a variety of languages. Massacres, pogroms, blood libels, terrorist attacks, or extermination attempts have colored every generation of Jewish existence since the destruction of the Second Temple in 70 C.E. Truth be told, however, living as a very small minority among non-Jews has also offered some mutual benefits for both sides, such as financial relationships and the sharing of scholarship and ideas. Certainly, the interaction between Jew and non-Jew has made its mark on the development of many Jewish customs, proving that Judaism is certainly not outside of historical influence. Today America boasts of the best relationship between Jew and non-Jew that history has ever seen in a non-Jewish country. Yet, there is another side to this success. Through intermarriage and assimilation, a great many Jews are losing the core of their unique religious identity and history.

The challenges of living in the Diaspora are underscored when we read or hear about the Jews in the Purim story living under Persian rule. The Scroll of Esther and much of the Rabbinic commentary about it foreshadow the very tensions that Jews continue to face wherever they are in the minority. These tensions are manifest in the fear of being unjustly blamed for the problems of non-Jews—an accusation that usually leads to violence—and in the fear of having to abandon Jewish identity to, at the least, fit in, and, at the most, not be killed.

Anti-Semitism

"There is certain people, scattered and dispersed among other peoples in all the provinces of your realm, whose laws are different from those of any other people and who do not obey the king's laws; and it is not in Your Majesty's interest to tolerate them."
—Esther 3:8

In Haman's words to King Ahasuerus, we see three of the most common attitudes found in anti-Semitism that have plagued Jews throughout the ages:

- hostility toward them as strangers when ruled by other nations,
- suspicion of their segregated customs and religious practices,
- fear of their disloyalty and harm to the state.[76]

Jews have witnessed the continuous ebb and flow of anti-Semitism (sad to say, most often flowing) century after century just about everywhere they have lived. Yet for Jews who have not lived directly in the shadow of anti-Semitism, the seeming realities of their own experience may cause them to regard anti-Semitism as unsubstantiated or not applicable to them. Perhaps because of their own notable, straightforward Jewish values of respecting differences, loving one's neighbors, and abiding by *dina de-malchuta dina* (loosely, "the laws of the land"),[77] they do not recognize the masked versions of anti-Semitism, such as hatred of the State of Israel.[78]

In the Talmud, three sages who lived during the 3rd to 4th centuries have a striking discussion about such a precarious Jewish attitude toward anti-Semitism. Their conversation regards the story of Purim. They ask why *Hallel* (a group of additional psalms of thanksgiving), which is usually said on festive occasions, is not included in the prayer service on Purim.

Rabbi Hiyya ben Avin said in the name of Rabbi Joshua ben Korcha [1st century Israel]: *"If for being delivered from slavery to freedom we chant a hymn of praise, should we not do so all the more for being delivered from death to life? If that is the reason, shouldn't we say* Hallel *also* [at Purim]*?"* ... *Rabbi Nachman said: "The reading of the Megillah is equivalent to Hallel." Rava said: "There is a good reason in that case* [of the Exodus from Egypt] *because it says* [in Hallel]*, O servants of the* LORD*, give praise,*[79] *who are no longer servants of Pharaoh. But can we say in this case, O servants of the* LORD *and not servants of Ahasuerus? We are sill servants of Ahasuerus!"*[80]

We learn specific and universal truths from that discussion. Even though Purim is a celebration of God's love of the Jewish people, wherein they are saved from death, God does not redeem them for national purposes, as occurs in the story of the Exodus from Egypt. The Exodus is an act of national redemption and, in turn, provides psychological freedom to a people thereby injected with self-determination. The salvation in the Purim account provides no reward of national freedom. In the end, the Jews are saved only to serve their non-Jewish ruler, Ahasuerus. They are still subject to his whim and that of the royalty who succeed him. For Rava in the Talmud, such a situation was a reality, because he actually lived under the continuing rule of the Persians. The point he makes about Purim should speak to all Jews, especially to those who live under any rule other than their own. History teaches that Jews can never become complacent about any government. As David Hartman, a modern Jewish philosopher explains, "We celebrate Purim, but without singing *Hallel*, because we are celebrating a reprieve from death in a world where murderous evil forces continue to be a threat."[81]

Intermarriage

When reading the Purim story, we might easily expect the subject of intermarriage between the Persian king, Ahasuerus, and the Jewish queen, Esther, to have been examined over the years, yet the topic tends to have been ignored. In today's world when intermarriage is particularly common and often considered the most significant contributor to the decreasing Jewish population,[82] the theme presented within Purim is ripe for examination.

Traditional Judaism has been able to generally overlook this issue because odd marriages occur with some frequency in the Bible, including that of Jacob and Leah (a marriage of a patriarch and a matriarch based on deception); Judah and Tamar (a marriage based on a man unknowingly impregnating his daughter-in-law), and David and Bathsheba (a marriage that grows out of adultery between a great king and the wife of his close friend). The most obvious parallel to the story of Esther is found in the behavior of the patriarch Abraham married to the matriarch Sarah. They are traveling together through foreign lands, and she is disguised as his sister. On two separate occasions, Abraham, to save his own life and ultimately both of their lives, has Sarah hide her identity. This action leads to her becoming a wife of the local king, first of Pharoah and then of Abimelech.[83] Abraham and Sarah are reunited and live to be the parents of the Jewish nation. In the Purim story, Mordecai, residing in a land ruled by strangers, advises Esther not to reveal her family origins or Jewish identity. She marries the local king, and this action saves that very same Jewish nation.

Rashi, the great medieval commentator, justifies the marriage between Esther and Ahasuerus by claiming that Esther went against her will and married the king only because she would receive the opportunity to help the Jewish people.[84] The mystical text of the Zohar goes so far to say that the *Shekhinah* (God's presence) concealed Esther's soul and sent another soul in its place; when the king slept with the queen, she was not the real Esther.[85]

The Talmud adds another twist. Esther was Mordecai's cousin, and we learn in chapter 2 of the Megillah that Esther's parents died. The Talmud is of the opinion that Mordecai took her for his wife,[86] which would lead to the shocking conclusion that Mordecai encouraged his own wife to marry the king. Therefore, we would have a situation even more similar to that of Abraham and Sarah. Not only is there a case of intermarriage between a Jewish woman and a non-Jewish king but Esther's adultery is at the instruction of her husband. Even the Greek translation of the Bible, the Septuagint, which preceded the Talmud, affirms this interpretation—further evidence that this view of the relationship is of ancient origin.[87]

In medieval times, many of the well-known rabbis and commentators, including Nachmanides (13th century; Spain and Israel) and Abarbanel (15th century; Spain) avoid these extremely difficult topics.[88] Those who do address the intermarriage and adultery found in the Purim story seem puzzled; they completely sidestep the personal aspect of such complex marital relationships by focusing their comments on the practical and halakhic (legal) issues surrounding the maintenance of two separate marriages.

In the 16th century, more attention was given to the complicated relationship of Esther and Ahasuerus. In the work called *Menot Ha-Levi*,[89] kabbalist Solomon ben Moses Ha-Levi Alkabetz directs himself to the line of thinking used by the Rabbis of the Talmud and found in midrashim. Exploring various nuances of Jewish law, he justifies and explains away the controversial and difficult aspects of the relationship between the Jewish queen and the gentile king.[90] Given our consideration today of the sociological effects of intermarriage in the current Diaspora, Alkabetz's technical approach does not provide a sufficient perspective. In contrast, during the season of Purim, we have begun to see the story of Esther as a holiday-based opportunity for discussing intermarriage and its impact on Jews personally and communally.

CHANCE, GOD, OR *MAZAL*

When we read through the Purim story, we notice the extraordinary number of times chance plays a part in the developments and the positive results it brings for the Jews. By chance, Esther becomes queen; by chance, Mordecai overhears the conspiracy against Ahasuerus; by chance, Ahasuerus stays up one night and happens to learn of the chronicle that recorded Mordecai's life-saving role; by chance, Haman enters just as Ahasuerus is thinking of how to reward Mordecai; and by chance, Ahasuerus is in a willing mood to receive Esther's every request. Chance seems to dictate the turn of every major event in the tale.

In his 1985 book on the Jewish holidays, Rabbi Michael Strassfeld interprets the role of chance as part of Purim's farcical nature, intended to contribute to the mood of fantasy and festivity. He writes: "The numerous plot devices also point to the whimsical nature of the story. Why does Vashti refuse to come before the king? Why is Esther told to keep her identity secret? Why is Mordechai not immediately rewarded for saving the king from the plot against his life? Why does Mordechai refuse to bow down to Haman? The answer, of course, is that without these contrivances the plot could not have reached its grand conclusion."[91]

We do not traditionally associate chance with God. In every book of the Bible, except the Scroll of Esther (and the Song of Songs), God orchestrates the outcome of each occurrence, either explicitly or from behind the scenes. But the Megillah makes absolutely no mention of God.[92] This characteristic has been interpreted in various ways. For example, if the Book of Esther is sending the message that luck is just as powerful as God, the story's outlook flies in the face of nearly all other perspectives of Jewish theology and by doing so must certainly be farce. Such a view—that the absence of God's name underscores the fantasy aspect of the story—echoes Strassfeld's point about the meaning of the nonsensical and ludicrous nature of Purim. Biblical scholar Adele Berlin, goes one step further, seeing the omission of God's name as intentional and preferable. She says: "The best explanation for [the omission of absence of sacred matters in the Book of Esther], especially the absence of God's name, is that, given that the story is so comic, at times bordering on lewd, such reticence about things religious is preferable, lest religion be debauched."[93]

Could it be, instead, that God's obvious absence from this biblical story actually underscores God's very presence in the world? Might this absence have spoken a clear and direct message to Jews living in the Diaspora, who were well versed in the biblical cautions about living outside the Holy Land under the rule of omnipotent kings? For example, in another book of the Bible, the First Book of Samuel, there is an explicit account of what happens to people who choose to follow an earthly sovereign rather than following God: "He [the king] will take your daughters as perfumers, cooks, and bakers. He will seize your choice fields, vineyards, and olive groves, and give them to his courtiers. He will take a tenth part of your grain and vintage and give it to his eunuchs and courtiers. ... He will take a tenth part of your flocks, and you shall become his slaves. The day will come when you cry out because of the king" (1 Sam. 8:13–8).

Along these lines, one might see Ahasuerus as personifying the worst possible representation of a king according to biblical standards. The reader of the story would be prompted to inquire about God's presence and wonder whether or not God will tolerate the sort of royal behavior described in the first chapter of Esther, in which there is a very lengthy wine orgy and a ridiculous decree that bans disrespect to husbands.[94] Jewish readers might thus see the actions of Mordecai and the crowning of Esther as God's merciful management from behind the scenes, with God's presence being manifest in the lives of these two people. For ancient Jewish audiences, this concept is rather boldly displayed: Esther and Mordecai were likely named after the two most popular Persian gods, Ishtar and Marduk. The choice of names is a comical wink at audiences, as if to say, "Of course God is present, even in the places you'd least expect it." Each seemingly chance encounter that favored Esther and Mordecai was actually a sign of God's influence.

Written in the Stars

Theologians continue to be concerned about ways to address the role of chance in life versus historical developments directed by an active God. The tension is never satisfactorily resolved in the Jewish tradition, but an examination of the word *mazal*, which in modern Hebrew is the word for "luck," may be helpful to our understanding. People are familiar with this word because of the common expression *mazal tov!* used to express congratulations or wishes for a successful outcome. Although the translation is "good luck" (literally, "luck good"), in fact the historical definition of the word *mazal* is "constellation" and is related to astrology. Thus, when Jews say *mazal tov*, they are pronouncing a relic of astrological beliefs. The expression announces that the moment is evident of a "good sign"—a sign that the event has been positively ordained in the stars.[95]

Astrology holds that a person's fate is determined and influenced by the constellation or sign under which he or she was born; and it has been a part of Judaism to greater or lesser degrees, depending upon place and time. In Israel, the ancient synagogues at Beit Alpha and at Tzipori[96] had zodiac calendars depicted in their mosaic floors (still extant); and Kabbalah, which became a thriving force in the 16th century, certainly took astrology as a possible avenue to divine secrets.[97] The mainstream tradition sometimes claims that astrology is in conflict with Judaism, although these concerns are primarily cautions against astrological soothsayers and divination.[98]

Even the Talmud, a work of intense religiosity, records a variety of opinions on divine guidance in the heavenly bodies. In one place it says that each human being is born under the providence of a planet and in another that a planet controls Israel's destiny.[99] In tractate *Shabbat*, a story is told that provides an example of the role of constellations—a story that concerns no less than the venerated Rabbi Akiva. In it, a soothsayer predicts that Rabbi Akiva's daughter will die from a snakebite on the night of her marriage.[100] After she gives her portion of the banquet meal to a poor person, a poisonous snake is found dead in the bridal chamber. Because of the soothsayer's thwarted prediction, Rabbi Yochanan (compiler of the Jerusalem Talmud, 3rd century) deduces from this incident that "there is no *mazal* for Israel (*ein mazal leYisrael*), but only for the nations that recognize the validity of astrology." To a certain extent, he is saying that Judaism has power greater than that of astrology. Yet tension and contradiction are inherent in that thought, because a person has to be a believer in astrology to be persuaded by Rabbi Yochanan's perspective.

DEBATE OVER THE SCROLL

Superstition and astrology pervaded the world for thousands of years. We can imagine how the Scroll of Esther, in which good fortune befalls the Jews without the openly visible involvement of God, may have played a role in the controversy that existed about its inclusion in the Bible. There is no scholarly consensus about when the canon (from the Greek for "model," or "standard") of the Bible was set; but most opinions date it between 200 B.C.E. and 200 C.E. Scholars generally hold that the third of the three sections, Kethuvim (The Writings), comprises the material that was accepted last. Among the decisions about what to include, the Song of Songs, Kohelet (Ecclesiastes), and Esther cause the most controversy in the Rabbinic discussions that take place in the Talmud. The probable reason is that these three books lack any expression of God's most sacred name—the Tetragrammaton (the four letters *yud, heh, vav, heh*).[101]

The Talmud, dating from approximately the 4th to 6th centuries, assumes the established canon of the Bible; and yet the Rabbis were later uncomfortable with the Book of Esther and debated its holy status. One remarkable talmudic legend, from the tractate *Megillah*, tells of Esther herself inciting the *chachamim* (sages) to include her book so that the events could be commemorated. The Rabbis seem to deny her request at first; they claim that her story may bring ill will from other nations, because it celebrates their downfall. Esther presses further and points out that the kings of Persia have already recorded the story. She contends that the sages should record her account not for its holy status but for the sake of posterity.[104] Although this explanation is folkloric, its presence in the Talmud tells us something about the Rabbis. It reveals that they themselves needed help comprehending the motivation for including the Scroll of Esther in the Bible.

What's in a Name?

To understand how the Jews, without explicit divine providence, could overcome Haman's evil scheme, the Rabbis ask a question: "From where does the Torah bring the name Esther?" The Talmud teaches that God is indeed present in the story of Purim, and the clue is in Esther's name. It has the same Hebrew root, *samech.tet.resh.* as the word for "hidden." The Rabbis' understanding comes from a verse in Deuteronomy: "Yet I will keep My countenance hidden on that day, because of all the evil they have done in turning to other gods."[102] With the name Esther thus derived from the phrase, "My countenance hidden" *(haster astir panai),*[103] we learn that God is present through Esther, but concealed, that the foreshadowing in the Torah validates having the book in the biblical canon, and that the Jews' suffering was God's punishment for idolatry.

Defiling the Hands

The tractate *Megillah* contains another debate over the canonization of certain books in Kethuvim. This argument may offer the most insight about the unique status of Esther:

> *Rabbi Judah* [3rd century, Israel] *said in the name of Samuel* [2nd to 3rd centuries; Babylonia], *"The Scroll of Esther does not defile the hands. Are we to infer from this that Samuel rules that Esther was not written under divine inspiration? How can this be, considering that Samuel himself said that Esther was written under divine inspiration? Rather* [Samuel rules] *that it was intended to be recited by heart and not written."*[105]

These few lines of Talmud are certainly riddled with questions. What is the meaning of "defiling the hands," and what does it mean for a biblical book to defile the hands? Furthermore, what does the defiling of hands have to do with canonization of a book, if anything at all?

Maimonides defines the concept of "defiling the hands" as a talmudic enactment used to physically preserve sacred texts.[106] During the time of the Temple (up until 70 C.E.), people were storing the *terumah* (the grain and produce given to the priests) next to sacred scrolls. As a result, mice, rats, and weasels scavenging for food ate their way through the scrolls as well. To prevent the storing of food and scrolls together, the Rabbis later initiated decrees that would act as deterrents. One decree was that sacred scrolls (e.g., biblical scrolls) defile the hands, meaning render the hands ritually impure. Since one must have ritually pure hands to handle the *terumah*, one could not safely touch the scrolls before touching the food; the scrolls would defile the hands and then the hands would defile the food, rendering it unusable. This decree provided a solution. Because no one wanted to ruin the *terumah*; they would not place the food anywhere near the scrolls. Thus the most sacred scrolls, the ones the Rabbis most wanted to protect from ruin, were considered to be the ones that defile the hands.[107]

For talmudists, a scroll's theoretical ability to defile the hands was one way to know whether it was part of the canon. In other words, the Rabbis held that the scrolls that defile the hands are the most sacred and are more likely to be part of the canon. In the discussion over Esther's status, they question whether or not her scroll is sacred enough to defile the hands. Rabbi Judah points out a seeming contradiction: The sage Samuel said that the Scroll of Esther does not defile the hands, yet Samuel also believed that Esther was "written under divine inspiration" and therefore, Judah says, would defile the hands.

Rabbis continued to have disputes about Samuel's position and how it should affect treatment of the book in Jewish law, and these arguments were filled with nuance and complexity on both sides.[108] Some notable halakhists, such as Maimonides who thought it did defile the hands, viewed the Book of Esther on a par with the rest of Kethuvim. Others, such as Moses Isserles, ruled to the contrary.[109] Ultimately, all these arguments over the status and canonization of Esther are *post facto,* because, as Rav Hai Gaon from 10th-century Babylonia conceded: "Does not all of Israel consider Esther to be in the Bible?"[110]

·✦— Purim —✦·
Pathways Through the Sources

Jerusalem Talmud
God's Acceptance of Purim

The Jerusalem Talmud, one of two versions of the Talmud, was written by Rabbinical scholars living in the northern part of Israel. They named it after their longed-for, beloved city of Jerusalem from which the Jews had been banished by the Romans. It was completed in the 5th century.

The Rabbis of the Talmud found it difficult to reconcile the differing opinions about biblical canonization of the Book of Esther. In this text, they pose a fascinating question: Is it worthwhile for Jews to dwell so much on the remembrance of oppression? Their discussion revolves around the layers of meaning concealed within the book itself.

> The Rabbis said: "Have we not had enough of impending oppressions? Do you want to increase them by recalling the oppression of Haman?" Rabbi Samuel ben Nachman [3rd century; Israel] said in the name of Rabbi Jonathan [Samuel's teacher], "Eighty-five elders, including more than thirty prophets have been unwilling to grant recognition to the Feast of Purim. They said, 'Moses told us that no prophet should add anything to the Law from now and henceforth; and yet Mordecai and Esther desired to create and establish a new institution!' They did not cease to ponder over it, until God opened their eyes and they found justification for it written in the Law, the Prophets and the Writings."
> —J. Talmud, *Megillah* 1:5

Babylonian Talmud
Recognizing the Limits

Judaism is not an ascetic religion, denying bodily pleasures. Wine and drink are recognized as legitimate expressions of delight and joy. For Purim, we are asked to go even further, beyond basic pleasure, and imbibe to the point where reality is blurred—perhaps because toppling our conventional mental order once a year can provide the freedom for deeper insight into life. Whatever the case, whether drinking is for joy on Shabbat or intoxication on Purim, we are always held responsible, always given limits. Drunkenness for adults may be condoned on Purim, but not a drunkenness of reckless abandon.

The most comprehensive version of the Talmud was completed in the 6th century by scholars living in Babylon, the center of world Jewry after 70 C.E.. One of its tractates is *Megillah,* which essentially deals with rules pertaining to the recitation of the Scroll of Esther. The following selection from this tractate is, however, more about the spirit and experience of Purim and less about the rules concerning its observance. The discussion involves three well-known talmudists of the 3rd to 4th centuries.

> Rava said: "It is one's duty to become intoxicated on Purim until he cannot tell the difference between 'cursed be Haman' and 'blessed be Mordecai.' "[111]
>
> Rabbah[112] and Rabbi Zeira got together for a Purim feast. They became intoxicated and Rabbah rose up and cut Rabbi Zeira's throat. On the next day he prayed on his behalf and revived him. The next year Rabbah asked, "Will your Honor come and we'll have a Purim feast together?" Rabbi Zeira replied, "One cannot count on a miracle happening every time."
> —B. Talmud, *Megillah* 7b

Babylonian Talmud
Manifold Irony

The Purim story is a satire. Within the story, everything that one expects to happen is turned on its head, resulting in a comedy of ironies. This *aggadah* (folkloric anecdote of an incredible event) from the Talmud expands upon the already inherent irony in the story to the point of hilarious absurdity. Despite the tragic ending, we must remember that the story was probably never taken as a historical reality. Awareness of its fictional characteristics allows us to laugh, because tragedy, especially when it befalls the wicked, is a major part of the spirit of comedy.

> *So Haman took the garb and the horse and arrayed Mordecai and paraded him through the city square* ... (Esther 6:11). Haman went and found Mordecai sitting with the Rabbis.... When Mordecai saw him approaching and leading the horse, he became afraid and said to the Rabbis, "This villain is coming to kill me. Get out of his way so that you won't get into trouble with him...."
>
> Haman then said to him, "Arise and put on this apparel and ride on this horse, for this is what the king desires of you."
>
> Mordecai replied, "I cannot do so until I have gone in the bath and cut my hair, for it would not be good manners to use the king's clothes as I am."

At this time, however, Esther had all the baths and barbershops closed [as part of the three-day proclamation for all to fast]. Therefore, Haman himself took Mordecai into the bath and washed him, and then went and brought scissors from his house and cut his hair. While he was doing so, he sighed and groaned.

Mordecai asked him, "Why do you sigh?"

He replied, "The man who was the king's most esteemed noble is now made to be a bath attendant and a barber…." After Haman cut Mordecai's hair and clothed him, he said to Mordecai, "Get up [on the horse] and ride."

Mordecai replied, "I can't. I'm too weak from the days of fasting."

So, Haman stooped down and allowed Mordecai to mount the horse from his back ….

As Haman was leading him through the street where Haman lived, his daughter who was standing on the roof saw him. She thought that the man on the horse was her father and the man leading the horse was Mordecai. So she took a chamber pot and emptied it on the head of her father. He looked up and when she saw that it was her father, she threw herself from the roof to the ground and killed herself.

—B. Talmud, *Megillah* 16a

Midrash

Darkness Must Precede Light

At times, the world can feel very unsafe, and we can easily fall into doubt and despair. Jews have experienced more grief over a longer period of time than any other people in history. Yet we have survived, maintaining faith in our relationship with God and a hope that we will achieve redemption. At its core, Purim is a holiday that teaches us hope. Even though darkness falls, we must remain strong and resolute in our knowledge that light does come.

Midrash, a term derived from the three-letter Hebrew root *dalet.resh.shin.*, meaning to "to seek" or "to investigate," is a collection of interpretations and explanations of biblical texts. The various collections were compiled and edited at different times; very often with the authors not identified. Midrash on Psalms *(Midrash Tehillim)* is a later collection (first known appearance in the 11th century) that comprises teachings and moral lessons based on verses in the Book of Psalms.

> In the verse "For the leader; on *ayyeleth ha-shahar* [the hind of dawn] (Psalms 22:1)," Scripture speaks of the generation of Mordecai and Esther [a time that was more dark than] the night. For though it was night, one has the light of the moon, the stars, and the planets. Then when is it really dark? Just before dawn! After the moon sets and the stars set and the planets vanish, there is no darkness deeper than the hour before dawn, and in that hour the Holy One answers the world and all that is in it: out of the darkness, he brings forth the dawn and gives light to the world.

> Then, too, why is Esther likened to the hind of the dawn? What is true of the light of dawn? Its light rays out as it rises; at the beginning, light comes little by little; then it spreads wider and wider, grows and increases; and at last it bursts into shining glory. So, too, Israel's redemption through Esther came about little by little....

> The sages said: When a hind is thirsty, she digs a hole, fixes her horns in it, and in her distress cries softly to the Holy One. The Holy One causes the deep to come up, and the deep causes water to spring up for her. So, too, Esther: when wicked Haman decreed cruel decrees against Israel, she, in her distress, began to cry softly in prayer to the Holy One, and the Holy One answered her.
> —Midrash on Ps., 22:13 [113]

Rashi on Ta'anit

Season of Miracles

Each season and month carries its own mood and character. Elul, for example, is the fall month that precedes Rosh Hashanah and Yom Kippur; and as such, it is building toward a time of self-assessment and judgment. At the opposite side of the Jewish year is the spring month of Adar and the holiday of Purim, a time for much gaiety. The different flavors of the yearly cycle of Jewish holidays help us to experience the wholeness of the human spirit.

The season of Purim is brought into focus here by the great commentator on the Bible and the Talmud, Rashi (acronymn for Rabbi Shlomo Yitzchaki). He was born in France in the 11th century, five centuries after the Babylonian Talmud was completed. With exceptional directness and clarity, Rashi's commentary explains the principles and concepts of daily prayers, commandments, and holiday celebrations.

> When the month of Adar begins we increase joy.
> Rashi 's commentary: *For these are the days that usher in the great miracles of Purim and Passover.*
> —B. Talmud, *Ta'anit* 29a

Maimonides

Reviving the Spirits of the Lowly

There is an aspect of Jewish law that emphasizes being thoughtful and considerate of people who are in need. This spiritual undercurrent, subtly present in the practice of Judaism, teaches that once we accept being responsible for one another, it is obvious that we must all share whatever material wealth we have—great or modest—with others. Maimonides, the 12th-century philosopher and legalist, was a champion at passing on this ideal. His *Mishneh Torah* incorporates the principles of Jewish faith and world outlook into the great body of talmudic literature. In *Hilkhot Megillah,* the section on the laws of Purim, he says that we best express our joy during Purim by giving to others, not by focusing extensively on our own pleasure and amusement.

> It is preferable for a person to be more liberal with his donations to the poor than to be lavish in his [preparation of the Purim] feast or in sending portions to his friends. For there is no greater and more splendid happiness than to gladden the hearts of the poor, the orphans, the widows, and the converts.
>
> One who brings happiness to the hearts of these unfortunate individuals resembles the Divine Presence, which [Isa. 57:15] describes [as having the tendency] of "reviving the spirits of the lowly, reviving the hearts of the contrite."[14]
> —Maimonides

Solomon Alkabetz

The Secret of Esther's Success

Jewish mysticism asserts that what happens in this world directly relates to what occurs in the heavenly realm. Such a perspective adds tremendous depth to our understanding of the lives not only of our ancestors but also of our own: What we do in our lives resonates all the way to God. Accordingly, if we carefully examine the words of the sacred text, we can discover profundity within the inner workings of the universe. This commentary by Rabbi Solomon Alkabetz, a 16th-century master kabbalist of Tzfat (in northern Israel), presents hidden levels of meaning from the Book of Esther that illustrate God's behind-the-scenes role in the world.

> *Then I shall go to the king* ... (Esther 4:16). Rabbi Yosef Gackon writes, concerning Esther's three-day fast that Esther had the following kabbalistic intention. Namely, that three days and nights contain seventy-two hours, and the word *b'chen* [translated as "then" in 4:16] has a numerical equivalence of seventy-two, corresponding to the [seventy-two-letter] Name of God....
>
> From that Name, the Divine life-force came to Esther's supernal *sefirah* [her corresponding divine emanation], for Esther was greenish in complexion [and green is the color for the *sefirah* of *chesed*, lovingkindness].
>
> Esther, with the power of these seventy-two hours, approached the King of the Universe in her prayers and could be sure of God's help. Then, in this physical world, she approached King Ahasuerus.[115]
> —Solomon Alkabetz

Sefat Emet
Out of Love Alone

Purim sits on the Jewish calendar on the opposite side of the year from Yom Kippur. The contrast is not only seasonal; the holidays also represent opposing spiritual identities. Yom Kippur is a day of physical abstention, whereas Purim is a day of physical indulgence. Yom Kippur is solemn, whereas Purim is merry.

The great Hasidic rabbi Yehuda Aryeh Leib Alter of Ger (b. 1847–d. 1904; Poland) was known by the name of his five-volume commentary on the Torah and holidays—*Sefat Emet* (literally, "The Language of Truth"). He makes the additional distinction that on Yom Kippur we are judged and must earn our merit, whereas on Purim our merit is simply given to us.

> [On Purim we sing:] "You have been their salvation forever; their hope from one generation to the next."

The salvation on Purim was eternal, for all generations. Just as the decree was "to destroy all the Jews" (Esther 3:13), so does the miracle apply to all generations. The Jewish people exist only by virtue of this miracle. It has been taught that in this case there was a heavenly decree against the Jews, but that God acted miraculously without regard to their merit.... That is why this holiday gives us such strength and hope, throughout the exile, to trust in God simply because we are joined to him.

This seems to be why one is obligated to become so drunk on Purim that one cannot tell the difference between "Blessed be Mordecai!" and "Cursed be Haman!" We thereby show that this day has nothing at all to do with our merit. It is called Purim because of the casting of lots; the fate [of destruction] was entirely natural and appropriate, the forces of evil having been strengthened by our own sins. God saved us out of love alone....

It is taught that Purim is like the Day of Atonement, called *Yom Ki-Purim*.[116] On Yom Kippur we reach beyond the natural state of negating our bodies, by abstaining from food and drink. This brings us to a certain freedom, one where transgressions are forgiven. On Purim we get to the same place by means of drinking and merrymaking, all with the help of God, not because of our own deeds.[117]
—Sefat Emet

Mordecai Kaplan
The Jewish Minority

For two millenia, most Jews have lived far outside of the Land of Israel in the Disapora, where they have been largely tossed about by whichever despot ruled the day. Now as ever before, the story of Purim continues to be understood as a paradigm for Jewish subjugation and anti-Semitism.

Rabbi Mordecai Kaplan, born in Lithuania in 1881, was ordained in New York in 1902 by the Jewish Theological Seminary. He would later develop his philosophy that Judaism is an "evolving religious civilization of the Jewish people" that must be continually reconstructed.[118] In the following paragraph from his 1937 book *The Meaning of God in Modern Jewish Religion*, Kaplan suggests that we should use the Purim celebration as a time to reassess the risks of living under the rule of any nation that is not the Jewish nation and to consider how we can be strong, overcome the dangers, and survive.

It is therefore necessary as it is appropriate, to make of the Feast of Purim, and of the special Sabbath preceding it, an occasion for considering anew the difficulties that inhere in our position as "a people scattered and dispersed among the nations." It is important that Jews know the nature of these difficulties in order that they may better equip themselves to meet them. Those days should make Jews conscious of the spiritual values which their position as a minority group everywhere in the Diaspora should lead them to evolve, and of the dangers which they must be prepared to overcome, if they expect to survive as a minority group.[19]
—Mordecai Kaplan

H. L. Ginsberg
The Intent of Esther's Author

Scholars essentially concur that the scroll of Esther is not a factual account. The book was probably written about 400–300 B.C.E. (toward the end of the Persian Empire) and likely based on a local legend about the characters Mordecai, Esther, and Haman. That legend was adapted to explain the origins of the Jewish observance of Purim, a holiday whose foundations had been heretofore obscure. Whatever the case, biblical scholar H. L. Ginsberg, in his introduction to the Book of Esther in *Five Megilloth and Jonah,* reminds us that the story must be taken seriously because of its spiritual and intellectual worth.

> According to [the Book of Esther] this feast of Purim originated in the escape of the Jewish people from a threat of total annihilation. From the way the story is told, however, it is fairly evident that though its core may well be such peril and deliverance, they cannot have happened exactly in the manner related. For the Book of Esther may be described, if one stretches a point or two, as a mock-learned disquisition to be read as the opening of a carnival-like celebration. ... Must we conclude, then, that our author was a religiously indifferent man? Not at all. The holiday whose cause he was pleading was, in his time no less than in ours, not one of solemnity but one of licit levity. ... If the book is read in the spirit in which it is written, all misgivings—on the scores of both credibility and spirituality—will be dissipated, the very extravagances and historical improbabilities will be relished, and the ingenuity of the plot will be admired.[120]
> —H. L. Ginsberg

·+— Purim —+·
Interpretations of Sacred Texts

The texts in these pages, each studied at multiple levels, are from three sources: the Book of Exodus, the Babylonian Talmud, and the Book of Deuteronomy. One of the *parshiyot* (weekly Torah portions) in Exodus is *Ki Tissa'*, which includes the commandment for a census. *Sotah* (literally, "Wayward Wife") and *Kiddushin* (literally, "Betrothal") are two tractates of the Babylonian Talmud, a work structured solely by free association among ideas, incidents, and personalities. Deuteronomy, the fifth book of the Torah, reviews much of the law and history recorded in the preceding four.

THE THREE LEVELS
Peshat: simple, literal meaning
Derash: historical, rabbinical inquiry
Making It Personal: contemporary analysis and application

A Half Shekel to Jewish Unity

The LORD [said]: When you take a census of the Israelite people according to their enrollment, each shall pay the LORD a ransom for himself on being enrolled, that no plague may come upon them through their being enrolled. This is what everyone who is entered in the record shall pay: a half-shekel by the sanctuary weight—a half-shekel as an offering to the LORD.... The rich shall not pay more and the poor shall not pay less than half a shekel when giving the LORD's offering as expiation for your persons. You shall take the expiation money from the Israelites and assign it to the service of the Tent of Meeting; ...
—Exod. 30:11–16

Peshat
During the times of the Temple, each Jew, rich and poor alike, was duty bound to contribute an annual half shekel (1 shekel equals 0.4 ounce of silver coin) for the upkeep of the Temple and for the communal sacrifices. The all-encompassing method of collection served as a way to count the nation, since taking a direct census was forbidden.[121] The amount was due on the 1st of Nissan (the month following Adar), the beginning of the new year for matters concerning the Temple[122] and a good time to ensure sufficient funds for Passover. (B. Talmud, *Megillah* 29b).

On the first Sabbath of Adar, this passage is read as the *maftir* (the supplementary Torah reading), in addition to a special haftarah (a reading from The Prophets) denoting the practice of contributing to the Temple treasury. The seasonal timing of the *maftir* and the haftarah reminded people of the need to donate funds (Mishnah, *Megillah* 1:1, 3:4). This *maftir* is the source for the ongoing Purim custom of collecting a half portion of the local currency from each Jew. Even though the Temple no longer exists, we use the money for upkeep of the synagogue or for donation to the poor.

Derash

From the Torah reading itself, the direct connection is not readily apparent between Purim and the collection of *mahatzit ha-shekel* (half shekel) for the month of Nissan. The Talmud associates the shekels mentioned in this text with those that Haman offers Ahasuerus for the right to eliminate the Jews.[123]

Reish Lakish[124] [3rd century, Israel] said: "It is obvious and known to He Who spoke the world into being that Haman was destined to weigh out shekels against Israel [to pay the king 10,000 talents[125] of silver to kill the Jews]. God therefore had His shekels precede those of Haman. And this is why the Mishnah teaches: 'On the first of Adar we announce the requirement to bring shekels'" (*Megillah* 13b).

According to the Talmud, the timing of the half-shekel payment for God's sanctuary and the timing of Purim are linked through the use of money. The tradition of the God-directed half-shekel donation was implemented before the time when Haman's evil plot was hatched and subsequently failed. Thus, the Rabbis tell us, the merit of the Jews' contribution protected them against the future evil designs of Haman—a sort of preemptive spiritual inoculation, goodness against evil.[126]

Making It Personal

Throughout the month of Adar and on Purim, we are bound together as a community. Yom Kippur, which falls on the opposite side of the calendar's cycle, is when we practice introspection; Purim is the holiday when we go outward. We put on costumes and act as something other than ourselves. Prayer is peripheral, whereas going out into the community, singing and dancing together, and giving to others, is core to observing Purim.

The giving of a half shekel or a half dollar has both straightforward and symbolic meanings. When everyone contributes the same modest amount, everyone is accounted for and everyone has an equal stake in the deed. Symbolically, each individual is represented by a half unit of currency, not a whole. The only way to become whole is by partnering and giving to the rest of the community. Indeed, we always retain our own individual half—a half that is between each of us and God; but the other half we give over to our people. The half-shekel lesson is that only by giving half of ourselves to our community do we become whole.

THE THREE LEVELS
Peshat: simple, literal meaning
Derash: historical, rabbinical inquiry
Making It Personal: contemporary analysis and application

The Anxiety of Redemption

Moses died on the seventh of Adar and was born on the seventh of Adar.

—B. Talmud, *Sotah* 12b

How do we know that he passed away on the seventh of Adar? Because it is said: *So Moses the servant of the LORD died there,* and it is written, *And the Israelites bewailed Moses in the steppes of Moab for thirty days* (Deut. 34:5–8). And it is also written: *After the death of Moses the servant of the LORD* (Josh. 1:1), as well as, *My servant Moses is dead. Prepare to cross the Jordan* (1:2) and, *Go through the camp and charge the people thus: Get provisions ready, for in three days' time you are to cross the Jordan* (1:11), and, *The people came up from the Jordan on the tenth day of the first month* [Nissan] (4:19). Subtract thirty-three days, and you arrive at the seventh of Adar as the date of Moses' death.

—B. Talmud, *Kiddushin* 38a

Peshat

The last chapter of the Torah, Deuteronomy, gives the account of Moses' death and the transfer of leadership to Joshua. Although many *midrashim* discuss how Moses died, little is mentioned about the date when Moses died. The Rabbis, however, poured over every detail of the Bible and deduced mathematically that Moses, who lived to be 120, was born and died on the same day, the 7th of Adar, precisely one week before Purim.

Derash

In the Book of Esther we learn how Haman cast lots to determine when to enact his evil plan to destroy the Jews.[127] The deciding lot fell upon the month of Adar, and the Talmud points out that this month was yet another example of irony in the story. Moses, the greatest Jewish figure, was born and died in Adar. Such focus on a very holy man implies that Adar was actually a month of good fortune for Jews (*Megillah* 13b). But Haman knew nothing about the date of Moses' birth and knew only that Adar was the month of Moses' death. He was happy, because he thought that Adar was a negative, unlucky month for the Jews. This ironic circumstance—that the month of planned annihilation could be the same as the month of good fortune—is reinforced in another place in the Talmud. Adar ultimately became a month of Jewish triumph; as the Talmud says, we must "increase our joy during the month of Adar" (*Ta'anit* 29a).

The Jewish legal codes seem to be split about the 7th of Adar—whether it is a day of celebration or a day of mourning. The *Tur* and Shulchan Arukh list the 7th of Adar among other sad days on which to fast (*Orach Chayyim* 580). Another authoritative source of customs, *Sefer Ha-Toda'ah,* points out that the 7th of Adar is a day of feasting and celebration for the *hevra kadisha* ("the burial society"). The burial society certainly cannot be celebrating its work, which would be inappropriate, having the effect of rejoicing over the anniversary of someone's death—in this case that of Moses. Moreover, Moses was buried not by humans but by God. The society is remembering and honoring the glory of this day—the 7th of Adar.

Making It Personal

Today, the month of Adar signifies the season of joy *par excellence* for Jews, since it brings the celebration of Purim's miraculous redemption story, along with the anticipation of Passover at the beginning of spring. This joy, however, masks a deep sadness. It is true that in Adar we recall an event of Jewish triumph and redemption but that redemption was born out of a nearly successful plan to exterminate us.

The 7th of Adar and the death of Moses also reflect these sorts of con-flicting feelings. We are grateful and happy to have had a leader such as Moses, but in remembering his birth we are overwhelmed by his death and the knowledge that "never again did there arise in Israel a prophet like Moses" (Deut. 34:10).

The joy of Purim is similarly not without sadness as witnessed by the elements of darkness in its comedy. During the Megillah reading, we titter at the story about the death of our enemies; and, during the *Purim-spiel,* we cackle at the silly and absurd antics of our usually dignified rabbis and teachers. These sensations are not the genuine joy we feel at a birth or a wedding. On some level, the laughter on Purim conceals our insecurity and the sadness we feel when we remember that as a people, Jews have often been in need of redemption. Even when we drink ourselves into a disconnection from reality, we are sobered by recognition of the romanticization in the Book of Esther— by the idealistic notion of a world where a secular ruler saves the Jews and a miracle occurs. After all, as the Talmud teaches about Purim, "one cannot count on a miracle every time" (*Megillah* 7b).

THE THREE LEVELS
Peshat: simple, literal meaning
Derash: historical, rabbinical inquiry
Making It Personal: contemporary analysis and application

The Root of Evil

Remember what Amalek did to you on your journey, after you left Egypt—how, undeterred by fear of God, he surprised you on the march, when you were famished and weary, and cut down all the stragglers in your rear. Therefore, when the LORD your God grants you safety from all your enemies around you, in the land that the LORD your God is giving you as a hereditary portion, you shall blot out the memory of Amalek from under heaven. Do not forget!
—Deut. 25:17–9

Peshat

These verses from Deuteronomy are the *maftir* (supplementary Torah reading) for *Shabbat Zakhor* (Sabbath of Remembrance), which immediately precedes Purim. It recalls the tribe of Amalek (ancestor of Haman), a nomadic group in the Sinai Desert we know only from the Bible. Given God's condemnation of the Amalekites[128] and the order to eradicate them, the Israelites must have regarded the tribe as a particularly grave threat.

In a sneak attack from the rear, the Amalekites killed the most defenseless of the Israelites, the stragglers weakened during the arduous Exodus from Egypt. The Torah views this action as a ruthless and indecent form of warfare, and it characterizes the entire tribe of Amalekites as people who are "undeterred by fear of God." Because they do not believe that committing a sin leads to consequences, the Amalekites deny the fundamental principle that underlies most religions or philosophies of ethics.

Derash

Besides being identified as Haman's ancestor, Amalek is mentioned as the grandson of Esau (Gen. 36:12), twin brother of the patriarch Jacob. The mishnaic Rabbis regard Esau as a terrible villain who is the progenitor not only of Amalek but also of the Roman Empire,[129] which was responsible for destroying the Second Temple and for dispersing the Jews from Israel in 70 C.E.[130]

The lines of ancestry in the Torah represent more than the physical characteristics of genetics. The Rabbis believe that moral disposition is transmitted from ancestors to descendants, and they identify the line of Esau as the one that transmits evil. The Zohar (the sacred book of

Kabbalah) even says that Esau/Amalek is associated with Satan and with things demonic.[131] It further explains that when God created the universe, Amalek was among the first nations created, and it represents the basis of individual and national evil.[132] Amalek is thus the physical manifestation of the *yetzer hara*,[133] the "evil inclination."[134]

Making It Personal

According to the Jewish tradition, the evil of Amalek and the corresponding evil inclination grow out of our own fears and doubts about the purposefulness of existence. The Midrash emphasizes that Amalek does not show up until the Israelites start to complain, to let in their doubts, despite their having just witnessed the miracle of Exodus: "Amalek came and fought with Israel" (Exod. 17:8).[135]

Although we often deny our fears and doubts about our purpose in life, our mortality, and our imperfections, most of us cannot fully silence or outrun them. It is difficult not to wonder whether life is truly meaningful or if it is simply the random result of the laws of physics and chemistry. Judaism asserts that we must remain faithful to the concept that life is completely meaningful in every aspect and that this life on earth leads to a life eternal. Judaism teaches that the alternative to having such faith can only be to believe that life is random. In that case, our inevitable demise awaits us

with the frightening reward of eternal nothingness. And if our end is so utterly hollow and meaningless, life itself is also futile and insignificant. After all, why should we behave morally if there is no true justice or consequence? What is to stop us from theft and murder if there is nothing to fear and no real love between people? If life is random, then aren't we all ultimately alone, sharing the same destiny of utter darkness no matter what we have done and how we have done it? These are important questions and asking them is to be expected; but if the doubts endlessly rule over us and guide our behavior, then we fail to end the existence of Amalek.

How do we continue asking these real questions while eradicating fear and the potential for evil? The answer is faith. We must find a balanced approach to faith that is neither blind to reason nor without real commitment. True faith, however, is not something that can simply be explained; it must be discovered by each individual.

·◆— Purim —◆·
Significance of the Holiday:
Some Modern Perspectives

From Reverence to Revelry

by Julie Pelc

In the story of Purim, a seemingly crazy, mixed-up series of events leads to the Jews of Persia triumphing over a plan to annihilate them. It is doubtful that these spectacular occurrences, described in the scroll of Esther, are historical in any way; rather, the Megillah represents an allegory of the miraculous survival of the Jewish people throughout history. The holiday may have its roots in ancient pagan celebrations. One theory suggests that it developed from a Persian spring masquerade or perhaps from a Babylonian New Year festival in which the god Marduk (could this be Mordecai?) and goddess Ishtar (Esther?) are triumphant over the foreign god, Humman (Haman?). Another theory contends that Purim originated in the five-day Persian Feast of Farwadigan, an event commemorating the dead. Supporters of this theory base their claim on the fact that both the ancient Greek version of the Bible, the Septuagint, and writings by the 2nd-century historian Flavius Josephus refer to Purim as "Furdaia," which some say is a distorted rendering of Farwadigan. Other theorists place Purim's origins in the Greek, rather than Persian, period of Jewish history—for example, finding the Hebrew word *purah* ("wine press") to be evidence of Purim's adaptation from the Greek festival of Pithoigia, or "Opening the Wine Casks."

Whatever the origins of the celebration, clearly Purim has developed into not only a much-loved but also an atypical Jewish holiday. In its festive manner of observance, Purim is reminiscent of Carnival, which occurs in the same season, and of Twelfth Night, which occurs at the end of the Christmas season. Purim contains a masquerade, burlesque entertainment, mockery, and a contest resulting in the election of a temporary ruler, or "Purim King," (inspired perhaps by the biblical beauty contest that made Esther a queen). Burning Haman in effigy is another Purim tradition that is similar to events during both Carnival and Twelfth Night.

As one of the most beloved communal celebrations in Judaism, Purim plays such a significant role in the Jewish calendar that by the 2nd century, an entire tractate of the Mishnah called *Megillah* was dedicated to discussing proper observance of the holiday. Yet the earliest descriptions of the festival from the eras of the Second Temple and the Misnah[136] offer no indication of the irreverence that we associate with Purim celebrations today. Instead, they primarily describe the laws about inscribing and reading the scroll of Esther.

Not until the talmudic era do we see the literary origins of the irreverent spirit we now associate with Purim. During this period, the Babylonian Talmud recorded the well-known dictum of the noted sage Rava: "One is obligated to get drunk on Purim to the point where he can no longer distinguish between 'Cursed is Haman' and 'Blessed is Mordecai' (*Megillah* 7b)." Gradually, the lighthearted and somewhat hedonistic celebration of Purim developed and became normative.

Intoxication, however, is not the sole manifestation of Purim's frivolity. Another universally recognized expression of the holiday is the *Purim-spiel*, a rowdy play based on the Megillah story or on other themes that lend themselves to mockery, complete with sarcastic, humorous, and iconoclastic entertainment. Although written evidence of the *Purim-spiel* exists in Europe only from the 14th century, Purim entertainment is likely of earlier origin. From the 12th century forward, Jews in Italy, southern France (Provence), and elsewhere were producing parodies wherein the actors poked fun at the Talmud, *halakhah,* liturgy, and other familiar pillars of Jewish life.

The Middle Ages also witnessed the development of the traditions, foods, and entertainment that we take for granted today. The early codes of Jewish law spend considerable amounts of time elucidating and detailing some of the most important Purim *mitzvot:* the festive meal and the customs of giving packages of food to friends and family (*mishloach manot*) and gifts of money to the poor (*matanot l'evyonim*).

From the 17th to 19th centuries, Purim customs continued to expand throughout Europe, where the now-famous Purim pastry, the hamantash, arose. The triangular cookie's name was adapted from the preexisting German *mahn-tash* ("poppy pocket"). The filled pastry, which represents either Haman's three-cornered hat or his ears, was given new significance as a motif for Purim. Also during this time, the role of children in the Purim celebration increased. The medieval practice of burning Haman in effigy to blot out his name evolved into the practice of having children write Haman's name on stones or wood blocks and then bang them together until the name was erased. The modern variation on this noise making is our custom of twirling *gragers* at the mention of Haman's name during the Megillah reading.

Despite Purim's historical development in customs and practices, the holiday has served since its inception as a lens through which we view the ways each generation of Jews has struggled with being a minority. The story of Purim presents the eternal story of the Jews living under threat in a strange land—a reality for two millennia. Therefore, the story's most profound significance may be in its spiritual and symbolic truth rather than in its historical certainty. For the Jews of each era, the transforming customs, traditions, and unique mood and spirit of Purim should reflect such truth. For as the Talmud tells us: "Whoever reads the Megillah backwards does not fulfill his obligation." Our sages explain that "backwards" here does not mean in reverse order; it means that whoever reads the Megillah merely as ancient history has missed the point. The Purim story, they argue, is still directly relevant to our contemporary world.

God, Are You There?

by Elie Kaplan Spitz

The stakes could not have been higher. The ruler of the largest empire of his day signed an edict calling for the destruction of the Jewish people on a set date chosen by lottery. Yet when the day arrived, it was not the Jews but their enemies who were vanquished. Not only were the Jews spared and allowed to defend themselves, they were honored by having the king elevate Queen Esther, who had finally revealed her true identity as a Jew, and her cousin Mordecai to the level of advisers who would help lead the empire. Through a series of perfectly timed, unanticipated events, the tables had turned.

In the Purim celebration, Jews annually recount these events through the reading of *Megillat Esther,* the scroll (or Book) of Esther, and by adding the following words to the day's *Amidah* prayer: "We thank you for the miraculous deliverance .... You, in great mercy, thwarted his [Haman's] designs, frustrated his plot and visited upon him the evil he planned to bring on others." Yet, in the detailed account in *Megillat Esther,* God's name is never mentioned. Why not? And in what sense did God perform a miracle?

Rabbi Shlomo Carlebach, the great spiritual songwriter of the modern Jewish community, taught that the absence of God's name is a reference to the way intimate relationships work. When you are in close proximity to a person, you do not need to use his or her name. For each of the players in the Book of Esther, God's immediacy makes the use of God's name unnecessary. In Carlebach's description, as well as that of most traditional commentators, God is the orchestrator of the events that unfold in the Book of Esther. In contrast, Professor

Richard Elliot Friedman in *The Disappearance of God: A Divine Mystery*[137] states that there is a progression throughout the Bible from a God who is actively present, "walking and talking with Adam in the Garden of Eden," to a God who is discreetly hidden. The circumstance is made apparent, Friedman writes, in God's addressing each of the three patriarchs, but then never speaking directly to their descendant Joseph. This phenomenon is also noteworthy in the later books of Hebrew Scripture, specifically Ezra, Nehemiah, and Esther, where there are no accounts of overt miracles. Most dramatic, God's name is not even mentioned in the Book of Esther. The author suggests that the shift from God's active engagement to apparent removal parallels a parent's allowing an offspring more control, honoring a growing maturity marked by greater responsibility and independence.

Yet God is not ignored by the participants in the story of Esther, as we see in many ways. Belief in God's supremacy is the reason why Mordecai refuses, as a Jew, to bow before human authority, specifically before Haman.[138] And Mordecai expresses faith in divine providence and in God's ultimate deliverance of the people when he says to Esther, "If you keep silent in this crisis, relief and deliverance will come to the Jews from another quarter, while you and your father's house will perish. And who knows, perhaps you have attained to royal position for just such crisis" (Esther 4:14).

In turn, Esther requests of Mordecai: "Go, assemble all the Jews who live in Shushan, and fast in my behalf … and if I am to perish, I shall perish!" (4:15–17). Fasting is a form of prayer. Through this action, the people beseech God to protect Esther. She is about to make her fateful appearance before King Ahasuerus, who has the authority to kill her just for showing up uninvited; this appearance will set the stage for having the king overturn his imperial decree.

Scholars have found no historical corroboration that the events described in the Book of Esther took place. The story reads like a *Purim-spiel,* a burlesque. The king is gluttonous and gullible; the bad guy and his wife are all bad; Mordecai saves the king's life; Esther, the young beauty, is chosen queen of the empire, while being able to hide her true origins until fate demands action; the Jews battle and kill hundreds of their enemies, but no mention is made of any Jewish losses; the Jews win and their enemies hang. Despite the fantastic plot and characters, this story fascinates us, because its central message rings true: those who have wanted to annihilate the Jewish people have repeatedly failed, and God's presence is evident in the mystery of our ongoing survival.

The Talmud, even as early as the 6th century, stated: "Do not rely on a miracle" (*Kiddushin* 39b; *Pesachim* 64b). We are empowered to take care of ourselves. Yet, looking back over our history, we cannot but marvel that we have survived and thrived as a religious people. Our wonder naturally translates as praise of a divinity who seems to be peering over our shoulders, simultaneously offering both providence and independence at the same time.

In our own time, we can identify with the sacred dance between uncertainty and faith that is embedded in the Book of Esther. Repeatedly, we have been left to wonder, as we look ahead in time, how will the State of Israel survive her enemies and what will keep the Jews from disappearing? Although God is not talking directly to us or performing overt miracles, we as a people continue to engage God with prayer and to hold onto the faith that we matter to God.

Self and Other

by Robert J. Cabelli

Megillat Esther and the holiday of Purim pose a number of ethical challenges as well as challenges to our sensibilities. The story is essentially a commentary on the corrupting influence of power. The king's easy arrogance in making life-and-death decisions and his inflated view of himself are woven together in both the excesses of his palace[139] and the series of edicts sent out under his seal. Instead of simply overturning the first edict, the king's advisers must construct a second one to counter it; the king's decree cannot be reversed, as if it were the product of a mortal—a fallible human. Rather, once established, it must remain in place forever, as if it were a divine judgment. The result is an appalling loss of life. With King Ahasuerus we see how power distorts perspective and corrupts, while with Haman we see how an insecure personality is drawn to power and to its malevolent abuse.

In retellings and spoofs of the Esther story, the king is often presented as a buffoon or as a pawn. This view differs from a story in the Babylonian Talmud,[140] which likens Ahasuerus to the owner of a field that contains a troublesome mound; he is only too happy to be rid of it, to let it go for free to his neighbor. What version of Ahasuerus is portrayed in the Megillah? Was the king an innocent man being duped into furthering the purposes of Haman or was he just casually complicit in his minister's desire to annihilate the Jews, as suggested by the metaphor offered in the Talmud? If we take the perspective of the Talmud (i.e., Ahasuerus was being complicit in accepting Haman's demands), then we must explore a fundamental question of ethical behavior: Can complicity ever be morally neutral, especially when the complicitous person is surrounded by actions of clear immorality?

The truth is, whenever evil and suffering are present, one need not look very far to find complicity or the failure to protest—the "sin of silence."[141] The words of German anti-Nazi theologian Pastor Martin Niemoeller[142] come to mind: "When they came for the Communists, I remained silent; I was not a Communist. When they locked up the Social Democrats, I remained silent; I was not a Social Democrat. When they came for the trade unionists, I did not protest; I was not a trade unionist. When they came for the Jews, I did not protest; I was not a Jew. When they came for me, there was no one left to protest." Niemoeller is quite clear about the role of complicity in his understanding of evil events and how self-interest (the "I") is central to its motivation.

Exploring a similar vein, we may consider Esther's moral position. Does self-interest govern her behavior? It would seem that Mordecai had trained her to see her Jewish identity as something problematic, something to be hidden in her pursuit of security and prestige. At the turning point in the story, however, Mordecai is able to convey another message to her. Mordecai says, "Do not imagine that you, of all the Jews, will escape with your life, by being of the king's palace" (Esther 4:13). His message is that she cannot dissociate her fate from that of her people. Of course, the converse is obviously true as well. If any one individual can be singled out because of her identity, then no one is safe and the entire community is at risk. In fact, this is what had already happened. Haman used his hatred for Mordecai as a springboard in seeking to wipe out the kingdom's entire Jewish population. By appealing to Esther's self-interest, Mordecai is able to broaden her sense of identity and help her recognize her responsibilities and obligations as a member of the Jewish community.

By the same logic, if any community, any ethnic or religious group, is singled out and no one comes to its defense, then all communities, all ethnic or religious groups, are at risk. Ahasuerus's kingdom is such a place. There are numerous peoples and numerous communities; as portrayed in the text, the tension among them is evident. For example, the opening chapter of the Book of Esther closes with these words from the king's edict: "that every man should wield authority in his home and speak the language of his own people" (1:22). We are continuously reminded of the 127 provinces in the kingdom and of the many different languages in use.[143] The Jews appear to be a minority dispersed throughout the realm,[144] but each provincial group of non-Jews is a minority as well. We may be helped in resolving some of these ethical issues by examining the idea of "community" as the fundamental unit of human society—as the basis of a secure and sustainable existence. In a polyglot society, a multicultural nation or world, two different implications emerge from this concept of community. The usual tension between "self" and "other" becomes magnified into a conflict between the community of "self" and the communities of "other." On the one hand, in the human psyche, the ingrained, perceived threat of the "other" to the "self" creates the impulse for the stranger to go under cover, to attempt to disappear—an exercise that Megillat Esther suggests is futile. On the other hand, as the book indicates, the ethic of mutual obligation within community, the foundation of communal survival and identity, when examined closely, extends to the individual's relationship to all communities. On this point rests our hopes for a humanistic balancing of our needs, for the mitigation of our self-destructive impulses, and for the acceptance of responsibility for the "otherness" of all of us.

She Makes Herself Seen: Gender and Power in Esther

by Alana Suskin

> Let Your deeds be seen by Your servants,
> Your glory by their children.
> —Ps. 90:16

Of the three female characters in Megillat Esther—Vashti, Esther, and the less-noted Zeresh (Haman's wife)—it is strange that Vashti is the one who, in modern times, first emerged as the hero of feminists. But as women see themselves more and more in political terms, Vashti's refusal to appear before the king, her husband, has seemed too radical.

Marilyn Frye says in her 1983 book *The Politics of Reality,* "Total power is unconditional access; total powerlessness is being unconditionally accessible. The creation and manipulation of power is constituted of the manipulation and control of access."[145] By this definition, Vashti's refusal of access looks far more expressive of having power than does Esther's meek submission to her kidnapping and marriage. However, there is another way of looking at the story. Over the course of the narrative, Esther develops from an initially weak, passive female to one who is genuinely an agent of power. She comes into her own strength, using only the limited tools at hand.

While Vashti, in contrast, appears at first to be powerful, she has, in fact, confused borrowed power with true agency. A midrash explains that Vashti was the daughter of Belshazzar, the tyrannical and impious king of Babylon, and the granddaughter of Nebuchadnezzar, the monarch who destroyed the First Temple.[146] The Rabbis of the Talmud relate Vashti's refusal as follows: "Thou son of my father's steward, my father drank wine in the presence of a thousand, and did not get drunk …" (B. Talmud, *Megillah* 12b); and, "You used to be the stable-boy of my father's house, and you were used to bringing in before yourself naked harlots, and now that you have ascended the throne you have not abandoned your evil habits" (*Midrash Rabbah, Esther Rabbah* 3:14). Unlike Esther, Vashti attempts to refuse by identifying with the power of her father. But borrowed power merely affirms women's lack of true agency. In using her father's identity as a source of power, Vashti validates the established hierarchies of patriarchy.

Vashti and Esther both struggle against what is known in feminist and post-modernist analyses as "the male gaze," which is a way of describing the interaction in art between subject and object. As John Berger wrote in *Ways of Seeing,* "according to usage and conventions which are at last being questioned but have by no means been overcome—*men act* and *women appear. Men look at women.*"[147] His argument states that looking is a demonstration of mastery and ownership over the subject of the gaze.

In *Megillat Esther,* the male gaze emerges in the act of Ahasuerus's order for Vashti to submit herself to being viewed—according to the Talmud—naked before others. In the ultimate exercise of power over another, this man has turned this woman into an object, a condition plainly seen in the midrash's description of the incident: "Said Ahasuerus to them, The vessel that I use is neither Median nor Persian, but Chaldean.[148] Would you like to see her? They said, Yes, but it must be naked" (*Megillah* 12b). The language, "*kli she'ani mishtamesh bo,*" is unambiguous: *kli* means "a vessel" (like a pot), and *mishtamesh,* means "use," just as one would use a hammer.

Vashti believes that she has the power to refuse and is proven wrong. First of all, she fails because she ultimately lacks the power to refuse. Second of all, she fails because removing herself from the male gaze, she becomes subjected to the general invisibility of women. Esther, in sharp contrast, does not absent herself. By appearing instead of disappearing, she seizes power and overturns the notion of power, which is typically based on male strength or upon connection to a powerful male. She goes from invisible to visible and recognizes that her salvation will not be achieved through the agency of a human being. At the same time, she does not make the mistake of becoming a gazed-at object. Rather, she transforms herself into an agent of power, and she gazes back.

How does this transformation happen? It is triggered at the moment in which Esther truly "sees" Mordecai. When he learns about the decree to destroy the Jews, Mordecai tears his clothes and wears sackcloth[149] so that Esther's servants will notice him and tell her about his appearance. Before this, "Mordecai would walk about in front of the court of the harem, to learn how Esther was faring and what was happening to her" (Esther 2:11). Notice that neither of them sees the other directly, nor does Mordecai have any notion of her having an active role in her own life. The language used by Mordecai, "what was happening to her" (*mah ye'aseh bah*), is completely passive, demonstrating her (assumed) lack of ability to control her own fate.

The second moment in Esther's transformation is when she does not simply go to the king to beg for mercy but makes him, and even Haman, actually "see" her by inviting them not once, but twice, to a private party in her chamber. This activity is the reverse of Vashti's actions; she held her own private party for women only and refused to come before the king when he called her. Esther brings the two powerful men to her court. By turning the tables, she transforms them from unassailable figures of power into her subjects. And when the king, angry with Haman, stalks out of the room, Haman grovels before Esther, just as she had gone in fear for her life before the king. This reversal is potent: She has taken as much power as she can and used it. She has forced these men to see her, and to see her not as a supplicant but as a figure of power. When, and in the same way, they look upon her, she looks back at them.

And within all the hidden faces in this story, there is one final secret: Esther symbolizes the people Israel. Israel is "the woman," tiny and humble, who is taken into captivity by those more powerful than she and forced to "submit" to a foolish master (another nation). The foolish master, King Ahasuerus (symbol of the other nation) to whom Esther submits both sexually and metaphorically, fails to protect her. Like Israel, Esther begins as an object, weak and unprotected—seemingly. But then Esther, the assimilated and meek, becomes a Jew and is revealed. And in becoming a visible Jew, both she and her nation are saved.

·◆— Purim —◆·
Alternative Meditations

A Purim Vision

by Michael Strassfeld[150]

Why must we seriously fulfill the commandment to be crazy on Purim?

The Jewish festival cycle is full of different moods—the bittersweet joy of Pesah, the mourning of the Three Weeks, the awe of Yom Kippur, the rejoicing of Simhat Torah, among others. Each of us in his or her own life experiences the same range of feelings, and part of the festival cycle's effort is to provide a context for those feelings. Each of us probably has difficulty in expressing one or more of them—for example, grief or joy or guilt. Surprisingly, perhaps, many people find it less difficult to feel contrite on Yom Kippur than to act the joyous fool on Purim. Purim calls upon us to give free rein to that dimension of our personalities signified by the phrase *ad de-lo-yada*. *Ad de-lo-yada*—the state of not knowing the difference between Haman and Mordechai—is a time when all our rules and inhibitions are swept away, when the superego is pushed aside by an untrammeled id. We enter the world of the drunk, a world of blissful ignorance of reality.

The state of *ad de-lo-yada* also enables us to see how easy it is to change from Mordechai to Haman, from crusader for justice into simply a crusader. That is why the Talmud says that we fully accept the Torah only on Purim, for only when we can mock the tradition can we fully accept it. Only then are we safe to do so; otherwise we make the tradition into an idolatry rather than a smasher of idols, into frozen-in-stone dogma of what once was rather than a living faith. The threat of the mountain of Sinai hanging over our heads evaporates as do all mirages at the laughter of the Jews on Purim. All the smoke and sound of Sinai vanishes and we see clearly the Torah, its great potentials and great dangers. We accept the Torah, knowing that once a year on Purim there will be a time to laugh at our own self-righteousness. We can live by that Torah all the rest of the year because for one day we can let out our repressed feelings as we overturn all the rules, even turning the Torah itself upon its head. Both for the sake of Torah and ourselves, we need Purim to laugh at what we value and thus paradoxically gain a real sense of self-worth.

Ad de-lo-yada has another level of meaning as well. It is not an animalistic state of stupor, but rather a higher degree of consciousness. It is a messianic/mystical moment when there is *no* difference between Haman and Mordechai, good and evil, for both are found in the Holy One "who created light and darkness, made peace and created evil" (Isa. 45:7).

Which is it then—Purim the nihilistic holiday of unbounded joy, or Purim the climax of the festival year by its fulfillment of the message of Pesah and Shavuot? Which is it, Haman or Mordechai? *Ad de-lo-yada*—I leave it to you to distinguish which is the real Purim.

When all the other festivals will be abolished [in messianic time], Purim will remain.[51]

Purim and the Nazis: Two Reflections

by Leslie Koppelman Ross and Philip Goodman

PURIM FEST 1946

[O]nly Holocaust revisionists would argue that the Nazis were not the embodiment of the depraved evil represented by Amalek and Haman. The Nazis themselves recognized the connection. In Poland, Hitler ordered synagogues closed for the entire day of Purim and prohibited the reading of the Book of Esther. Secular journalists wrote that the story of Purim foreshadowed the end of Hitler, who himself said in a 1944 speech that if the Nazis went down in defeat, the Jews would celebrate a second triumphant Purim. Indeed, on October 16, 1946, ten sons of Haman were hanged at Nuremberg, the fulfillment of Esther's image of the ten sons of Haman hanged again, as she had requested in Persia (Esther 9:13). As reported in news publications of that day, on his way to the gallows, Julius Streicher shouted "Purim Fest, 1946!"

—Lesli Koppelman Ross[52]

THE TASTE OF DELIVERANCE

When Hitler was delivering one of his infamous speeches in a large hall in Munich at the start of the Nazi ascent to power, he could not help but notice that a man in the front row was making facial contortions of derision and joy marked with an occasional outburst of laughter.

The man's behavior resulted in bringing confusion to Hitler midst his anti-Semitic invectives and causing annoyance to the *Fuehrer*. When the speech was concluded, Hitler in great ire sent for the one who disturbed him and indignantly inquired who he was.

"I am a Jew," he said innocently.

"Then you should be taking my address more seriously," warned Hitler. "Do you not believe that I will fulfill my threats to bring about the destruction of the Jews?"

"You should be aware," the Jew replied, "that you are not the first anti-Semite who sought to destroy us. You may recall that the great Pharaoh of Egypt sought to enslave the Jews. To commemorate his defeat and our redemption, we eat tasty Matzot and observe the festival of Passover. Haman was another enemy of ours who brought about his own downfall. The delicious Hamantashen we eat and the jolly festival of Purim recall our deliverance from him. While listening to your venomous diatribe, I wondered what kind of delicacy would the Jews invent and what kind of holiday they would establish to celebrate your downfall."
—Philip Goodman[153]

Laughter

by Lawrence Kushner[154]

There can be joy in silence or with tears, just as there can be laughter in terror or in pain. When people are joyous, they are at their best: they are generous, kind, grateful, and reverent. Happy families are just that; if they don't actually laugh, they smile a lot. They laugh at jokes, the state of the universe, and above all, they laugh at themselves. I am not talking here about ridicule or jest, nor laughter from embarrassment or anxiety. It is a joy to be alive.

I'm talking about learning how to discern the humor in even our "holiest" undertakings. If by the word "sacred" we mean that we cannot laugh at it, then it is less than sacred. But conversely whatever occasions joyous laughter turns out to be sacred.

Rabbi Nahman of Bratslav used to counsel his students that depression was the most clever disguise of the *yetzer hara,* our evil impulse, and we must fight with every weapon in our power, even simply having friends tell us one joke after another.

Laughter is so important that Jews have institutionalized it into a holiday. Purim does more than celebrate the foiled attempts of anti-Semites everywhere, it makes us laugh at ourselves. The head of the famous Slabotka Yeshiva, on Purim, would dress up like a horse.

It is interesting furthermore that we have made Purim, which celebrates the foiling of our enemies, into a time for laughter by dressing up like them. Zalman Schachter-Shalomi used to say that when the Purim play is over, all the actors get applause, but Haman, the villain, gets the most. Access to the most joyous part of ourselves comes through ritualized reminders that we are as bad as our enemies. On Purim we are enjoined to get so drunk we cannot even tell the difference. Indeed, only our ability to laugh at ourselves keeps us sane and from becoming like them....

I remember how my father used to love to sing "The Red River Valley." He never missed an opportunity to offer a solo. To this day I cannot hear it without crying. Only once did it make me laugh. The organist at the temple in Detroit where he worked played it as a prelude to the funeral. Amazed, people picked their heads up from their tears and one by one, as they recognized the melody, began to smile.

Laughter at sad times does more than relieve tension, it initiates healing. Laughter reminds us of another dimension of our psyche. I suspect that laughter may be able to banish the fiery sword that guards the entrance to the Tree of Life. This may be why the Hasidim were fond of punning that *Yom Kippurim* could also be mistranslated not as the Day of Atonement but a day like Purim. According to one tradition, after the Messiah comes, observance of all the holidays will be abrogated except the day when we laugh at our enemies and ourselves.

A woman I know had a son who was killed in the Israeli army. She tells of the funeral and a joke she found herself thinking at that terrible time. "Please don't think me escapist or irreverent. But there I was, walking in the cortege to the cemetery, with my brother and other son, right behind the jeep carrying the casket and flanked by six soldiers. I wanted so much to reach out and touch the coffin one last time but the procession was so military, I was afraid. And suddenly I found myself thinking, 'I know parents have to let go of their children, but this is just ridiculous!' And at that moment, she confided, "I realized that I was going to make it."

PART 5

Guidance along the Way

If two sit together and are engaged in the study of the Torah,
the presence of God comes to rest between them.

— Mishnah, *Pirke Avot* 3:6

The Holy Conversation

I N THE JEWISH TRADITION, the study of sacred texts is not done alone but in a pair,[1] because learning is conversation. Such a pair is known as a *chevruta* (literally, in Aramaic, "friendship"). When we participate in a *chevruta*, we multiply the number of questions and interpretations that are generated and expand our perspective beyond our own set of life's experiences. As a team, we are able to learn much more than we would by ourselves. In humble acknowledgment that our individual insights are limited, we reap the benefits of our partner's thoughts, in concert with feeling the pressure to clarify our own opinions and beliefs. The forum is bound together by lively debate. For all these reasons, the Rabbinic tradition repeatedly states that the process of studying in a *chevruta* is itself holy and beneficial.

When we study sacred texts in Judaism, we encounter a multiplicity of voices and thoughts. On the traditional page used for Torah study, a few verses of Torah are surrounded by the commentary of medieval scholars such as Rashi, Ramban, and Ibn Ezra. On a page of Talmud, the words of text are framed by Rashi's explanations and the insights of the Tosafot. All of the commentators together provide a density and breadth of examination. We see their questions on the text, the thoughts of their teachers about the same topics, and the commentators' own interpretations. With these writings together in one place, laid out before the partners' eyes, a *chevruta* is automatically plugged into a conversation that has been going on for millennia, the "grand conversation." As Mimi Feigelson, a professor of Rabbinic literature at the American Jewish University says, "Some of my best friends are dead rabbis!"

Each time we read a text, we unearth and engage all of the questions and learning that came before us. And then we sustain and expand the conversation by injecting our own queries and observations. In this way the Torah remains alive and vibrant—an eternal Tree of Life. So, too, does the tradition itself remain vital when we observe a law or custom—another form of the ongoing conversation. For example, each time we light Shabbat candles, we carry the weight and power of the tradition that has defined holy Jewish living for many hundreds of generations. And while we take in the luminescence of the flames, we merge the tradition with our own unique spiritual force.

Practicing the *mitzvot* and studying the sacred texts are in and of themselves holy experiences, not necessarily because they intrinsically contain some unidentifiable, purifying component but because the process of our doing these things makes them holy. They enrich our lives and hallow our experiences as we attach our souls to the grand conversation, infusing these moments with our spirituality, our scholarship, our heritage, and the very core of our being.

Exploring Traditional Sources

With the complexities and nuances that permeate all aspects of our Jewish lives, we can have difficulty defining Judaism and its spiritual essence. Contemporary scholar Rabbi David Wolpe does so by offering a fitting and inspiring metaphor. He says that the Jewish religion is the continual dialogue between God and the Jewish people.

The metaphor works well in two ways. First, "dialogue" implies that activity and reciprocity are present in our relationship with God. Indeed, the concert of voices in the Jewish tradition resound with vibrancy and with ongoing passion for our unique covenant with the Creator. These voices include the diverse ideas in the books of the Bible, the arguments in the Talmud, and the responsa of rabbis and Jewish scholars— all of which are threaded through time. The questions that lie at the heart of Torah remain alive in every generation, and it has been the prerogative of Jews to examine and reexamine those questions together. As a community of learners, we are defined by the way we ask, discuss, debate, and respond, using every facet of our minds and hearts, constantly seeking to know God so that we can fulfill our responsibilities in our relationship with the Holy One.

The second noteworthy aspect of the metaphor is its emphasis on the ever-continuing nature of this dialogue. The chain of the tradition expands, in the same way the seeds of the Torah, from which the garden of Jewish thought and life grows, sprout and flourish. In fact, any relationship needs a continuous conversation filled with examination in which we reapply the truth and knowledge gained from the past to all of life's new experiences and perspectives. If we speak only of what was and not of what is or will be, the relationship becomes irrelevant and obsolete.

Today we look upon the rabbis and scholars of both the past and present as critical links in the Jewish chain. With their writings and teachings, they all become our friends and a part of our *chevruta*. Because of them, we have the magnificent opportunity to join the continuous dialogue that has existed since the dawn of civilization. And by combining their wisdom with our own understanding and experience, we can be confident that another link has been attached to the chain, ensuring that our unique spiritual essence moves forward into the next generation.

Alkabetz, Solomon ben Moses Ha-Levi

(b. circa 1505–d. circa 1576, Greece, Turkey, and Israel) One of the great kabbalists of Tzfat. He is most famous as the author of the mystical Shabbat hymn *Lekhah Dodi* wherein his initials begin each stanza. He also composed a commentary on the Book of Esther called *Menot Ha-Levi* (loosely, "Portions of the Levites") as well as commentaries on the Song of Songs, the Book of Ruth, and the Passover Haggadah. Alkabetz (sometimes transliterated as Alqabitz) was the brother-in-law and teacher of Moses Cordevero (b. 1534–d. 1572), a leader of the Tzfat kabbalists.

Apocrypha

(literally, "Hidden Writings" in Greek) A collection of books that is part of Jerome's Vulgate translation of the Christian Bible but not part of the Hebrew Bible (TANAKH). All 15 books are now canonized except for Prayer of Manasseh and 1 and 2 Esdras, which are a part of the Christian Bible appendix. The Apocrypha was a part of the Greek Bible used by Jews in Egypt, and today scholars question why these books did not become part of the TANAKH. Most scholars say that the books were written too late to be included and that 2 Maccabees and Wisdom of Solomon, in particular, were composed in Greek rather than Hebrew. Among the titles included in the Apocrypha are 1 Maccabees, Ben Sira, Tobit, Judith, Baruch, Susanna, and Bel and the Dragon.

Arukh Ha-Shulchan

(literally, "Laying the Table") A comprehensive code of Jewish law compiled by Rabbi Yechiel Michel Halevi Epstein (b. 1835–d. 1905, Russia). This code attempts to update the Shulchan Arukh (literally, "Set Table") by Joseph Karo and claims to be the final authority on many customs.

Baal Shem Tov

(b. 1698–d. 1760, Ukraine) Yisrael ben Eliezer, known as the Baal Shem Tov ("Master of the Good Name"), is understood to be the founder of Hasidism. Most of the biographical information about him is in the form of stories and legends passed on by his disciples. They describe the Baal Shem Tov (also referred to by the acronym Besht) as coming from a poor and simple family. His special abilities related to mysticism began at an early age, and legend claims that he worked miracles and battled demons. His teachings emphasize the spiritual, through joy in living and through the power and transcendence of prayer.

Ben Ish Chai

(b. 1833–d. 1909, Persia) Yosef Chaim ben Eliyahu Al-Hacham, influential teacher and chief Rabbi of Baghdad. He was known by the same name as his major work, the *Ben Ish Chai,* which discusses the weekly portion of the Torah mixed with both Kabbalah and the daily practices of *halakhah.* He authored more than 60 books on all aspects of Judaism, and some of his poems became part of the liturgy used by the Jews of Baghdad.

Bible See TANAKH

Books of the Maccabees

Four books not included in the Scriptures, but found in the Apocrypha. The first two are the primary sources for the celebration of Hanukkah. Book 1 gives an historical account of the Hasmonean war from the beginning of the revolt until the death of Simon. Book 2 fills in the story of Judah Maccabee and covers the theme of the Jews' adherence to Judaism in all circumstances. The last two books deal with two very different topics. Book 3 tells of the persecution of the Jews in Egypt; book 4 discusses chiefly the dominance of reason as the basis of reverence for God and the means to the mastery of passion.

Buber, Martin

(b. 1878–d. 1965, Austria) Renowned religious philosopher. His translations and organization of Hasidic parables and anecdotes, such as *The Legend of the Baal Shem Tov, The Tales of Rabbi Nachman,* and *Tales of the Hasidim,* helped introduce the Western world to Eastern European Jewry. His greatest philosophical discourse is the book *I and Thou.*

Buber, Solomon

(b. 1827–d. 1906, Russia) Scholar, editor, independent researcher, bank employee, and philanthropist. He lived in Lemberg, now Lviv, in Ukraine. Buber was particularly interested in midrash, to which he devoted a very high level of systematic research.

Chemdat Yamim

(literally, "Treasure of Days") A collection of kabbalistic texts and writings about customs that was edited in Izmir, Turkey, in the early 18th century. Because it was clearly influenced by the Shabbateans, the largest messianic movement in Jewish history, Nathan of Gaza (a great supporter of the false Messiah, Shabbetai Tzvi) was rumored to be the author. (Modern scholars contend that his authorship is highly unlikely.) Shabbateanism severely disappointed the Jewish people; and thus this work, when originally published, was denounced. *Chemdat Yamim* did not resurface until scholars in the 20th century developed renewed interest in it. Significant works such as *Pri Etz Hadar* (literally, "The Fruit of the Lovely Tree") and *Ma'aseh Yehudit* (The Account of Judith) originate in *Chemdat Yamim.*

Cordovero, Moses ben Jacob

(b.1522–d. 1570, Israel) One of the preeminent kabbalists of 16th-century Tzfat. Cordovero's country of birth is not known, but he was likely the scion of a family that had fled Spain or Portugal for the Land of Israel. He studied with Joseph Karo and Solomon Alkabetz. Cordovero authored several important kabbalistic works, including *Pardes Rimonim* (literally, "Orchard of Pomegranates") and *Tomer Devorah* (known in English as *Palm Tree of Deborah*). His most significant book is *Or Yakar* (Precious Light), which is an extensive commentary on the Zohar and the Torah, among other sacred texts. He is also known by the acronym Ramak.

Flavius Josephus See Josephus.

Gaster, Theodor H.

(b. 1906–d. 1992, Romania and United States) Outstanding 20th-century biblical scholar and expert on comparative religions and mythology. He is noted for his English translation of the Dead Sea Scrolls and his books *Myths, Legends, and Customs in the Old Testament* and *Festivals of the Jewish Year.* His middle initial stands for Herzl; Gaster was named after Theodor Herzel, the founder of modern political Zionism, who died in 1904.

Gemara

Usually referred to as the Talmud, even though this description is technically erroneous. Written in Aramaic, the Gemara (literally, "Learning") is the discussion of and commentary on the laws of the Mishnah by the Rabbinic sages of the 2nd through 5th centuries C.E., who are known as *amoraim*. In their explanation and elucidation of the Mishnah, the *amoraim* draw from other sources, including the Midrash, the Tosefta, and postbiblical works (e.g., *Ben Sira*, also called *Ecclesiasticus*). Two 5th-century Babylonian sages, Ravina and Rav Ashi, have traditionally been given credit for finalizing the Gemara; modern scholars believe that it did not reach its present form until the end of the 7th century.

Guide of the Perplexed See Maimonides.

Theodor Herzl

(b. 1860–d. 1904, Hungary and Austria) Statesman, writer, visionary of an independent Jewish state, and founder of the political Zionist movement. His arguments for the urgent need for a Jewish national home, preferably in the Land of Israel, were outlined in his 1896 work called *Der Judenstaat* (The Jewish State).

Heschel, Abraham Joshua

(b.1907–d. 1972, Poland, Germany, and United States) One of the most prominent and most widely quoted Jewish religious philosophers in the modern era. Born in Warsaw, he was descended from Hasidic dynasties on both sides of his family. He studied Talmud in the school for *Wissenschaft des Judentums* (Science of Judaism) in Germany and philosophy at Berlin University. With the rise of Nazism, he was brought to the United States as a teacher by the Hebrew Union College. Later he was a professor of Jewish ethcis and mysticism at the Jewish Theological Seminary. He is known for having been extremely active in the civil rights movement and for having served as a leader in the Jewish–Christian interfaith movement. His best-known books are on theology and include *The Sabbath*, *God in Search of Man*, and *Man Is Not Alone*.

Hirsch, Samson Raphael

(1808–1888, Germany) The founder of contemporary Orthodox Judaism and one of the preeminent rabbis, preachers, and philosophers in Jewish history. His writings often reflect his strong opposition to the current of Reform Judaism and modernization that was sweeping through Western Europe, especially Germany, during his lifetime.

Ibn Ezra, Avraham

(1089–1164, Spain) A poet, grammarian, and astronomer, known best for his commentary on most of the TANAKH. His commentary is unique in its grammatical analysis and independent ideas. After his son converted to Islam in 1140, Ibn Ezra went into self-chosen exile, traveling through North Africa and Europe.

Isserles, Moses

(b. circa 1525–d. 1572, Poland) One of the outstanding *posekim* (rabbinic descisors). He was an authority on Kabbalah, philosophy, astronomy, and history. Among his best-known work is *Mapah* (see Shulchan Arukh) and *Darkhei Moshe*, his commentary on the *Tur.* Isserles was called Rema or Rama, two acronyms of his name.

Isserlin, Israel

(b. 1390–d. 1460, Germany, Italy, and Austria) Rabbi Israel ben Petahiah Isserlin, best known for his book of Jewish law, *Terumat Ha-Deshen* (literally, "Removing, or Lifting, the Ash"). This work served as one source for several of the codes, including *Ha-Mapah*, the Ashkenazic gloss to the Shulchan Arukh.

Jerusalem Talmud See Talmud.

Josephus

(b. circa 38–d. 100 C.E., Israel) An Israelite general during the Great Jewish Revolt (66–70 C.E.). When his fortress was conquered, he traded sides and changed his name from Yosef ben Matityahu Ha-Kohen to Flavius Josephus (or Josephus Flavius in Jewish circles) and became an adviser to emperors Vespasian and Titus. As a historian, his works are the principal and, for certain periods, the only source of knowledge about events in the late Second Temple era, from the establishment of the Hasmonean rule until the destruction of the Temple. His books were written in Greek when he was living in Rome and were intended to be read by non-Jews as well as Jews who were estranged from their people. Scholars attach the most importance to *The War of the Jews* (against Rome) and to his comprehensive work *The Antiquities of the Jews.*

Judith

One of the books in the Apocrypha about the heroine Judith (Yehudit in Hebrew— literally, "Jewess"), who lived during the reign of the Assyrian emperor Nebuchadnezzar. The book, preserved in Greek, tells of the Assyrian subjugation of the Jews and how Judith seduced the Assyrian General Holofernes, intoxicated him, and chopped off his head. The themes relate well to Hanukkah and thus have become a story retold during the holiday. The legend also exists in medieval midrashim.

Kaplan, Mordecai Menachem

(b. 1881–d. 1983, Lithuania and United States) A highly influential and controversial rabbi in the Conservative stream of Judaism. He founded the Teachers Institute in 1909 at the Jewish Theological Seminary and would later develop a philosophy leading to the establishment of the Reconstructionist movement. Kaplan's theology held that in light of the advances in philosophy, science, and history, it would be impossible for modern Jews to continue to adhere to many of Judaism's traditional theological claims. Among his works are *Judaism as a Civilization* and *The Meaning of God in Modern Jewish Religion.*

Karo, Joseph See Shulchan Arukh.

Kethuvim

(literally, "The Writings") The third of the three sections of the TANAKH. It was the last to be canonized and consists of Psalms, Proverbs, Job, the Song of Songs, Ruth, Lamentations, Ecclesiastes, Esther, Daniel, Ezra, Nehemiah, 1 Chronicles, and 2 Chronicles. It is also known by its Greek rendering, "Hagiographa."

Kitzur Shulchan Arukh

An abridgement *(kitzur)* of Joseph Karo's Shulchan Arukh, by Solomon Ganzfried (b. 1804–d. 1886, Hungary). Ganzfried was a firm traditionalist and fought to preserve traditional observance amid the rapid changes of modernity. In this abridgement, Ganzfied tended to select the most stringent views and eliminate minority or alternative opinions on Jewish law.

Klein, Isaac

(b. 1905–d. 1979, Hungary and United States) Author of *A Guide to Jewish Religious Practice,* one of the most popular and expansive books of customs and observances written in English. Rabbi Klein's work is considered authoritative by the modern Orthodox, Conservative, and Reform streams of Judaism.

Levush

A collection of laws and customs, including elements of the *Tur* and the Shulchan Arukh, by Rabbi Mordecai ben Avraham Jaffe, also known as Baal Ha-Levush (b. circa 1535–d. 1612, Prague). A very popular, authoritative source that gives the rationale for many of the customs, it was referred to frequently by the scholars who came after him. This work can be found in the back of many traditional volumes of the *Tur.*

Luria, Isaac Ashkenazi

(b. 1534–d. 1572, Israel) Renowned teacher of Kabbalah and *halakhah*. Born in Jerusalem, he grew up in Egypt and later settled in Tzfat, northern Israel. His teachings inspired a school of thought; and although Luria himself really did not write much, his followers produced volumes of material representing his teachings. "Lurianic Kabbalah" basically teaches that the purpose of creation is to have the community and each individual heal the world (*tikun olam*, literally, "fixing the world"), thus gradually reuniting and perfecting the divine realms (see *sefirot*), as well as humanity.

Maccabees See Books of the Maccabees.

Magen Avraham

A popular commentary on the *Orach Chayyim* section of the Shulchan Arukh, which seeks to harmonize differences between Moses Isserles and Joseph Karo as well as uphold the authority of the Shulchan Arukh over the *Tur*. It was written by Rabbi Avraham Abele Gombiner (b. circa 1637–d. circa 1683, Poland).

Maharal of Prague

The commonly used name of Rabbi Yehudah Loew ben Betsalel (b. 1525–d. 1609), one of the most prolific of Ashkenazic writers, legal authorities, and mystics. His birthplace is unknown, but it was probably Poland. Maharal is the Hebrew acronymn of Moreinu Ha-Rav Lowe ("Our Teacher the Rabbi Loew"). For many years the Maharal held the post of chief rabbi of Prague, a city that was then the capital of Bohemia. His work, much favored in Hasidic learning, can be found in *Gur Aryeh* (literally, "Young Lion"), a commentary on the Torah. In his pedagogical approach, he held that children should be taught the Torah in a systematic, gradual manner rather than the rigid system of the day. He is perhaps most widely known, however, as the legendary creator of the magical *golem*, a clay figure that is slave to its master's commands.

Maharil

(b. circa 1360–d. 1427, Austria) Rabbi Jacob Ha-Levi of Moelin, sometimes referred to as the "Father of Ashkenazic Customs." He wrote a compendium on the yearly customs of Ashkenazic Jewry called *Minhagei Maharil*. He is widely quoted by many Ashkenazic codifiers, including Moses Issereles. Maharil is an acronym for "Our Teacher, the Rabbi, Israel Levi." (The patriarch Jacob was known by the name Israel.)

Maimonides

(b. 1135–d. 1204, Spain and Egypt) Rabbi Moses ben Maimon, a physician and possibly the greatest Jewish thinker of all time. He wrote many important works, including legal codes and philosophical expositions. Among them are the *Mishneh Torah*, the first written Jewish legal code, which is composed in remarkably clear Hebrew, and the *Guide of the Perplexed* (*Moreh Nevuchim*), a work showing a tremendous Aristotelian influence) which interprets the Torah with the objective of eliminating apparent contradictions with philosophy. Maimonides is also known by the acronymn Rambam.

Midrash

(literally, "Elucidation" or "Exposition") A body of work that combines the theological, homiletical, and ethical lore of the Rabbis in the Land of Israel from the 3rd through 10th centuries. The word midrash is derived from the three-letter Hebrew root *dalet.resh.shin.* (*lidrosh*), meaning to search for, which denotes searching out and discovering other meanings and information from Scripture.

Midrash Rabbah

An important series of books that expounds upon and further illustrates each book of the Torah as well as the *megillot* (five historical tales that are part of the biblical book called The Writings): the Song of Songs, Ruth, Esther, Ecclesiastes, and Lamentations. Each volume is identified by the name of the corresponding book from the Bible, followed by the word *Rabbah* ("Great"), for example, *Exodus Rabbah* and *Song of Songs Rabbah*. As a series, these works were edited and redacted between the 5th and 10th centuries. Final touches to *Numbers Rabbah* and *Esther Rabbah* were made as late as the 13th century. *Genesis Rabbah*, the oldest (425 C.E.) of the series, includes material from the Apocrypha, Philo, and Josephus.

Mishnah

(literally, "Teaching") The first compilation of the Oral Law and the foundational text for the Talmud and for the Rabbinic tradition. Most scholars attribute it to Rabbi Yehudah Ha-Nasi (Rabbi Judah the Patriarch, who lived in Judea under control of the Roman Empire) and date its final editing to circa 200 C.E. There are six "orders," or volumes, of the Mishnah categorized by different areas of Jewish law: *Zera'im* (laws governing agriculture and farm products), *Mo'ed* (laws relating to seasons and holidays), *Nashim* (laws relating to women and family life and to marriage and divorce),

Nezikim (summaries of Jewish civil and criminal law), *Kodashim* (laws relating to holiness in matters of sacrifices and ritual slaughter), and *Toharot* (laws about purity). The word mishnah is derived from the three-letter Hebrew root *shin.nun.heh.,* "to repeat," which indicates the primary method for learning and oral study at that time.

Mishnah Berurah

One of the most authoritative commentaries on the part of the Shulchan Arukh that is devoted to everyday Jewish life, *Orach Chayyim.* It was written by Rabbi Yisrael Meir Ha-Kohen (b. 1838–d. 1933, Poland), who is known by the name of his first book, *Chofetz Chaim* (which primarily deals with the laws of *loshon ha-ra* or guarding one's speech).

Mishneh Torah See Maimonides.

Nachman of Bratzlav

(b. 1772–d. 1810) One of the most influential and fascinating of all Hasidic rebbes (masters). The great-grandson of the Baal Shem Tov (founder of Hasidism), Nachman did not believe he was a worthy heir to the leadership of the Hasidic dynasty and chose to embark on a path of deep, and often dark, introspection and self-denial. Born in Ukraine, he traveled to the Land of Israel in 1798–99, but his time there was limited by the Napoleonic wars. Returning to Russia, he moved from Zlatipolia to Bratzlav. Upon his death, Rebbe Nachaman's followers—distinguished to this day by their intense loyalty to their *admor* (spiritual leader)—have established the tradition of not naming a successor. His teachings and stories were posthumously published in *Likkutei Moharan* (literally, "Collection of Teachings by Our Teacher Rabbi Nachman") and a book of his tales called *Sippurei Ma'asiyot.* They are still widely read.

Nachmanides/Ramban

(b. 1194–d. 1270, Spain and Israel) Rabbi Moses ben Nachman, a physician and one of the most important scholars in Jewish history. He is most well known for his commentary on the Torah, but he was also an important halakhist, kabbalist, and poet. Between 1263 and 1265, he represented Spanish Jewry in an official debate between Christians and Jews about religious truths. Victorious in his aggressive refutations of Christianity, he recorded the points of the debate in *Sefer Ha-Vikkuach* (literally, "The Book of the Dispute"), a publication that led to a papal warrant for his arrest; he escaped to Israel.

Nevi'im

(literally, "Prophets") The second of the three parts of the TANAKH. It is often further divided into its first set of books, *Nevi'im Rishonim* (Former Prophets), which are primarily historical in nature, and its second set, *Nevi'im Acharonim* (Latter Prophets), which are the speeches of the prophets whose names they bear. One or two chapters from Nevi'im are read each Sabbath and on most holidays. Called *haftarot* (plural of haftarah), they each have particular relevance to the Torah reading for that day.

Pesikta de Rav Kahana and *Pesikta Rabbati*

Two versions of Palestinian midrashim written about parts of the TANAKH: The Five Books of Moses and The Prophets. (*Pesikta* means "section" in Aramaic.) *Pesikta de Rav Kahana* was probably completed by the 5th century C.E., while the *Pesikta Rabbati*—a later version that draws upon the former—was completed after the 9th century and includes glosses from the 13th century. A critical edition of the work was translated into English by William G. Braude in 1968.[2]

Pirke de Rebbe Eliezer

Narrative midrash, or exposition, on biblical stories, falsely attributed to the 2nd-century sage Eliezer ben Hyrcanus. Modern scholars claim that this work was probably written in the Land of Israel in the 8th century. It has furthered Rabbinic thought and is the basis for many customs. (*See* Pseudepigrapha.)

Pri Etz Hadar

(literally, "Fruit of the Lovely Tree") Part of an 18th-century compendium of kabbalistic customs, *Chemdat Yamim* (literally, "Treasure of Days"). Considered significant enough to be printed also as a separate pamphlet (as early as 1728), it is the primary source for the details and meaning of the Tu b'Shevat seder. Dr. Miles Krassen, scholar of Kabbalah and Hasidism, provided the first translation of *Pri Eitz Hadar* into English, which can be found in *Trees, Earth and Torah: A Tu B'Shvat Anthology*, published by The Jewish Publication Society.

Prophets, The See Nevi'im

Pseudepigrapha

A postbiblical (circa 200 B.C.E.–200 C.E.) collection of works, literally named "False (from *pseudo*) Writings (from *graph*)." These books were falsely attributed to ancient heroes to gain in authenticity and authority and possibly to coerce biblical canonization. Nonetheless, these works are highly significant for Jews and Christians. Examples of the Pseudepigrapha are Jubilees, I Enoch, 2 Enoch, Life of Adam and Eve, and Joseph and Asenath.

Rabbenu Gershom

(b. 960–d. 1028, Germany) Gershom ben Yehuda, the leading halakhic and talmudic authority of his time and head of a prominent Jewish academy. Rabbenu (literally, "Our Rabbi") Gershom was nicknamed *Me'or Ha-Golah* ("Light of the Diaspora"). Certain of his decrees were revolutionary, particularly the prohibitions against polygamy, against divorcing a woman against her will, and against reading someone else's mail. These laws became binding for Ashkenazic Jews. Modern scholars challenge whether they were decreed by Rabbenu Gershom himself; but, no matter what, they marked a major shift in German Jewry's reliance on Babylonia, which had been the major center of Jewish learning and authority from about 220 C.E. until the 10th century.

Rabbenu Nissim

(b. circa 1315–d. 1375, Spain) Rabbi Nissim ben Reuven of Gerondi, a great talmudist, *rosh yeshivah* (head of a Jewish school of higher learning) and court physician. Rabbenu (literally, "Our Rabbi") Nissim is best known for his discourse on Judaism called *Derashot* (loosely, "Interpretations") and for his commentary on the Rif's *Sefer Ha-Halakhot* (The Book of Laws). He is also referred to by the acronym of his name, Ran.

Rambam See Maimonides.

Rashbam

(b. 1080–d. 1174, France) Rabbi Shmuel ben Meir, one of the great Bible and Talmud commentators (*see* Tosafot) commonly referred to by the acronym of his name. He is known for his direct style that sticks to a very close reading of the text. The Rashbam was the grandson of the renowned commentator Rashi and was not shy about arguing with his grandfather.

Rashi

(b. 1040–d. 1105, France) Hebrew acronym for Rabbi Shlomo ben Yitzchak, generally regarded as the greatest commentator on both the Torah and the Talmud. Without his explanations, both would be much more difficult to understand. His commentary on the Torah was the first book to be printed in Hebrew; the semicursive typeface, which the printer created to distinguish the explanations from the biblical text, is called "Rashi script" and is still used today.

Rosh

Hebrew acronym for Rabbi Asher ben Yechiel (b. circa 1250–d. 1327, Germany and Spain), leading student of Rabbi Meir of Rothenburg. Rabbenu (literally, "Our Rabbi") Asher is recognized as one of the top halakhic authorities, and his work *Rabbenu Asher* was one of the primary sources for the *Tur* (written by his son Jacob ben Asher) and for the Shulchan Arukh. His explanations on the Talmud were collected and appear in the back of most traditional volumes of the Talmud.

Scholem, Gershom

(b. 1897–d.1982, Germany and Israel) Founder of the modern and scholarly approach to studying Jewish mysticism. A professor at Hebrew University for 40 years, he wrote dozens of books, including *Major Trends in Jewish Mysticism, Origins of the Kabbalah,* and *Sabbetai Tsevi: The Mystical Messiah.*

Sefat Emet

A five-volume work (The Language of Truth) that contains some of the most creative and enriching commentaries on the Torah and on the holidays. Written by Rabbi Yehuda Aryeh Leib Alter of Ger (b. 1847–d. 1904, Poland), it is still widely studied. In 1998, parts of it were published in English, translated by Arthur Green.

Sefer Abudraham

A comprehensive commentary on synagogue ritual and prayers, composed by Rabbi David ben Joseph Abudraham (lived 1300s, Spain). Abudraham culled from many sources to explain the differences between local customs and the calendar.

Sefer Ha-Bahir

(literally, "The Book of Brightness") The earliest source of kabbalistic literature, written in the form of midrash by an unknown author from either Spain or southern France. The work itself attributes sections to the early Rabbis of the Mishnah, but scholars have shown that it is clearly influenced by the later terminology of 12th-century thinkers (e.g., Abraham ibn Ezra) and the medieval collection of midrashim called *Pirke de-Rebbe Eliezer. The Bahir,* as it is commonly known, introduces core kabbalistic concepts, such as the *sefirot* (the 10 emanations of God) and the femininity of the *Shekhinah* (the presence of God).

Sefer Ha-Hinnukh

(literally, "The Book of Education") An anonymous work from the 13th century, intended to be a simple guide to Jewish belief and practice. A 16th-century author attributed it to the talmudist Aaron ben Joseph Ha-Levi (b. 1235–d. 1300, Spain), and this attribution has generally been accepted. *Sefer Ha-Hinnukh* is an enumeration of the 613 *mitzvot*, arranged according to the order of the Torah portions (*parshiyot*), which includes their halakhic and ethical aspects.

Sefer Ha-Manhig

(literally, "The Guide Book") One of the earliest books on Jewish customs. Written by Rabbi Abraham ben Nathan of Lunel (b. 1155–d. 1215, France), this particular work describes the customs of various Jewish communities, as well as the rationale for their practice.

Sefer Ha-Minhagim

A highly popular work in its time, created by Rabbi Isaac of Tyrnau (b. end of 14th century–d. 15th century; Hungary). It describes the customs (*minhagim*) of different Ashkenazic communities. Moses Isserles, the Ashkenazic authority on *halakhah*, often refers to Tyrnau's work in his additions and comments on the Shulchan Arukh.

Sefer Ha-Toda'ah

A popular 1962 work by Rabbi Abraham Eliyahu Ki Tov (b. 1912–d. 1976, United States) that concentrates on the holidays and seasons and includes halakhic and folkloric material. Published in English as *The Book of Our Heritage: The Jewish Year and Its Days of Significance.*[3]

Sefer Mordechai

A work that discusses halakhic teachings and many customs of Ashkenazic Jewry, written by Rabbi Mordechai ben Hillel (b. circa 1250–d. 1298, Germany). It records many doctrines of the author's principal teacher, Rabbi Meir ben Baruch of Rothenburg, as well as those of the Rif (Rabbi Yitzchak Alfasi). Many subsequent codes quote this work, and it appears in the back of the traditional Talmud.

Septuagint

(literally, "The Seventy") The oldest version of the Bible in Greek (3rd century C.E.). Legends from the *Letter of Aristeas* and the Talmud (*Megillah* 9a) surround the birth of the translation. According to legend, it involved 72[4] simultaneous and equal translations of the Bible from Hebrew to Greek. The Septuagint played a pivotal role in hellenized Jewry. In addition to the Hebrew Bible, the Septuagint also includes several translations of the books of the Apocrypha.

Sforno, Ovadiah ben Yaakov

(b. 1475–d. 1550, Italy) One of the great Bible commentators and medieval Jewish philosophers, a physician by trade. Sforno's commentary is usually on the plain meaning (*peshat*) of the biblical text and grammar. He also authored a commentary on *Pirkei Avot* (literally, "Chapters of the Sages," commonly known as *Ethics of the Fathers*) and a philosophical treatise called *Or Ammim* (literally, "Light of Nations").

Shulchan Arukh

(literally, "Set Table") The standard code of Jewish law, first published in 1565. It was compiled by Rabbi Joseph Karo (b. 1488–d. 1575, Spain, Turkey, and Israel). Karo, clearly one of the greatest legal authorities and mystics in Jewish history, followed the style of Jacob ben Asher's *Tur*. He devised the Shulchan Arukh as a key for and synopsis of his own magnificent commentary and elucidation of the *Tur*, known as *Beit Yosef*. The Shulchan Arukh includes the gloss of Rabbi Moses Isserles, also known as Rema (b. circa 1525–d. 1572, Poland), which is titled the *Mapa* (literally, "Tablecloth"). The Shulchan Arukh emphasizes Sephardic customs and practices, while the *Mapa* treats those of the Ashkenazim.

Sifra

(literally, "Book" in Aramaic) Also known as *Torat Kohanim*, a midrash that focuses on the halakhic aspects of the Book of Leviticus. The material comes primarily from the *tannaim* (the Rabbis quoted in the Mishnah). Most scholars believe the final redactor of the work to be a student of Yehudah Ha-Nasi, either Abba Aricha (known as "Rav")[5] or Rabbi Chiya.

Sifrei

(literally, "Books" in Aramaic) Midrash, mostly halakhic in nature, from the school of Rabbi Ishmael that offers verse-by-verse Hebrew exegesis of the biblical books

Numbers and Deuteronomy. Parallel works exist from a rival midrashic school (the school of Rabbi Akiva), which are called *Sifrei Zuta* for Numbers and *Mekhilta de'Rabbi Shimon Bar Yochai* for Deuteronomy.

Sofer, Moses

(b. 1762–d. 1839, Germany and Austria-Hungary)   An outstanding rabbi and halakhic authority, known for his gentleness and peace-loving nature. Nonetheless, he found himself in the forefront of the struggle against the *Hashkalah*, the Jewish movement that favored adopting the vaolues of the Enlightenment. He fought for strict observance of all Jewish customs and forbade his students to read secular literature. He wrote more than 100 works, the best known being the six volumes of his responsa (answers to questons of *halakhah*) and his Bible commentary, which were given the overall title *Hatam Sofer*, the acronym by which the author is generally known.

Talmud

The central and most important body of Rabbinic literature. Combining the Mishnah and Gemara, the Talmud contains material from the Rabbinic academies that dates from sometime before the 2nd century C.E. through the 6th century. It includes halakhic and midrashic expositions, wisdom, personal stories, and arguments. There are two versions: (1) the Jerusalem (*Yerushalmi*), or Palestinian, Talmud and (2) the Babylonian (*Bavli*) Talmud. When people speak of the Talmud generically, they are referring to the *Bavli*, as it is more extensive and widely used. There are 63 areas of study that make up the Talmud, called tractates (*masechtot*). The Talmud serves as the primary source for all later codes of Jewish law.

TANAKH

An acronym for the three books that make up the cornerstone of Jewish beliefs: Torah (the Five Books of Moses); Nevi'im (The Prophets); and Kethuvim (The Writings). When Jews speak of the Bible, they are referring to the TANAKH.

Tanchuma or *Tanchuma Yelamednu*

A collection of midrashic literature, including large sections from *Midrash Rabbah* and *Pesikta Rabbati*, based on the triennial cycle of Torah readings. Much of it is attributed to the 4th-century Palestinian sage Tanchuma ben Abba, hence the name *Tanchuma*. It is distinguished by repetition of an opening phrase, *yelamednu rabbenu*, "Let our master teach us." Scholars are unsure of the date for the final version of *Tanchuma*; the first printed edition appeared in approximately 1521. This work is sometimes confused with a different collection of midrashic material called *Tanchuma Buber* published in 1875 by scholar Solomon Buber (b. 1827–d. 1906, Ukraine).

Tanna de-be Eliyahu[6]

An aggadic midrash narrated in the name of the prophet Eliyahu (Elijah). It has two sections: *Seder Eliyahu Rabbah* and *Seder Eliyahu Zuta*.[7] These comprise teachings on the rationale for mitzvot and morality. Scholars put its start date in the 3rd century with final redaction in the 10th century. The identity of the author is unknown, although his location has been attributed to Jerusalem, Babylon, or Italy. *Tanna de-be Eliyahu* purports to narrate the memoirs of a wise man who tells of all that occurred to him as he traveled from place to place.

Tosafot

(literally, "Additions") Additions to and continuations of Rashi's talmudic commentary and the talmudic process in general. They were written between the 12th and 14th centuries in France and Germany by many scholars, including Rashi's grandchildren, for example, Rashbam. An indispensable part of Talmud study, the Tosafot are printed in the margins of teach page of Talmud, opposite Rashi's commentary. The phrase "The Tosafot" is used as a group name for the rabbis who wrote these additions.

Tosefta

(literally, "Supplement") A collection of additional teachings and statements by the Rabbinic sages organized in the same arrangement as the Mishnah. Scholars debate whether the Tosefta comprises solely tannaitic material (circa 2nd century C.E.) or if it includes material of a later date. Either way, Tosefta is considered authoritative, and much of it is quoted in the Gemara. The Tosefta can usually be found in the back of traditional volumes of the Talmud.

Tur

A book also known as *Arba'ah Turim* (literally, "Four Columns"). It was created by Rabbi Jacob ben Asher (b. circa 1270–d. circa 1340, Germany and Spain), who was known also as the Baal Ha-Turim ("Master of the Columns"). This ambitious work attempts to bridge the gulf between Ashkenazic and Sephardic laws and opinions in force at the time. The legal decisions of great rabbis are divided into four main topics, called columns, or *turim*. The Baal Ha-Turim emphasizes the work and thought of Maimonides and even more so of the "Rosh" (an acronym for the name of his own father, Rabbenu Asher). Joseph Karo's Shulchan Arukh, the fundamental code of Jewish law, follows the basic structure of the *Tur*.

Writings, The *See* Kethuvim.

Yalkut Shimoni

An anthology of midrashim on all portions of the TANAKH. Rabbi Shimon Ha-Darshan of Frankfurt compiled it in the 13th century as a handbook on religious beliefs for Jews throughout the Diaspora. With midrashim culled from 50 different sources, it is very useful for critical analysis.

Yehuda Ha-Levi

(b. 1075–d. 1141, Spain) An important and influential Jewish poet and philosopher who was a physician by profession. His poetry, tending toward the mystical, has been placed in the liturgy (including the *Yamim Noraim*); but his most famous work is the *Kuzari*, written in Arabic and given a structure similar to a platonic dialogue. The *Kuzari* describes the conversion of the king of Khazars (a seminomadic people from Central Asia). Ha-Levi uses the dialogue to argue three things: faith is not inconsistent with reason, revelation is superior to reason, and both of the preceding ideas are proven by looking at Jewish history.

Zohar

(literally, "Illumination") A book of mystical commentaries on the TANAKH that mixes together theology, psychology, myth, ancient Gnosticism, and superstition. The objective is to uncover the deepest mysteries of the world—namely, why God created the universe, how God is manifest in the world, and what the forces of life are. Although some accept the claim that the Zohar was authored by Rabbinic sage Shimon bar Yochai (lived 2nd century C.E., Israel) and his saintly contemporaries, most scholars believe it to have been largely written by Moshe de Leon (b. 1240–d. 1305, Spain).

Endnotes

Introduction

1   Abraham Joshua Heschel, *God in Search of Man* (New York: Farrar, Strauss, and Giroux, 1955), 16–7.

2   Gregory Bateson, *Mind and Nature: A Necessary Unity* (New York: Bantam Books, 1979), 14.

3   Nina Beth Cardin, *The Tapestry of Jewish Time* (Springfield, N.J.: Behrman House, 2000), 1.

Part 1: Eternal Moments of Jewish Time

1   Literally, "Lord of the World." Liturgical poem composed in the Middle Ages. It is sung to various melodies at the close of many religious services.

2   Ole J. Thienhaus, "Jewish Time: Ancient Practice, Hellenistic and Modern Habits, Freud's Reclaiming," *Judaism* v. 48, no. 4 (fall 1999), 442–9.

3   Abraham Joshua Heschel, *The Sabbath* (New York: Farrar, Strauss, and Giroux, 1951), 96.

4   Ibid., 8.

5   In Judaism, the dates as established by Christianity are referred to as B.C.E. (Before the Common Era) and C.E. (Common Era).

Part 2: Hanukkah

1   *The Antiquities of the Jews*, 12:7:7 in *The New Complete Works of Josephus*, trans. William Whiston, ed. Paul L. Maier (Grand Rapids, Mich.: Kregel, 1999), 409.

2   The first day of Hanukkah, the 25th of Kislev, sometimes occurs in very late November. If it falls in the last week of December, the holiday continues into January. In any case, all or most of the holiday always occurs in December.

3   The date for Christmas is December 25 on the Gregorian calendar. In countries that celebrate holidays according to the Julian calendar, such as Russia and Serbia, the corresponding date is January 7 (not to be confused with January 6, the original date for celebrating Jesus' birth on the Gregorian calendar).

4   Two theories have been presented as to why Hanukkah is scarcely mentioned in the Mishnah: (1) Rabbi Yehudah Ha-Nasi, who is attributed with the editing of the Mishnah, purposely excluded the story of Hanukkah. Yehudah Ha-Nasi was of Davidic ancestry and regarded the Hasmoneans as usurpers, since they were not of the Davidic line; and (2) it was an intentional political move not to include the Maccabees for the sake of safety from the ruling Romans. There may have been a serious concern for what the Romans would do if word came to them that the Jews were studying and celebrating a successful rebellion for independence. *See* Isaac Klein, *A Guide to Religious Jewish Practice* (New York: Jewish Theological Seminary, 1979), 227.
Brief mention of Hanukkah occurs in the Mishnah as follows: (1) *Ta'anit* 2:10 and

Mo'ed Katan 3:9, where it is simply listed as a day on which mourning is forbidden; (2) *Bava Kama* 6:6, which discusses the possible liability that may be incurred by people who light candles outside; and (3) *Megillah* 3–4, which lists the holiday's Torah readings.

5 B. Talmud, *Shabbat* 21b.

6 The word "deuterocanonical" comes from the Greek, meaning "belonging to the second canon." It is indicative of a dispute in the early church over acceptance of these books as scriptural texts. Even today, Catholics and Protestants do not classify these texts in the same manner.

7 No one knows why there is a discrepancy between the numbers 70 and 72. We are relying upon legend, which is repeated verbatim by Flavius Josephus, our historian of the time. Most scholars offer the explanation that 70 is the closest round number, which in Roman numerals is LXX.

8 The midrashic account of Judith first appears in printed form in *Chemdat Yamim*, an 18th-century kabbalistic collection.

9 Assyria was an ancient country in what is now northern Iraq. From the early part of the 2nd millenium B.C.E., Assyria was the center of a succession of empires; it was at peak in the 8th and late 7th centuries B.C.E., when its rule stretched from the Persian Gulf to Egypt. It fell in 612 B.C.E. to a coalition of Medes and Chaldeans.

10 Judges 16.

11 Chapters 4 and 5.

12 Most modern scholars believe the date was in the 6th or 7th centuries, and the language was likely Aramaic before translation into Hebrew. The scroll is first mentioned in a Babylonian legal work *(Halakhot Gedolot)* circa 825 C.E.; and Saadia Gaon, the 10th-century leader of Babylonian Jewry, referenced it extensively. In recent times, scholars have come to view the scroll as historically unreliable.

13 Scholars recognize many historical contradictions in the work. They date its authorship to the late 2nd century B.C.E.

14 To create this summary, in addition to the first two Books of the Maccabees and the works of historian Josephus, I used Solomon Zeitlin, *The Rise and Fall of the Judean State* (Philadelphia: The Jewish Publication Society, 1962), 1:1–131. *See also* Theodor H. Gaster, *Festivals of the Jewish Year* (New York: Morrow and Quill, 1952), 233–53; and Solomon Grayzel, "Hanukkah and Its History," in *The Hanukkah Anthology*, ed. Philip Goodman (Philadelphia: The Jewish Publication Society, 1976), 3–26.

15 Macedonia was an ancient country in southeastern Europe, at the northern end of the Greek peninsula. Today the region is divided among Greece, Bulgaria, and the Republic of Macedonia.

16   Antioch is now a city in southern Turkey called Antakya.

17   These groups should not be confused with Hasidism, the mystical religious movement started by the Baal Shem Tov (Rabbi Yisrael ben Eliezer) in 18th-century Eastern Europe).

18   Mattathias's great-grandfather was named Hasmon, believed to be a descendant of the priestly family Joarib. Variations of the name are Jarib and Jehoiarib.

19   I Maccabees 4.

20   *Antiquities of the Jews* 12:7:7 in *The New Complete Works of Josephus*. *See* Al Wolters, "Halley's Comet at a Turning Point in Jewish History," *Catholic Bible Quarterly* 55 (1993): 687–97. Professor Al Wolters from the Redeemer University College in Ontario, Canada, suggests that Josephus might have called it the Festival of Lights because Halley's comet was visible at that exact time in Jerusalem. Wolters cites the claims of astronomers who say that the comet was visible in the ancient Near East in the year 164 B.C.E. from September through December.

21   Because Hanukkah lasts for eight days, it always coincides with one Shabbat. The haftarah (specified weekly reading from The Prophets) is Zechariah 2:14–4:7, which concludes with the phrase quoted here.

22   *Orach Chayyim, Beit Yosef* 670.

23   Arukh Ha-Shulchan 670:3–5.

24   Maimonides, *Mishneh Torah, Hilkhot Hanukkah* 3:2; *Sefer Ha-Toda'ah*, vol. I, 268–70. This reasoning does not stand up to the test of nature, as it is quite possible to produce olive oil from olives in the Jerusalem area in less than eight days.

25   *Pesikta Rabbati* 2:1.

26   I Macc. 4:39–59.

27   2 Maccabees was intended to be an abbreviated version of a five-volume historical account of Jason of Cyrene (*see* ch. 2:19), which was lost over time. Unlike I Maccabees, which was originally written in Hebrew (although, only a Greek version survived antiquity), 2 Maccabees was composed in Greek.

28   Translation from *The Oxford Study Bible: Revised English Bible with Apocrypha*, ed. M. Jack Suggs, Katharine Doob Sakenfeld, and James R. Mueller (New York: Oxford University Press, 1992), 1247–8.

29   I Macc. 13:51.

30   Rabbinic literature even compares the *lulav* to a victory baton (Midrash on Ps. 17:5).

31   I Macc. 4:52–54; II Macc. 10:4–5.

32   This talmudic text is used to illustrate this exact same point. *A Different Light: The Big Book of Hanukkah*, ed. Noam Zion and Barbara Spectre (Jerusalem: The Shalom Hartman Institute, 2000), 247.

33   A well-known mosaic at the Vatican, in the so-called grotto beneath St. Peter's Basilica, is commonly referred to as a depiction of Jesus riding in a chariot and appearing as the sun god Helios.

34   The Eastern Orthodox Church did not move the date to December 25 until the 5th century, and it has continued to retain January 6 as the day that Jesus' baptism is celebrated. The Armenian Church is an exception to this practice, because it still uses January 6 as the date for both birthday and baptism.

35   The competition worked both ways. With the coming of Christianity, the ancient pagan festival of Yule, celebrated according to the lunar calendar in Anglo-Saxon, Germanic, and Scandinavian cultures, was moved to December 25.

36   The date change also helped dilute the popularity in the Near East of the winter solstice holiday for the Persian god Mithra. The attraction to Christmas was even further enabled by the similarities between the stories of Jesus and Mithra. Born of a virgin birth, Mithra was the son of the great Persian deity, Ahura Mazda. Both Jesus and Mithra raised the dead, performed miracles, and were killed and resurrected after a springtime meal with 12 disciples.

37   As described in Exodus 37:17–24, a "menorah" is a candelabra that has seven branches.

38   B. Talmud, *Shabbat* 24a; Maimonides, *Mishneh Torah, Hilkhot Hanukkah* 3:3; *Tur*/Shulchan Arukh, *Orach Chayyim* 671: 5–7.

39   B. Talmud, *Shabbat* 21b.

40   B. Talmud, *Shabbat* 21b; Maimonides, *Mishneh Torah, Hilkhot Hanukkah* 4:5; *Tur* 672:1; see also *Beit Yosef* there. A dispute occurred between the Rambam and the Ba'al Ha-Turim about what the Talmud meant when it said that the lights should be kindled at sunset and about how to best exemplify *pirsumei nissah*. In other words, when is the best time to show off the lights to passersby? The *Tur* understands it to mean after sunset and therefore after the evening prayer (*Ma'ariv*), while the Rambam maintains that we should light them right at the time of sunset. This dispute is somewhat irrelevant today when we consider modern conditions, such as living in the age of electricity with business hours that extend well beyond sundown. That being said, most people follow the Rambam.

41   Additional oil or larger candles (tea lights work well) should be used for the Hanukkah lights to make sure they will last a full half-hour after sunset.

42   The Rema, in both *Darkei Moshe* and the *Mapa* (*Orach Chayyim* 273:1), says he learned the preference of olive oil from the Maharil, while *Sefer Mordechai* (*siman* 268) cites learning it from Rabbi Meir ben Barukh of Rothenberg.

43   Klein, 229.

▲   ▲   ▲   ▲   ▲   ▲   ▲   ▲   ▲   ▲   ▲   ▲   ▲   ▲

44   B. Talmud, *Arakhin* 13b.

45   *Tur*/Shulchan Arukh, *Orach Chayyim* 676.

46   *Terumat Ha-Deshen*, 106; see *Beit Yosef* 676 for summary of *Terumat Ha-Deshen.*

47   Shulchan Arukh, *Orach Chayyim* 676:5.

48   *Hatam Sofer, Orach Chayyim* 187.

49   B. Talmud, *Shabbat* 21b.

50   Maimonides, *Mishneh Torah, Hilkhot Hanukkah* 4:1–3.

51   The Talmud uses the word *ha-mehadrin,* which is translated here as "The Zealous." Instead of *ha-mehadrin,* Maimonides uses the expression *ha-mehader et ha-mitzvah* (literally, "one who beautifies the mitzvah").

52   The Talmud uses the words *mehadrin min ha-mehadrin,* which are translated here as "The Very Zealous." Maimonides, however, uses the expression *ha-mehader yoter* (literally, "one who beautifies more").

53   The Rema claims that this is the common custom among Ashkenazic Jews, *Mapa, Orach Chayyim* 271:2.

54   According to Maimonides, "Sephardic" refers to people in Spain. Today Sephardic is often used as an umbrella term to mean all non-Ashkenazic Jews (Ashkenazim are the Jews of Central and Eastern Europe and their descendants). The name derives from Sepharad, most likely Sardis in Asia Minor, which became home to exiles from Jerusalem after the destruction of the First Temple. The first known appearance of the word "Sepharad" is in the Bible, in Obadiah 1:20. This Aramaic translation of the Bible (attributed to Yonatan ben Uzziel) identified the term as "Spain." The word later came to apply to the Jews who were expelled from Spain in 1492 (many of whom moved to Portugal, the Mediterrean Basin, North Africa, and the Middle East).

55   This is the custom quoted by Joseph Karo in the Shulchan Arukh, *Orach Chayyim* 271:2.

56   David Golinkin, "Hanukkah Exotica," in *A Different Light: The Big Book of Hanukkah,* edited by Noam Zion and Barbara Spectre (Jerusalem: The Shalom Hartman Institute, 2000), 177–8. *See also* Philip Goodman, *The Hannukkah Anthology* (Philadelpha: The Jewish Publication Society, 1992), 265–6.

57   The Jews of medieval France and Italy seemed to have called this game—which was apparently not even connected to Hanukkah—by other names: *tam v'hetzl* or *tam v'kes* both meaning ("whole and half") and *tam v'khazer* ("whole and missing").

58   In Yiddish, the word is *dreyen.*

59   Arukh Ha-Shulchan 670:9. See also *Be'ur Halakhah* 670:2 in which the author, Yisrael Meir Ha-Kohen (the Chofetz Chaim), uses very strong language to condemn card playing during Hanukkah.

▲   ▲   ▲   ▲   ▲   ▲   ▲   ▲   ▲   ▲   ▲   ▲   ▲

60   From an online essay by Professor Eliezer Diamond of the Jewish Theological Seminary.

61   This practice is still followed in some circles, for example, among the Hasidim.

62   Mishnah, *Sanhedrin* 3:3. *See also* Mishnah, *Rosh Hashanah* 1:8, where it says that gamblers are not reliable as witnesses of the new moon.

63   B. Talmud, *Sanehdrin* 24b. Rami bar Chama offers the opinion that gambling is like stealing, because one is entering into an agreement (*asmachta*) in which each party erroneously expects the outcome to work favorably for them. Therefore, because the gamblers do not truly expect to lose, the losers have their money taken from them against their will (i.e., stealing from them). Rav Sheshet argues that gambling is not an *asmachta*, because the outcome is determined by skill as well as chance and therefore the players know that they have a chance to lose. Rather, he argues, gambling is not good because it is a futile occupation. Both arguments are understood to be consistent with Rabbi Yehudah in the Mishnah, and both Rami bar Chama and Rav Sheshet understand gamblers to be untrustworthy. However, since Rav Sheshet does not see gambling as an *asmachta* and sees it as demeaning those who contribute nothing to the world, he would seem to permit occasional gambling by those who have other jobs and contribute to the world.

64   Maimonides, *Mishneh Torah, Hilkhot Geneivah* 6:8–11.

65   Tosafot, on *Sanhedrin* 24b *d''h: kol ki ha'I gavna lav asmachta hee*, Rif on *Sanhedrin* 4b, Rosh on *Sanhedrin* 3:7, and *Sefer Mordechai* on *Sanhedrin* 690 all side with Rav Sheshet (in contrast to Rambam, who is unclear) and would thus permit gambling on a casual basis as long as the gamblers had other occupations and contributed to society. When explaining Rav Sheshet's position in *Sanhedrin* 24b, Rashi, as well as Rabbenu Tam (Tosafot on *Bava Metzi'a* 74a *d''h: hakha lav beyado*) states that an *asmachta* does not apply in situations where there is more than one person, as both parties must accept the possibility of losing in exchange for the possibility of winning (prohibited on the basis of stealing).

The *Mapa* and *Beit Yosef* (*Choshen Mishpat* 207:13) further the position of Rav Sheshet, allowing only gambling that involves certain skill and where players openly put their money up front (so they show they have already relinquished it in some way, precluding Rami bar Chama's idea of it being stolen).

The Israeli government made an amendment in 1964 that punishes professional gamblers with up to one year of imprisonment and a fine of up to "5,000 pounds." (In 1948, the newly established State of Israel inherited the Palestinian pound, soon renamed the lira and, within a few years, no longer pegged to the British pound. The currency of Israel became the shekel in 1980.) For a good summary of Jewish law and gambling, which mentions this fine, see *The Principles of Jewish Law*, ed. Menachem Elon (Jerusalem: Keter Publishing, 1974), 511.

66 "Hanukkah Exotica" by David Golinkin in *A Different Light*, 178.

67 *Mapa, Orach Chayyim* 670:2. The Rema quotes the Kol Bo and the Ran. The *Mishnah Berurah* (Rabbi Yisrael Meir Ha-Kohen, the Chofetz Chaim, 1838–1933), commenting on the Rema in 270:2, adds, "She was the daughter of Yohanan the High Priest. There was an edict that every engaged woman should sleep with a nobleman first [*prima nocte*], and she fed the head of the oppressors cheese to make him drunk, and cut off his head, and everyone fled."

68 A medieval midrash, *Ma'aseh Yehudit*, says that Judith "opened the milk flask and drank and also gave the king to drink, and he rejoiced with her greatly and he drank very much wine, more than he had drunk in his entire life." This text, translated by David Golinkin, implies that Judith gave Holofernes (here referred to as the king) both milk and wine.

69 *See* Gil Marks, *The World of Jewish Cooking* (New York: Simon and Schuster, 1999), 220–4. Although I have not found one definitive source that says potatoes latkes evolved from cheese latkes, there is considerable evidence in various fields to support this idea.

70 Matthew Goodman, "Toasting Triumph over Tyranny with Foods Cooked in Oil," *Forward*, December 7, 2001.

71 The name is based on the Greek *sufgan*, meaning "puffed" or "fried."

72 Philip Goodman, *The Hannukkah Anthology*, 268.

73 Shulchan Arukh, *Orach Chayyim* 273:1.

74 Professor Eliezer Segal from the University of Calgary claims that this custom is mentioned in *Chemdat Yamim*. He quotes: "In some communities, the custom has arisen of having the children distribute coins to their teachers along with other gifts. Other beggars make the rounds then, though the mitzvah is intended primarily for the benefit of impecunious students."

75 Rabbi Yisrael ben Eliezer, the Baal Shem Tov, was born in 1698 in a village on the Russian-Polish border. He died in 1760.

76 Philip Goodman, 268.

77 Alternative spellings of Lag b'Omer, Yom Ha-Atzmaut, and Tu b'Shevat.

78 Ron Wolfson, *Hanukkah, 2nd Edition: The Family Guide to Spiritual Celebration* (Woodstock, Vt.: Jewish Lights Publishing, 2001).

79 Literally, "bread of faces"; 12 cakes or loaves of bread prepared and presented before God on the golden table. Each Sabbath, new loaves replaced the old, which were then eaten by the priests as holy bread.

80 Bar Kokhba revolt (132–5 C.E.).

81 Web site of the Jewish Outreach Institute.

82   According to *The Oxford Study Bible*, 1198, the author's "143" is 169 B.C.E. by today's reckoning.

83   *The Oxford Study Bible*, 1198–9.

84   B. Talmud, *Sanhedrin* 82a, states that although God's law finds what Phinehas did acceptable, it should not be followed: "The law may permit, but we do not follow that law!" Moreover, the J. Talmud, *Sanhedrin* 27b, says that the Rabbis would have excommunicated Phinehas for what he did, had it not been for God's acceptance of him.

85   *The First Book of Maccabees*, ed. Solomon Zeitlin, trans. Sidney Tedesche (New York: Harper & Brothers, 1950), 79–89. Also appears in Goodman, 38–40.

86   Literally, the "Scroll of Hidden Things." This work is mentioned elsewhere by other Rabbinic scholars from the 11th and 12th centuries and probably refers to an anthology of biblical explanations and Jewish philosophy. It has been lost over the course of time.

87   *Sefat Emet, D'rash Le-Hanukkah* 1:211. Translation from Arthur Green, *The Language of Truth* (Philadelphia: The Jewish Publication Society, 1998), 381–2.

88   Translation by Nachman Bulman in *The Book of Our Heritage* (New York: Feldheim, 1997), 295–6.

89   Chabad is a Hebrew acronym for three intellectual faculties: *hokhmah* ("wisdom"); *binah* ("comprehension"); and *da'at* ("knowledge"). Lubavitch is the name of the town in White Russia where the movement was based for more than a century. The movement was nearly decimated during the Holocaust but was expanded greatly during the 1940s in the United States by Rabbi Yosef Yitzchak Schneersohn.

90   From *Sichot Ha-Rebbe* (literally, "Talks of the Rebbe"). This source is quoted in Zion and Spectre, 36.

91   Theodor H. Gaster, *Festivals of the Jewish Year* (New York: William Sloane Associates, 1953), 244–6.

92   Yehezkel Kaufmann, trans. Moshe Greenberg, "The Biblical Age," *Great Ages and Ideas of the Jewish People*, ed. Leo W. Schwartz (New York: Random House, 1956), 91–92.

93   There are two versions of the Talmud: Jerusalem Talmud (completed in the 5th century in northern Israel) and the more extensive Babylonian Talmud (completed in the 6th century in Babylon).

94   Translated by Reuven Hammer in *Or Hadash* (New York: The Rabbinical Assembly, 2003), 307.

95   The Second Temple was completed in 515 B.C.E. on the site of the First Temple, which had been destroyed by the Babylonians. More than 500 years later, in 70 C.E., the very large and magnificent Second Temple was destroyed by the Roman general Titus in response to the Jews' unsuccessful Great Revolt. The Western Wall in Jerusalem is

revered today because it is a remnant of the "mount" (or base) of the Second Temple.

96   Rav Kook is explaining the Talmud on Hanukkah (*Shabbat* 21b). Translated by Sam Shor.

97   *See* Tosafot in B. Talmud, *Shabbat* 21b, *d'h: V'mehadrin min ha-mehadrin.*

98   Today Judaism almost exclusively follows Hillel's practice, adding one light per night, from one to eight, rather than Shammai's, which started with eight the first night and decreased to one. As on frank scholar put it: *chet neirot v'halakhah k'Beit Hillel* or "[There are] eight lights, and the law follows the Beit Hillel" *(Sefer Abudraham. Seder Hadlakat Ner Hanukkah).*

99   If the sixth stanza is included, it is usually done without translation.

100 Maimonides, introduction to first mishnah of 10th chapter of tractate *Sanhedrin.* For an English translation see *Fundamentals of the Rambam,* trans. and annotated Avraham Yaakov Finkel (Scranton, Pa.: Yeshivath Bet Moshe, 2005), 2:336–8.

101 A commentary on *Pirkei Avot* ("Ethics of Our Fathers"), probably composed in the late 3rd century.

102 *The Language of Truth, The Torah Commentary of the Sefat Emet,* trans. and interpreted Arthur Green (Philadelphia: The Jewish Publication Society, 1998), 379.

103 Written at the founding of Kibbutz Maale Ha-Hamisha.

104 *Leviticus Rabbah, Shemini* 11.

105 Gen. 1:3.

106 Noam Zion, "How Hanukkah Became a Home Holiday," in Zion and Spectre, 164–7.

107 Theodor Herzl, "The Menorah," in *The Jewish Spirit: A Celebration in Stories & Art,* ed. Ellen Frankel (New York: Stewart, Tabori and Chang, 1997), 31–3.

108 "Lights by Night" in *The Eternal Journey,* Jonathan Wittenberg, (New York: Aviv Press, 2003), 105–7.

109 Nick Naydler, "Like a songbird in its cage," in *For Anne Frank* (Bristol: Loxwood Stoneleigh, 1991).

110 From Wayne Dosick, *Dancing with God: Everyday Steps to Jewish Spiritual Renewal* (San Francisco: HarperCollins, 1997), 134–5.

Part 3: Tu b'Shevat

1   Arbor Day is an American holiday founded in Nebraska in 1872 as a day for massive tree planting. It is now observed on the last Friday of every April (except in Louisiana, which observes it on the first Friday of January). The purpose of the celebration is to encourage people to plant and care for trees.

2   Georges Roux, *Ancient Iraq* (London: Penguin Books, 1964), 40–7.

3   David Rindos, *The Origins of Agriculture: An Evolutionary Perspective* (Burlington, Mass.: Academic Press, 1987), chaps. 1–2; Colin Tudge, *The Time before History* (New York:

Touchstone Books, 1997), 264–79.

4 Arthur Waskow, "Growing Tu B'Shvat: The Life-Juice of the Tree History," in *Trees, Earth, and Torah: A Tu B'Shvat Anthology*, ed. Ari Elon, Naomi Mara Hyman, and Arthur Waskow (Philadelphia: The Jewish Publication Society, 1999), 5.

5 Gen. 2:7.

6 Gen. 2:5.

7 Gen. 3:17–9.

8 In this case (Lev. 19:23), the Hebrew *va'araltem arlato*, which the JPS TANAKH translates as "you shall regard its fruit as forbidden," literally means "you shall trim its fruit in the manner of a foreskin." See *Etz Hayim: Torah and Commentary*, ed. David Lieber (Philadelphia: The Jewish Publication Society, 2001), 698.

9 My colleague Rabbi Baruch Zeilicovich inspired me to see this connection.

10 Nogah Hareuveni, *Nature in Our Biblical Heritage* (Kiryat Ono, Israel: Neot Kedumim, 1980), 106–9. This source draws a parallel between Tu b'Av (15th of Av), which is exactly six months on the other side of the calendar year. Accordingly, Tu b'Av is the date on which sunlight begins to diminish in strength.

11 Deut. 8.8.

12 Hareuveni, *Nature in Our Biblical Heritage*, 109–13.

13 The Shulchan Arukh, *Orach Chayyim* 572:3 states that fasting is prohibited on Tu b'Shevat thus placing it in the same category as festivals. *Sefer Mordecai* (13th century) on tractate *Rosh Hashanah* 701 provides the rationale for this fasting prohibition, claiming that since all of the New Years are listed in the same Mishnah (i.e., *Rosh Hashanah* 1:1), they are equal to each other in some respects, including prohibitions on fasting. Also, Rabbi Meir of Rothenburg provides a proof-text equating Tu b'Shevat to a proper festival in the name of Rabbenu Gershom *Meor Ha-Golah* (960–1028)—*see* Rabbi Shlomo Yosef Zevin, *The Festivals in Halakhah* (New York: Mesorah Publications, 1999), 1:481–2.

14 For a good introduction and translation, *see* Joyce Galaski, "Shemoneh Esrei for the New Year of the Trees: A Medieval Amidah for Tu B'Shvat," in *Trees, Earth, and Torah*, 71–82.

15 Gershom Scholem, *Major Trends in Jewish Mysticism* (New York: Schocken Press, 1941), 244–51.

16 For a superb description of the Lurianic conception of creation, *see* Lawrence Fine, *Physician of the Soul, Healer of the Cosmos: Isaac Luria and His Kabbalistic Fellowship* (Stanford, Calif.: Stanford University Press, 2003), 124–49. In short, the Lurianic myth begins with a universe having been composed solely of God and God's infiniteness. Then, God chose to create the world, either because God wanted to benefit something other than God's Self or because God wanted to self-improve and cleanse God's Self from the element of stern judgment *(din)*.

Therefore, God withdrew *(tsimtsum)* in order to create room for the creation of the universe. After God withdrew, what was left was an unformed mass *(golem)* from which the four worlds would develop. God then sent forth God's own energy and light back into the unformed mass, forming vessels or containers for the light, which then animated them. The energy and light came in the form of 10 emanations called *sefirot*, and each of the *sefirot* was to be contained in each of the vessels. Because the intensity of the light of the "higher" *sefirot*, it spread beyond their own vessels and most of the others shattered, unable to contain it. This resulted in the separating and scattering the *sefirot* and elements of compassion and judgment, along with the broken shards of the vessels. Had the vessels been strong enough to contain the *sefirot* and highest forms of divine energy, then divine order and harmony would have been established. However, the shattering ended that process; and, even though they were separated and scattered, many of the pieces remained attached to shards of broken vessels. Those shards make up our world. Furthermore, the higher forms of light such as lovingkindness and benevolence became attached to the broken vessels, along with elements of evil, i.e., derivatives of the *sefirah* of *din.* Therefore, through both our internal and our external lives, our purpose is to actually release the divine light from the shattered vessels, allowing for God's reunification and regaining of harmony. This process of releasing the divine sparks is called *tikun olam* (healing the world).

17   A kabbalistic teaching in *gematria* claims that because the adult has 32 teeth and God's name *(Elohim)* appears 32 times in the Bible's account of Creation, chewing has the potential to heal the world *(tikun olam)* when done with proper concentration.

18   *Otzar Yisrael*, ed. Judah David Eisenstein (New York: privately printed, 1913), 10:34; available to download for free at www.hebrewbooks.org/. This popular encyclopedia notes that on Tu b'Shevat in 1890, a group of teachers took their students to Motza to plant a tree in honor of the day. This may be the origin of the contemporary custom.

19   *Magen Avraham* 131:16.

20   B. Talmud, *Ta'anit* 23 a.

21   Herbert Dobrinsky, *A Treasury of Sephardic Laws and Customs* (New York: Yeshiva University Press, 1988), 376–80; Rabbi Shlomo Yosef Zevin, *The Festivals in Halakhah*, 1:484.

22   Michael Strassfeld, *The Jewish Holidays: A Guide & Commentary* (New York: HarperCollins Publishers, 1985; HarperResource Quill, 2001), 180.

23   This translation was guided by that of William G. Braude in *The Book of Legends, Sefer Ha-Aggadah*, ed. Hayim Nahman Bialik and Yehoshua Hana Ravnitzky (New York: Schocken Press, 1992), 11.

24   Translated by David Seidenberg.

25   *Sefer Hachinuch: The Book of Education*, no. 529 (New York: Feldheim Publishers, 1989).

26   Translation by Daniel Matt in *The Zohar: Pritzker Edition* (Stanford, Calif.: Stanford University Press, 2004), 2:128–9.

27   *Yah* is one of the names of God derived from the Hebrew letters *yud* and *heh*. Rather than using the more commonplace translations for the Hebrew word for God, this translation uses the name *Yah*.

28   Translated by Zalman Schachter-Shalomi; found in *Trees, Earth, and Torah*, 153. Note: the blessing with which the reading begins is Reb Zalman's alternative translation to the traditional blessing for seeing trees blossom for the first time in the year.

29   This piece is based on *Tanchuma Buber* with adaptations; Adam Fisher, *Seder Tu Bishevat: The Festival of Trees* (New York: CCAR Press, 1989), 41.

30   Martin Buber, *I and Thou* (New York: Scribners Classics, 1958), 7–8.

31   Ismar Schorsch, "Trees for Life," in *Trees, Earth, and Torah*, 238–40.

32   Deuteronomy is a Greek word that means "Second Law," derived from the Hebrew term *mishneh Ha-Torah*, "copy of this Teaching" (Deut. 17:18). In the Septuagint (the Bible translated into Greek) each of the Five Books of Moses was given a new name. Deuteronomy was imposed on top of the original Hebrew name, which is *Devarim* ("Words") from the first sentence, beginning: "These are the words that Moses addressed to all Israel . . ." (Deut. 1:1).

33   The word *mishneh* comes from the three-letter Hebrew root *shin.nun.heh.*, or *lishnot*, which means "to repeat/recycle." Because *lishnot* means to repeat, it has a connection to the concept of learning, which is something done through repetition. Thus *Mishneh Torah* means a repetition of the Torah. The name Mishnah, the body of work that is the core of the Talmud, comes from the same root.

34   *A Person Is Like a Tree, A Sourcebook for Tu BeShvat*, trans. guided by Yitzhak Buxbaum, (Northvale, N.J.: Jason Aronson, 2000), 94.

35   *See also* I Chron. 29:20 for an example of the origin of this formula in the Bible.

36   B. Talmud, *Menachot* 43a.

37   For a comprehensive guide to rules over food blessings see Naftali Hoffner, *Guide to Blessings* (Union of Orthodox Jewish Congregations of America, 1997).

38   Abraham Joshua Heschel, *God in Search of Man* (New York: Farrar, Straus, and Giroux, 1955), 356.

39   *Etz Hayim: Torah and Commentary*, ed. David Lieber (Philadelphia: The Jewish Publication Society, 2001).

40   *See* Maimonides, *Mishneh Torah, Hilkhot Yesodei Ha-Torah* 2:2 in which he says, "What is the path of love and fear of God? When a person contemplates God's wondrous and great deeds and creations and appreciates God's wisdom that surpasses all comparison, he will

immediately love, praise, and glorify God, yearning with tremendous desire to know God's great name, as David [Psalms] stated: 'my soul thirsts for God, the living God' (Ps. 42:3)."

41 These were the four tithes:

(1) *Terumah*—annually, a total of $\frac{1}{60}$ to $\frac{1}{40}$ of one's crop was given as a gift to the *Kohanim*;

(2) *Ma'aser rishon* (first tithe)—annually, a total of $\frac{1}{10}$ of the portion of the produce left over after *terumah* had been taken was given as a gift to the Levites. The Levites, in turn, gave $\frac{1}{10}$ of this gift to the *Kohanim*;

(3) *Ma'aser sheni* (second tithe)—during the first, second, fourth, and fifth years of the seven-year cycle, $\frac{1}{10}$ of the remaining produce was brought to Jerusalem to be eaten there by the owner of the crop; and

(4) *Ma'aser oni* (tithe of the poor)—during the third and sixth years of the seven-year cycle, $\frac{1}{10}$ of one's crop was given for the poor. It replaced the second tithe in those years.

42 The laws for the *shemitah* are in Lev. 25. There it prohibits reaping the harvest from the land in the seventh year, allowing the land "a year of complete rest." Perhaps there was an agricultural benefit from doing this (e.g., reducing sodium in the soil), though most scholars understand the benefits to be ethical (e.g., reducing economic competition, because rich and poor alike were under the same restrictions). Some farmers in modern-day Israel still observe the laws of *shemitah*.

43 *See* Harold S. Himmelfarb, *Jewish Education for Naught: Education the Culturally Deprived Jewish Child* (Washington, D.C.: Institute for Jewish Policy and Planning and Research of the Synagogue Council of America, 1975); Geoffrey Bock, *Does Jewish Schooling Matter?* (American Jewish Committee, 1977); Ariela Keysar and Barry Kosmin, *Research Findings on the Impact of Camp Ramah* (National Ramah Commission of the Jewish Theological Seminary, 2004).

44 *Tomer Devorah*, chap. 9; *see* English translation, *The Palm Tree of Deborah*, trans. Moshe Miller (Southfield, Mich.: Targum Press, 1993).

45 Gen. 2:15 states that Adam's purpose is both to work the earth and to watch over it. Also, the laws of the sabbatical year in Lev. 25:1–7 are intended to allow the earth to replenish itself, ensuring that it is not abused intentionally or unintentionally.

46 As evidenced by the law in Deut. 22:10 that forbids yoking an ass and ox together and by the thrice-repeated law prohibiting boiling a kid in its mother's milk (Deut. 14:21; Exod. 23:19, 34:26).

47 Hareuveni, *Nature in Our Biblical Heritage*, 118.

48 For a more detailed treatment of *bal tash'hit* as a legal principle, *see*, for example, Norman Lamm and Jonathan Helfand in *Torah of the Earth: Exploring 4,000 Years of Ecology in Jewish Thought*, vol. I, ed. Arthur Waskow (Woodstock, Vt.: Jewish Lights Publishing, 2000).

49   *Shabbat* 67b.

50   Samson Raphael Hirsch, *Horeb: A Philosophy of Jewish Laws and Observances,* trans. I. Grunfeld (New York: Soncino Press, 1981), 279–80.

51   Ibid.

52   Ps. 24:1.

53   *Rosh Hashanah* 31a.

54   Buxbaum, *A Person Is Like a Tree,* 63–4.

55   *Midrash Rabbah, Ecclesiastes Rabbah* 7:28.

56   Citrus is a wholly edible fruit, because we can use the peel for food, and probably fits best at this third level. But some people place citrus at the first level, that of fruit with a shell.

57   For collections of useful texts and ideas, *see* the Web site neohasid.org and also the Web site of the Coalition on the Environment and Jewish Life, www.coejl.org/.

58   In the anthology *Trees, Earth, and Torah,* 276–81

59   Alternative transliteration of the name of the holiday.

60   *See* Deut. 24:19–22; Ps. 24:1; Lev. 25:23–4.

61   Translation from *Haggadah Shel Tu-Bi'Shevat,* The Jewish National Fund, 11.

62   Matt Biers-Ariel, Deborah Newbrun, and Michal Fox Smart, *Spirit in Nature* (Springfield, NJ.: Behrman House, 2000), 10.

63   In Yitzhak Buxbaum, *A Tu BeShvat Seder: The Feast of Fruits from the Tree of Life,* (New York: Jewish Spirit Publishing, 1998), 26.

64   Alternative transliteration of the name of the holiday.

65   *Sarei Ha-Maiya,* 3:168.

Part 4: Purim

1   *The Hasidic Anthology,* ed. Louis I. Newman (Northvale, N.J.: Jason Aronson, 1963), 42. Although the word "laughing" is not used, there are references to "happy to be alive" and "cheerful without cause." Nonetheless, I have heard this sequence offered by various teachers, who included "laughing" as the third lesson.

2   Maimonides, *Mishneh Torah, Hilkhot Megillah* 2:8–11; Shulchan Arukh, *Orach Chayyim* 690:3.

3   B. Talmud, *Megillah* 4a; Maimonides, *Mishneh Torah, Hilkhot Megillah* 1:3; *Tur*/Shulchan Arukh, *Orach Chayyim* 687:1.

4   *Midrash Rabbah, Esther Rabbah* on 1:11 says Ahasuerus wanted Vashti to show up wearing nothing but the royal diadem so the men could ogle her.

5   The Bible gives several examples of permitting Jews to bow to superiors (Gen. 23:7; 43:28; Exod. 18:7; I Kings 1:23). Mordecai refused in this case for ethnic reasons, as it would be offensive to bow to a descendant of Agag, the Amalekite king and sworn

enemy of Israel (I Sam. 15, and cf. Exod. 17.14–6; Deut. 25.17–9). Rabbinic interpretations give additional reasons. One claims that Haman was wearing an idol around his neck; and if Mordecai had bowed to Haman, he would have bowed to an idol. Another suggests it is inappropriate to bow to anyone other than God.

6   Shulchan Arukh, *Orach Chayyim* 686:2.

7   Bathing is forbidden on both Yom Kippur and Tisha b'Av; working is forbidden on Yom Kippur only.

8   Shulchan Arukh, *Orach Chayyim* 686:2; *Mapa.*

9   Ibid.

10   B. Talmud, *Megillah* 2a. *See* Shlomo Yosef Zevin in *The Festivals in Halakhah*, which cites this discussion of the Talmud with regard to how that discussion evolves into the basis for the Fast of Esther. As Zevin points out, when the Talmud says, "The thirteenth [of Adar] is a time of gathering for everyone," the commentary *She'iltot*, in the section discussing *parashat vayakhel*, interprets the term "gathering" as "fast day."

11   The source in the Torah is Exod. 17:10: "Joshua did as Moses told him and fought with Amalek, while Moses, Aaron, and Hur went on the top of the hill." Although this verse hardly implies that Moses fasted, the Rosh is basing his interpretation on the teaching in the *Mechilta, Amalek* chapter 1 (*see also* Rashi), which interprets this to mean that Moses fasted and recited *selichot*, "penitential prayers."

12   Rosh on *Megillah* 2a, 1:8. *See also* Ran on *Megillah* 2a; Tosefot, *Ta'anit* 18a, *d"h: Rav;* Beit Yosef, *Orach Chayyim* 686:2. My translation was guided by Rabbi Shlomo Yosef Zevin in *The Festivals in Halakhah*, vol. 2 (New York: Mesorah Publications, 1999), 574–5.

13   Isa. 51:1–13.

14   Chap. 3. *See also* B. Talmud, *Yoma* 81a.

15   Maimonides sums it up well in the *Mishneh Torah* when he says, "This practice [fasting] is one of the paths of repentance, for when a difficulty arises and the people cry out to God and sound the trumpets, everyone will realize that the difficulty occurred because of their evil conduct, and it states, *Your sins have withheld the bounty from you* [Jer. 5:25]. This [realization] will cause the removal of this difficulty" (*Hilkhot Ta'aniyot* 1:2).

16   Maimonides, *Hilkhot Ta'aniyot* 5.

17   This is also related to the reason for fasting on one's wedding day, one of the most jubilant and profound days of a person's life. *See* Rama in Shulchan Arukh, *Even Ha-Ezer* 61:1, also *Be'er Hetev* there, and Rama *Orach Chayyim* 562:2; Arukh Ha-Shulchan, *Even Ha-Ezer* 61:21. Hasidic thought, which is inclined toward the spirituality of joyfulness, is particularly keen on this purpose for fasting. *See* Nachman of Bratslav, *Likutey Mohoran* 77.

18   Esther 4:16.

19   Esther 9:16.

20   *Mishnah Berurah*, 686: 2, *se'if katan* 2.

21   *See* B. Talmud, *Megillah* 19a where it mentions fasting the day of a battle as a means to avert any tragedies that may occur.

22   Maimonides, *Hilkhot Megillah* 1:1; *Tur*/Shulchan Arukh, *Orach Chayyim* 687:2, 696:7.

23   B. Talmud, *Megillah* 4a states that the reading must be fitting for all times (it is a statement of God's praise), including the night. Since the Mishnah (*Megillah* 2:6) does not mention the nightly reading, some authorities have deduced that it was a later institution. *See also* Maimonides, *Hilkhot Megillah* 1:3; *Tur*/Shulchan Arukh, *Orach Chayyim* 687:1.

24   B. Talmud, *Megillah* 4a.

25   Judaism has both positive and negative commandments. A positive, time-bound commandment is a commandment to do something, such as praying, at a specific time. A negative commandment is a prohibition against an activity. In traditional Judaism, women are not mandated to fulfill certain positive commandments. The reason generally offered is the overriding need to fulfill obligations of domesticity and child-rearing that are time-bound.

26   Maimonides, *Hilkhot Megillah* 1:1; *Tur*/Shulchan Arukh, *Orach Chayyim* 689:1.

27   B. Talmud, *Megillah* 4a; *Tur*/Shulchan Arukh, *Orach Chayyim* 689.

28   *Levush, Orach Chayyim* 693:3. B. Talmud, *Megillah* 14a argues that *Hallel* should not be recited for events that took place outside the Land of Israel.

29   B. Talmud, *Megillah* 14a.

30   Mishnah, *Megillah* 1:1; Maimonides, *Mishneh Torah, Hilkhot Megillah* 1:4–5; *Tur*/Shulchan Arukh, *Orach Chayyim* 688.

31   *Sefer Abudraham* 230.

32   *Beit Yosef, Orach Chayyim* 688.

33   The demarcation of 3,000 years refers to the time of Joshua, as opposed to that of Mordecai and Esther, as it was Joshua who initiated the drive to annihilate the descendants of Amalek (Haman's ancestor). See *Sefer Abudraham*, 230. The story of Joshua is also related to the conquest of the Land of Israel, which gives those cities a certain level of importance—see *Beit Yosef, Orach Chayyim* 688.

34   Authorities identify the following cities in the Land of Israel as walled at the time of Joshua: Jaffa, Akko, Gaza, Lod, and Tiberias (although the Talmud, *Megillah* 5b, expresses some doubt over Tiberias). In another category are cities whose walled status is uncertain: Shechem (Nablus), Hebron, and Tzfat. *See* Shlomon Yosef Zevin, *Festivals in Halachah*, vol. 2 (Brooklyn, N.Y.: Mesorah Publications, 1999), 508.

35   Deut. 16.

36   This is Hillel Ha-Nasi (the Patriarch), son of Rabbi Judah Ha-Nasi. Rabbi Shlomo Yosef Zevin, *The Festivals in Halakhah*, vol.1 (New York: Mesorah Publications, 1999), 81. Zevin cites Nachmanides' *Sefer Ha-Zechut* concerning chapter 4 of B. Talmud *(Gittin)* as the source of the date (359 C.E.). He also notes other medieval rabbis, namely Ha-Levi, emphasize that Hillel II only innovated the permanence of the months and leap years, but the methods and structure of the calendar were previously established by the Sanhedrin.

37   B. Talmud, *Megillah* 6b.

38   Shulchan Arukh, *Orach Chayyim* 568:7, 55:9–10.

39   B. Talmud, *Pesachim* 64b, *Megillah* 6b.

40   B. Talmud, *Megillah* 6b; Shulchan Arukh, *Orach Chayyim* 697:2. *See* range of opinions in *Tur* and *Beit Yosef, Orach Chayyim* 697. Baal Ha-Turim (Rabbi Jacob Ben Asher) permits fasting and eulogies on the 14th and 15th of Adar I, while Rambam, Rosh, and Rif write of increasing joy on those days.

41   B. Talmud, *Megillah* 7a specifies that it is "two gifts to two men." See also *Tur*/Shulchan Arukh, *Orach Chayyim* 694:1.

42   I Cor. 13:3.

43   2 Cor. 9:7; Gal. 6:2, 5; Mark 12:41–4; Luke 11:4, 12:35, 21:1–4.

44   Acts 20:35.

45   B. Talmud, *Gittin* 7a, and *Bava Kama* 119a.

46   *Orhot Zadikkim,* trans. Seymour J. Cohen (New York: Feldheim Publishers, 1969), 303. *Orhot Zaddikim,* "Ways of the Righteous," is an anonymous medieval work, reflecting the values of Hasidism.

47   B. Talmud, *Sukkah* 49b.

48   It is permitted to have the feast in the morning. If Purim falls on Friday, the feast should ideally be held before noon because of the impending onset of Shabbat.

49   Eliyahu Kitov, *The Book of Our Heritage*, vol. 2 (New York: Feldheim Publishers, 1997), 433–4.

50   It has been said that in ancient Persia the ears of the condemned criminal were cut off before the public hanging. This would have been the case with Haman. However, even if that were true, Haman was impaled in our story.

51   Philip Goodman, *The Purim Anthology* (Philadelphia: The Jewish Publication Society, 1973), 415.

52   Esther 9:22.

53   B. Talmud, *Megillah* 7a–b; Maimonides, *Mishneh Torah, Hilkhot Megillah* 2:15; *Tur*/Shulchan Arukh, *Orach Chayyim* 695:4.

▲   ▲   ▲   ▲   ▲   ▲   ▲   ▲   ▲   ▲   ▲   ▲   ▲   ▲

54   *Mapa, Orach Chayyim* 695:4 notes the masculine language of *ish* and *re'aihu*. Here Moses
     Isserles infers that a woman, who is also obligated to perform this mitzvah, must there-
     fore give to another woman. The concern is that a man will give to a single woman
     (*almanah*) and raise doubts about their sexual relationship (see *Mishnah Berurah, se'if katan*
     26). Elsewhere, the *Mapa* limits the scope of such concerns where it would seem not to
     include *mishloach manot* (*Even Ha-Ezer* 45:1). Nevertheless, in today's world, with the many
     different kinds of relationships between men and women, some people maintain that
     such concern is not necessary—men and women should give gifts freely to one another
     without worry of sexual undertones.

55   Maimonides, *Mishneh Torah, Hilkhot Megillah* 2:15; Shulchan Arukh, *Orach Chayyim* 695:4.

56   From a speech by Ben Gurion quoted in Noam Zion and David Dishon, *A Different
     Night: The Family Participation Haggadah* (Jerusalem: Shalom Hartman Institute, 1997), 39.

57   Exod. 17:8–16.

58   Aaron was Moses' brother and the High Priest. Hur, according to Flavius Josephus, was
     Miriam's husband (*Antiquities of the Jews*, bk. III, 2:4). Although Hur is hardly mentioned
     in the Bible, he must have been an important person in his time.

59   Deut. 25:17–9.

60   The inner impulse toward good is known as the *yetzer ha-tov*.

61   Zohar 2:65a–b, 3:281b. *See also* David Golinkin, "The First Word: Are Jews Still
     Commanded to Blot Out Amalek?" *The Jerusalem Post*, March 9, 2006.

62   *Etz Hayim: Torah and Commentary*, 420–1. *See also* Zohar 2:194b, where it describes Amalek
     as a spiritual force that is to be battled.

63   *Targum Sheini* 4:15. Louis Ginzberg, *Legends of the Jews* (Philadelphia: The Jewish
     Publication Society, 1968) also cites an alternative version presented by Philo, wherein
     God tells Samuel to allow Agag to impregnate his own wife: "Suffer Agag and his wife
     to come together this night, and slay him tomorrow; but preserve thou his wife until
     she has given birth to a male child, and then she, too, shall die. The child born of her
     shall be an offense to Saul" (6:233–4). According to that legend, the child conceived
     was Edad, the very arms-bearer that delivered the final blow to Saul in 1 Sam. 31. *See
     also* B. Talmud, *Megillah* 13a.

64   Saul Austerlitz, "Groggers Defame Villain, Ennoble Twirler," *The Forward*, March 18, 2005.

65   *Mapa, Orach Chayyim* 690:17; Philip Goodman, *The Purim Anthology*, 324.

66   The Talmud teaches us that there are parameters to this experience, and we still must
     follow basic guidelines of common decency. This thought seems to be the moral of the
     talmudic story in which Rava becomes intoxicated on Purim and kills Rabbi Zera. B.
     Talmud, *Megillah* 7b.

67   B. Talmud, *Shabbat* 88a.

68   For a similar transfer of dates by the Roman Catholic Church, *see* "The December Connection" in part 2 of this book in reference to Christmas.

69   The word "carnival" has passed into the vernacular and taken on a secular meaning in most of the Western world.

70   Deut. 22:5.

71   *Mapa, Orach Chayyim* 696:8.

72   B. Talmud, *Chullin* 139b.

73   *The Purim Anthology*, 357–67.

74   B. Talmud, *Megillah* 7b.

75   Alexander Ziskind, *The Foundation and Root of Worship (Yesod v'Shoresh Ha-Avodah)*, as discussed by Rabbi Tzvi Hersh Weinreb, March 15, 2005, press release from the Orthodox Union: "It Is *Not* a Mitzvah to Get Drunk on Purim!"

76   Also exhibited by Egypt in Exod. 1:10.

77   Exod. 22:21–3; Lev. 19:18; B. Talmud, *Nedarim* 28a, *Gittin* 10b.

78   Even after the major ingathering of Jews to the State of Israel in the second half of the 20th century, anti-Semitism did not abate. Instead, it was redirected and disguised worldwide by both demagogues and academics as defamation of Zionism, of the State of Israel, of any group or country supporting it, and of the Israeli people.

79   Ps. 113:1.

80   B. Talmud, *Megillah* 14a.

81   David Hartman, *A Living Covenant: The Innovative Spirit in Traditional Judaism* (Woodstock, Vt.: Jewish Lights Publishing, 1997), 220.

82   *See* Egon Mayer, Barry A. Kosmin, and Ariela Keysar, *American Jewish Identity Survey 2001* (Graduate Center of the City University of New York, 2001). Any interpretation of the demographic studies of the Jews in the United States describes a very bleak picture of seriously declining numbers of Jews over several generations, especially when focusing on the liberal streams of Judaism. We have become especially aware that intermarriage, in addition to Jews marrying at later ages and having fewer children, all add up to zero population growth.

83   Pharaoh in Gen. 12:10–20 (at which time Sarah was still named Sarai and Abraham was still named Avram). and Abimelech of Gerar in Gen. 20.

84   Rashi on Esther 2:11.

85   Zohar *Ki Tezte* 276a.

86   B. Talmud, *Megillah* 13a; *see also* Rashi on Esther 2:7. When the Scroll of Esther says Mordecai took Esther for his daughter (*bat*) in 2:7, the Talmud reads it as *bayit*—literally

meaning "house." But in the patriarchal terminology of the Talmud, the word *bayit* is often used for wife (i.e., the woman is defined by her household duties).

87   The Talmud (*Megillah* 13a) addresses this problem—namely, that only virgins were admitted into the contest. In other words, how could Esther be allowed to marry if she was already married and presumably not a virgin? The Talmud maintains that married women were in fact allowed in the beauty contest and that Ahasuerus desired not a virgin but the "taste of a virgin."

88   For a comprehensive discussion of the biblical commentators and how they address this issue, see Barry Dov Walfish, "Kosher Adultery? The Mordecai-Esther-Ahasuerus Triangle in Midrash and Exegesis," *Prooftexts: A Journal of Jewish Literary History* 22, no. 3 (2002), 305–33.

89   Loosely translated, "Portions of the Levite."

90   Barry Dov Walfish, "Kosher Adultery?"

91   Michael Strassfeld, *The Jewish Holidays: A Guide & Commentary* (New York: HarperCollins Publishers, 1985; HarperResource Quill, 2001), 188.

92   In the Septuagint, the Book of Esther does include God's name.

93   Adele Berlin, "Esther," in *The Jewish Study Bible* (New York: Oxford University Press, 2004), 1624. *See also* David R. Blumenthal, "Where God Is Not: The Book of Esther and Song of Songs," *Judaism: A Quarterly Journal of Jewish Life and Thought* 44, no. 1 (winter, 1995), 80–93. Blumenthal argues that the strong sexual undertones are the reason for the name's omission.

94   *See* Sabine M. L. Van Den Eynde, "If Esther Had Not Been That Beautiful: Dealing with a Hidden God in the (Hebrew) Book of Esther," *Biblical Theology Bulletin* (Seton Hall University: December 2001), vol. 35, 145–50.

95   For that reason, the response among traditionalists to *mazal tov!* is a hearty repeat of *mazal tov!* rather than thank you.

96   Tzipori was home to the Sanhedrin (highest judicial council of the ancient Jewish nation) in the first half of the 3rd century. The Sanhedrin, headed by Rabbi Yehudah Ha-Nasi, moved there from the settlement of Beit Shearim (now Kiryat Tivon), southeast of modern Haifa.

97   Other great medieval Jewish philosophers and scholars openly endorsed astrology, such as Sa'adia Gaon, Ibn Ezra, and Nachmanides. See also *Tur, Yoreh De'ah* 179, which seems to support Nachmanides' view of astrology.

98   Lev. 19:26; Deut. 18:9–12. Examples of Rabbinic rejection of soothsaying can be found in B. Talmud, *Sanhedrin* 65 and *Pesachim* 113b, and *Deuteronomy Rabbah* 8:6. Maimonides takes this talmudic rejection to the extreme when he says, "These and similar things are all lies and deceit. ... It is not fitting for Israel to be attracted by these follies or to believe they

have any efficacy. Whosoever believes that they are possible, though the Torah has forbidden their practice is but a fool," *Mishneh Torah, Hilkhot Avodat Kochavim* 11:16.

99   B. Talmud, *Shabbat* 53b, 146a, and 156a.

100   B. Talmud, *Shabbat*, 156a.

101   It is worth noting that Esther was the only canonized book not found among the Dead Sea Scrolls (literature from the Jewish sect of the Essenes, who flourished from the 2nd century B.C.E. to the 1st century C.E.).

102   Deut. 31:18.

103   B. Talmud, *Chullin* 139b.

104   B. Talmud, *Megillah* 7a.

105   Ibid.

106   Maimonides, *Mishneh Torah, Hilkhot She'ar Avot Ha-Tuma* 9:3–6.

107   B. Talmud, *Shabbat* 14a–b.

108   *See* Michael Broyde, "Defilement of the Hands, Canonization of the Bible, and the Special Status of Esther, Ecclesiastes, and Song of Songs," *Judaism: A Quarterly Journal of Jewish Life and Thought* 44, no. 1 (winter, 1995), 80–92. I am indebted to Broyde for the insight and textual references given in this article as well as the expansive discussion on the topic of the treatment of the Book of Esther in Jewish law.

109   Maimonides, *Hilkhot Avot Ha-Tuma* 9:4. Isserles, *Mapa* on *Orach Chayyim* 691:2 discusses how the Scroll of Esther does not maintain the same ritual status of other books. The Broyde article cited in note 108 also discusses and references numerous opinions from medieval halakhists.

110   *Otzar Ha-Geonim*, ed. B. M. Levin, (Haifa: Hebrew University Press, 1938) on *Megillah* 7a, cited in Broyde.

111   Both phrases have the same numerical equivalence (*gematriya*) of 502.

112   Rabbah bar Nachmani.

113   Translated by William G. Braude; see *The Book of Legends*, ed. Hayim Nahman Bialik and Yehoshua Hana Ravnitzky (New York: Schocken Press, 1992), 152–3.

114   *Mishneh Torah, Hilkhot Megillah* 2:17.

115   Solomon Alkabetz, *Menot Ha-Levi*, 263.

116   The use of the phrase *Yom Ki-Purim* is a midrashic move that plays off of the biblical name *Yom Ha-Kippurim*, found primarily in the Book of Leviticus.

117   *Sefat Emet, Derush le-Purim.*

118   In 1938, his closest disciple and son-in-law, Ira Eisenstein, founded the Reconstructionist Rabbinical College, which promotes Kaplan's philosophy as a separate religious denomination.

119 Mordecai Kaplan, *The Meaning of God in Modern Jewish Religion* (New York: Reconstructionist Press, 1937), 361–2.

120 H. L. Ginsberg, *Five Megilloth and Jonah: A New Translation* (Philadelphia: The Jewish Publication Society, 1969), 82–84.

121 In the Talmud, Rabbi Eleazar bases this prohibition on a biblical verse from Hosea 2:1. "The number of the people of Israel shall be like that of the sands of the sea, which cannot be measured or counted."

122 As the Rabbinic sages teach us, throughout the year there are truly four new years. One falls upon the first day of the spring month of Nissan. It commemorates the day when the princes of the Jewish tribes brought offerings for the dedication of the Tabernacle (the portable sanctuary the Israelites used in the wilderness). Another is the New Year for the Trees, Tu b'Shevat (which usually falls in February), on the 15th of the winter month of Shevat. A third new year, falling in late summer, signifies the annual renewal of tithing of cattle, on the 1st of Elul. The fourth is Rosh Hashanah (literally, "The Head of the Year"), which takes place in the autumn.

123 Esther 3:9.

124 Reish is a contraction of "Rabbi Shimon" ben Lakish. He was a 3rd-century talmudic sage who lived in the Land of Israel.

125 The talent, also known as a "kikar," was the largest unit of monetary weight in the Bible. The relation between the talent and the shekel is defined in Exod. 38:25–6. The half shekel brought by 603,550 men amounted to 100 talents and 1,775 shekels. By this calculation, a talent was equal to 3,000 shekels. *The Oxford Study Bible*, 1630, estimates that 10,000 talents of silver equals 333 tons or 302 metric tons, which would be close to the annual tribute of the entire Persian Empire.

126 The Jerusalem Talmud (*Pe'ah* 2) explains that the specific amount of a half, rather than a whole, shekel also functions as counterbalance to evil by atoning for the sin of worshiping the Golden Calf. Accordingly, because the Israelites sinned for half of a day, they must give half of a shekel back to God.

127 Esther 3:7.

128 Amalekites are a nation descended from of a common ancestor, the mysterious Amalek. Because of the role of Amalek in the Exodus narrative, Rabbinic literature uses the name to represent evil; however, there is no specific image of exactly who Amalek is or what form this evil takes.

129 Esau and the country where he settled (Edom) are demonized in the Midrash. The Rabbis explain that the Edomites are the progenitors of the Roman people.

130 *Midrash Rabbah, Genesis Rabbah* 67:4. Amalek's line, which seems to have been responsible for many horrors perpetrated upon the Jews, is associated with Esau. The account of Esau in the Torah alone, however, portrays a reasonable person who was able to forgive and love his brother Jacob after being wronged by him; *see* Gen. 33.

131 Zohar 1:65a.

132 Zohar 125a–b, 2:65a

133 In the Jewish tradition, the *yetzer ha-ra* is the opposite of the *yetzer ha-tov*, the inclination to do good. These impulses are believed to exert influence over everyone.

134 Zohar 3:160a.

135 *Midrash Rabbah, Exodus Rabbah* 19:20; 24. *See also* Zohar 2:65–6a.

136 The period of the Mishnah extends from the early 1st century to the early 3rd century and is so named in recognition of the Mishnah's role in the implementation of Rabbinic Judaism. In this complex and turbulent transitional era, new systems replaced the Temple-centered religious and political structures that had endured during the previous millennium. These years are also known as the late Hellenistic, or the Roman, or the Early Christian period, depending on the context of the reference.

137 Richard Elliot Friedman, *The Disappearance of God: A Divine Mystery* (New York: Little, Brown, 1995).

138 Esther 3:2–6.

139 The extreme decadence of the king's party and the description of the furnishings of his palace, with its similarity to the colors and materials used in the Tabernacle, may similarly reflect a critique of the idolatrous wish of a human king to invite comparison with the Divine.

140 B. Talmud, *Megillah* 13b–4a.

141 E. W. Wilcox, "Protest," in *Poems of Problems* (London: Gay and Hancock, 1914), 154–55.

142 Martin Niemoeller (b. 1892–d. 1984) was imprisoned in concentration camps from 1937 to 1945 for his opposition to the nazification of German Protestant churches. He is best known today for the poem "First They Came for the Communists." Nonetheless, some scholars put him in the category of an anti-Semite for positions he took in the early 1930s.

143 Esther 1:1; 1:22; 3:12; 8:9.

144 Esther 3:8.

145 Marilyn Frye, *The Politics of Reality: Essays in Feminist Theory* (Freedom, Calif.: The Crossing Press, 1983), 103.

146 Esther 3:8ff.

147 John Berger, *Ways of Seeing* (London: Penguin Books, 1972), 45, 47.

148 Media was a region of Asia to the southwest of the Caspian Sea, corresponding approximately to present-day Azerbaijan. Persia is now Iran. Chaldea was a country making up what is now southern Iraq.

149 Esther 4:1.

150 Michael Strassfeld, *The Jewish Holidays: A Guide & Commentary* (New York: HarperCollins Publishers, 1985; HarperResource Quill, 2001), 197–8.

151 *Midrash Rabbah, Proverbs Rabbah 9:2.*

152 Lesli Koppelman Ross, *The Lifetime Guide to the Jewish Holidays* (Aventura, Fla.: Jewish Legacy Press, 2003), 502.

153 Philip Goodman, *The Purim Anthology*, 384.

154 Lawrence Kushner, *The Book of Words* (Woodstock, Vt.: Jewish Lights Publishing, 1993), 63–5.

Part 5: Guidance along the Way

1 Although the traditional style is to study in pairs, *chevruta* learning can also be done in small groups.

2 *Pesikta Rabbati: Homiletical Discourses for Festal Days and Special Sabbaths 1 & 2*, Yale Judaica Series (New Haven, Conn.: Yale University Press, 1968).

3 Eliyahu Kitov, *The Book of Our Heritage: The Jewish Year and Its Days of Significance*, trans. Nachman Bulman, revised and adapted by Dovid Landesman and Joyce Bennett (Jerusalem and New York: Feldheim Publishers, 1997).

4 The number varies by source, with 5 and 70 being other variations. The latter perhaps gave rise to the Latin name Septuagint, which is the accepted name today.

5 The Talmud refers to the work as *Sifra de-be Rav.*

6 *Tanna* is the Aramaic term for a rabbi who lived at the time of the Mishnah. The name of the midrash, *Tanna de-be Eliyahu*, is translated as "The Lore of the School of Elijah" in a book by William G. Braude and Israel J. Kapstein, *Tanna Debe Eliyyahu* (Philadelphia: The Jewish Publication Society, 1981).

7 According to Rashi, the midrash has the two names, "Rabbah" for the earlier, and "Zuta" for the later lectures.

Glossary

Adar
The 12th month of the Hebrew calendar. Purim falls on the 14th of Adar.

Adar Sheini (literally, "Second Adar")
A leap month. During Jewish leap years, which occur 7 out of every 19 years, a 13th month is added—Adar Sheini, which is positioned adjacent to the regular, or first, Adar. During a leap year Purim is observed in Adar Sheini.

Aggadah
The nonlegal portions of Rabbinic literature, including moral lessons, prayers, legends, and folklore. Their analysis and explication of the Bible are primarily homiletic.

Ahasuerus
The king of Persia who marries Esther and plays a significant role in the story of Purim. He is believed by many scholars to be the historical emperor of Persia known as Xerxes the Great who reigned from 485–65 B.C.E.

Al Ha-Nissim (literally, "For the Miracles")
A thanksgiving prayer added to the *Amidah* and to the *Birkat Ha-Mazon* (the prayers said as grace after meals), summarizing the key theological elements of the holiday for which it is said—Hanukkah or Purim.

Alexander the Great
Greek (Macedonian) general (356–323 B.C.E.) who rapidly conquered the ancient Near East, all the way from Turkey and Greece to India. He was well known as a student of philosopher Aristotle. Alexander built a vision known as Hellenism, which favored a world unified by the Greek culture and language. His succeeding generals struggled over and divided the world he left behind. Their dynasties were defeated by Rome 300 years later.

Amalek
As described in Exodus, the tribe that attacked the Israelites as they left Egypt. In Deuteronomy, the Torah says the Amalekites attacked the weak and weary among the

Israelites, and it mandates that Jews never forget that tribe or its descendants. Rabbinic literature identifies the mysterious "Amalek" as the manifestation of evil on earth.

Amidah (literally, "Standing")

The central Jewish prayer that is said silently and while standing. It is also referred to as *Ha-Tefilah* (The Prayer) and as the *Shemoneh Esrei* (Eighteen Blessings).

Antiochus IV

Ruler of the Greco-Syrians and the Seleucid dynasty from 175 to 164 B.C.E. Known in his domain as Epiphanes, Greek for "god manifest," he was responsible for the edicts that caused the Hasmonean rebellion in the Hanukkah story.

Aramaic

An ancient Semitic language closely related to Hebrew. Jews are understood to have adopted Aramaic during the Babylonian exile, thus leading to the use of Aramaic in parts of the TANAKH (e.g., Daniel) and all of the Talmud and the Zohar.

Ashkenazim

Jews with long-ago ancestors from Germany or France. Throughout the medieval period of persecution, many Ashkenazim migrated to other parts of Europe, especially Poland and Russia.

assiyah

The world of action in Kabbalah. The lowest of the four worlds within the universe.

atzilut

The world of emanation or nearness in Kabbalah. The highest of the four worlds within the universe.

bal tash'hit (literally, "do not destroy")

The Jewish prohibition against wanton destruction. The phrase is derived from the law in Deuteronomy that forbids cutting down an enemy's trees during a siege.

beriyah

The world of creation in Kabbalah. The second of the four worlds within the universe.

Book of Esther

One of the *hamesh megillot* (five scrolls) in a part of the TANAKH (Bible) called Kethuvim (The Writings). Known in Hebrew as *Megillat Esther* (the Scroll of Esther), it is the basis for the holiday of Purim.

derash (literally, "inquiry")

An interpretation of a text in contrast to *peshat*, which is the plain meaning of a text.

Diaspora (from the Greek for "Dispersion")

The Jewish communities outside of the Land of Israel. The concept and term originated in the 6th century B.C.E. when the Second Temple was destroyed by the conquering Babylonians, who forced the Israelites to leave their country and settle in new places. The Hebrew equivalent for Diaspora is *galut* (literally, "exile").

dreidel

Yiddish term for the four-sided spinning top used as a game during Hanukkah. Each side of the top denotes a result, indicated by four different Hebrew letters. Although the game actually developed over time in different places, it is associated with a Hanukkah legend, memorializing the bravery of the Jewish soldiers. The modern Hebrew word for dreidel is *sevivon*.

Esther

The heroine of the holiday of Purim and the biblical book named after her. The name in Hebrew is Hadassah.

Etz Hayim (literally, "Tree of Life")

A well-known metaphor for the Torah itself. In kabbalistic thought, *Etz Hayim* represents the divine emanations of God into the universe, which are known as the *sefirot*.

Fast of Esther

A minor fast day commemorating the fast that Esther proclaimed in the story of Purim. It generally falls on the 13th of Adar, the day before Purim, unless Purim falls on a Sunday, in which case the fast occurs on the preceding Thursday. The Hebrew name is *Ta'anit Esther.*

Festival of Lights *See* Hanukkah.

Four Worlds

The kabbalistic concept that there are spiritual levels of creation, each representing a rung on the continuum of consciousness or awareness of God. The four basic worlds are *atzilut, beriyah, yetzirah,* and *assiyah.* These four worlds, however, originate from a fifth, higher world, known as *adam kadmon* (literally, "primordial mankind"). All 10 of the *sefirot* (emanations of God into the world) are manifest in each world, but a particular *sefirah* dominates in each world.

gelt

Yiddish word for money. It is also the term used for the foil-wrapped chocolate coins that are given to children on Hanukkah.

gematriya

The system that creates parallels between the Hebrew alphabet and numbers—that is, each Hebrew letter is equal to a number. The Jewish tradition has long sought meaning in numbers through their word equivalence and in words through their numerical equivalence.

grager (Yiddish, from the Polish word for "rattle")

The noisemaker used on Purim to drown out the sound of Haman's name when it is read from the *Megillat Esther.* In Hebrew, the noisemaker is called a *ra'ashan.*

haftarah; pl. *haftarot*

A selected portion from the biblical Book of Prophets that is read following the Torah reading (*parashah*) on Shabbat and most holidays.

Hag Ha-Urim (literally, "The Celebration of Lights")

One of the alternate names for Hanukkah, often also called The Festival of Lights.

halakhah (literally, "the way"); pl. *halakhot*

Jewish law, including the rules, observances, and requirements of Jewish life, which originated in the Torah. The Rabbis organized the laws into the Mishnah and Talmud. The term is derived from the three-letter Hebrew root *heh.lamed.khaf.,* or *lalekhet,* meaning "to go" or "to walk."

Hallel (literally, "Praise")
Psalms 113 to 118 recited on festivals and Rosh Hodesh as a display of joy and gratitude.

Haman
Villain in the Purim story and chief advisor to King Ahasuerus.

hamantash (literally, "Haman's hat"); pl. **hamantashen**
Yiddish term for the triangular, filled cookies traditionally eaten on Purim.

Ha-Nerot Hallalu (literally, "These Lights")
A prayer, also referred to as "We Kindle These Candles," customarily recited or sung after the kindling of the Hanukkah candles and followed by the hymn *Ma'oz Tzur* ("Rock of Ages").

Hannah
In the Midrash, the name given to the mother who witnessed her seven sons tortured and killed for refusing to commit idolatry. (In the versions of this story in the Second Book of the Maccabees and in the Babylonian Talmud, the woman is unnamed.) This Hannah is one of the earliest recognized Jewish martyrs and not to be confused with the mother of Samuel in the Bible.

Hanukkah (literally, "Dedication")
The winter holiday that commemorates the rededication of the Temple during the Maccabees campaign against the Greek Syrians. The story is told in the nonbiblical First and Second Books of the Maccabees and in *Megillat Antiochus*. The dedication occurred on the 25th of Kislev, but the holiday is observed for eight days to memorialize a the miracle that one day's worth of oil lasted for eight days.

hanukkiah; pl. *hanukkiot*
The nine-branched candelabra that holds the Hanukkah candles. It has one branch for each day and a ninth one, the raised *shamash*, which is a servant candle used to light the other eight. The word *hanukkiah* is modern Hebrew. The candelabra is often referred to as a Hanukkah menorah.

Hasidim (literally "Pious Ones")

Primarily, this term identifies the followers of Hasidism, the Jewish religious movement founded in the 18th century by the Baal Shem Tov. In the context of Hanukkah, however, the term refers to the Jewish zealots who revolted against the Greek Syrians in the 2nd century B.C.E.

Hasmoneans

The family descended from the Jewish priest Hasmon. Made famous by Mattathias and his sons (the Maccabees), it became a dynasty that ruled over Israel for more than 100 years before being defeated by the Romans. The name in Hebrew is *Chashmona'im.*

Hellenism

The term used to describe the process of spreading Greek culture and thought across the ancient Near East. Hellenism began with Alexander the Great in the 4th century B.C.E.

Judah Maccabee

The principal hero of the Hanukkah story. Son of Mattathias the Hasmonean, Judah became the military leader who led the Jews to victory over the Greek Syrians. The term Maccabee is a nickname, which tradition holds was derived from the Hebrew word *maccaba,* "hammerhead." The choice of nickname may have been related to the shape of Judah's forehead. The warriors who fought alongside Judah were known as Maccabees.

Kabbalah (literally, "Reception")

The tradition of Jewish mysticism, which maintains that there are hidden truths within the Torah. The primary resource for Kabbalah is the Zohar. Hasidism bases many of its teachings upon Kabbalah.

Kiddush (literally, "Sanctification")

The blessing recited over wine. It is said every Sabbath, on Jewish holidays, and before celebratory meals to sanctify these occasions.

Kislev

The ninth month of the biblical calendar. Hanukkah begins on the 25th of Kislev.

Kohen Gadol (literally, "Great Priest")
The leader of all the *kohanim* (priests), who were the direct descendants of the first priest, the patriarch Aaron, brother of Moses. The priests' sacred duties were inherited by birthright and included the ritual offering of sacrifices and the burning of incense. During the era of the First Temple, the Kohen Gadol had special duties such as instructing the nation in the Torah and serving as a judge in legal matters. During the period of the Second Temple, the Kohen Gadol became more involved with issues of state and less concerned with the moral guidance of the nation.

latkes (literally, "pancakes")
Yiddish term for pancakes, usually referring to potato pancakes, which are an especially popular food on Hanukkah. They are fried in oil—a reminder of the Hanukkah miracle.

levivot (literally, "pancakes")
The biblical term for pancakes in general and the modern Hebrew term for potato pancakes *(latkes)* specifically.

lulav (literally, "palm branch")
One of the group of four plants that symbolize joy for life and dedication to God when used in Sukkot rituals, The *lulav* is also a symbol of military victory.

Maccabees
In the Hanukkah story, family members and soldiers who followed the leadership of Judah Maccabee.

maftir
From the three-letter Hebrew root: *fey.tet.resh.,* meaning "to end." The additional Torah reading added to the seven basic divisions of each parashah. On Shabbat, the last few verses of the weekly portion are repeated as the *maftir.* On holidays and special *Shabbatot,* verses related to that particular day are read. The term also refers to the person who both recites the blessing over that portion of the Torah and chants the haftarah.

mahatzit ha-shekel (literally, "the half shekel")
An expression that refers to the custom of giving charity *(tzedakah)* during the

month of Adar. Originally each person gave a half shekel to the priests for the offerings at the Tabernacle (later, for the upkeep of the Temple) and as a tax. The custom today of giving three coins is derived from the three-time repetition of the word *terumah* ("donation" or "offering") in the verses in the Torah that discuss the half shekel (Exod. 30:11–6). The final date for giving this charity is the 1st of Nissan (the month that follows Adar). However, we remind ourselves to give well in advance, at Shabbat Shekalim, which falls on the Shabbat before the 1st Adar. Some people have the custom of then giving the three coins specifically on the Fast of Esther or on Purim.

Ma'oz Tzur (literally, "Fortress Rock" or "Rock of Ages")
An Ashkenazic hymn sung each night of Hanukkah at the conclusion of candlelighting.

Mattathias
Member of Hasmonean priestly family and father of sons who came to be known as the Macabees. In the Hanukkah story, Mattathias's act of zealotry initiates the revolt against the Greek Syrians, which ultimately leads to the rededication of the Temple.

Megillah (literally, "Scroll")
Short reference to the scroll of Esther *(Megillat Esther)* that is read on Purim.

Megillat Esther See Book of Esther.

megillot (literally, "scrolls")
Reference to five books, the *hamesh megillot,* found in Kethuvim (The Writings), the last part of the TANAKH (Bible). Each of the *megillot* is assigned to be read on a specific holiday: the Song of Songs on Pesach; the Book of Ruth on Shavuot; Lamentations on Tisha b'Av; Ecclesiastes on Sukkot; and the Book (or scroll) of Esther on Purim.

menorah (literally, "lamp")
The seven-branched, golden candelabra used in the Tabernacle in the wilderness and later, in the Temple in Jerusalem.

minhag (literally, "custom"); pl. *minhagim*
A custom observed and transmitted by the Jewish people. *Minhagim* often reflect the time and place of the Jews who first kept them. For many people, adherence to Jewish customs is maintained as strictly as adherence to Jewish law *(halakhah)*.

mishloach manot (literally, "delivery of portions")
The festive practice of sending gifts of food to friends and relatives on Purim.

mitzvah pl. **mitzvot;** (literally, "commandment")
One of the religious obligations detailed in the Torah, the majority of which fall into the positive category of religious, ethical, or moral obligations. The Torah also contains negative mitzvot, which are prohibitions.

Modi'in.
The village in northern Israel where Mattathias and his sons lived. In the Hanukkah story, it was here that the Jewish revolt against the Greek Syrians began.

Mordecai
A cousin of Queen Esther and a hero of the Purim story.

orlah (literally, "hindered" or "restricted")
A tree within the first three years after planting. Fruit from such a tree may not be eaten or any benefit derived from it, in accordance with the biblical commandment in Leviticus (19:23).

oznei Haman (literally, "Haman's ears")
The modern Hebrew name for the Purim cookies that are called hamantashen in Yiddish.

parashah (literally, "portion"); pl. *parshiyot;*
The weekly Torah portion, also called *sidrah.* The Torah is divided into 54 of these portions—one section for each week of a leap year on the Hebrew lunar calendar. In non-leap years some of the portions are combined to create double *parshiyot* that compensate for the reduced number of weeks.

Passover

The spring pilgrimage festival commemorating the Israelites' Exodus from Egypt. It is also known as the Feast of Freedom or the Feast of Matzot. The Hebrew name is Pesach. Its Hebrew calendar date is the 15th of Nissan, which corresponds to late March or early April.

peshat (literally, "simple")

The plain meaning of a text in context in contrast to *derash*, which is the homiletical meaning.

pirsumei nissah (literally, "publicizing the miracle")

The expression for the guiding principle behind why we light the Hanukkah candles and why we place them in a location visible to passersby.

Purim (literally, "Lots")

The festive holiday that falls in the Hebrew month of Adar and recalls the events in the biblical Book of Esther. In that story, the evil Haman, adviser to the king of Persia, casts "lots" to decide the date for destroying all the Jews.

Purim *katan* (literally, "little Purim")

The 14th of Adar I, a day that anticipates and mirrors the festive spirit of Purim. During a leap year, Purim *katan* stays in Adar I, while "regular" Purim is celebrated in Adar II.

Purim-spiel

A Purim *spiel* (Yiddish for "play") in which actors dance, sing, and mock society. Often the play relates to the story and characters in the Book of Esther.

Rabbinic era

The time of greatest Rabbinic development, when Rabbinic Judaism evolved to become normative Judaism. The first division of this era was that of the sages. It was called *tannaim*, a word that comes from the Aramaic word for "repeat," for which the Aramaic root (a language written with Hebrew characters) *tav.nun.alef.* is equivalent to the Hebrew root *shin.nun.heh.* That Hebrew root is also the basis for the word "Mishnah" (the foundational text of the Oral Torah); thus the *tannaim* were "Mishnah teachers" who repeated and passed down the Oral Torah. Most of the *tannaim* lived in the period between the destruction of the Second Temple (70 C.E.) and the Bar Kochba Revolt (135 C.E.). The second division of the Rabbinic era is that of the *amoraim*, a word that comes from the Aramaic word for "speaker." The *amoraim* continued to interpret and transmit Jewish law, thought, and practice expanding upon the foundations laid by the *tannaim*. This work occurred at academies in Israel (Tiberias, Caesarea, and Tzippori) and in Babylonia (Nehardea, Pumpeditha, and Sura). The Talmud, which was primarily compiled about 400 C.E. in Israel and about 500 C.E. in Babylonia, provides the fullest expression of the *amoraim*.

Rosh Hashanah La-Ilanot (literally, "New Year for the Trees")
One of the names for Tu b'Shevat.

Rosh Hodesh (literally, "Head of the Month")
The new moon and the beginning of each Hebrew month. While it is marked today as a special occasion with distinctive liturgy, in biblical times Rosh Hodesh was celebrated more elaborately, as an outright festival. During the early Diaspora, when long-distance communication became more difficult, two days of Rosh Hodesh celebration became customary for some months in certain years, as the custom remains today.

sages
A descriptive term to indicate those rabbis who contributed the greatest insights and developments in Jewish thought and practice. Most occurences of the term refer to Rabbis of the Rabbinic era, but sometimes the term is used for rabbis from the medieval period (for example, Nachmanides).

Sanhedrin
The highest court of the Land of Israel from mid-2nd century B.C.E. to 425 C.E. At its height, the Sanhedrin did more than make judicial rulings on civil, criminal, and ritual matters; it also functioned to a large extent as a legislature, involved in the major communal issues of the day. The name comes from the Greek term for "Council of Elders" *(Synedrion)*.

sefirah (literally, "portion"); pl. sefirot
One of the 10 emanations, or varying aspects, of God in the universe. The *sefirot* play a central role throughout kabbalistic doctrine and teachings. Each *sefirah*

embodies a divine quality and, according to Kabbalah, the *sefirot* are the underlying forces in the world and in the Torah.

Sephardim

Jews who trace their ancestry back to Spain before the expulsion in 1492. (*Sepharad* is the Hebrew name for Spain.) Sephardic holiday customs, cuisine, liturgy, and even Hebrew differ in some ways from those of the Ashkenazim, the name of the group of Jews who trace their family history back to France and Germany. (*Ashkenaz* is the Hebrew name for Germany).

se'udah

A feast.

Shabbat; pl. *Shabbatot*

The Sabbath, or day of rest. It begins at sunset on Friday night and ends about 25 hours later, after sunset on Saturday night. (The extra hour ensures that the full 24-hour period is observed.)

Shabbat Zakhor (literally, "Sabbath of Remembrance")

The Shabbat preceding Purim. The *maftir* begins with the word *Zakhor* and recounts the Israelite war with Amalek (Haman's ancestor). The haftarah for this Shabbat tells the story of King Saul and King Agag (a descendant of Amalek).

shamash (literally, "attendant" or "servant")

The ninth candle on the *hanukkiah* that is used to light each of the eight Hanukkah candles. The holder for the *shamash* is positioned noticeably higher than those of the other candles.

Shavuot (literally, "Weeks")

One of the three pilgrimage festivals. Also known as the Feast of Weeks and as the Harvest Festival, it commemorates the giving of the Torah at Mount Sinai and celebrates the first harvest of the fruits of spring. The seven-week period that falls between Shavuot and Passover is called the Omer. The Hebrew calendar date for Shavuot, which usually falls in May or June, is the 6th of Sivan.

Shekhinah (literally, "Dwelling")
One of the names for God, and explicitly the presence of God, commonly described as a light or radiance that illuminates the world. The word *Shekhinah* has the same root as *lishkon*, which is *shin.khaf.nun.*, meaning "to dwell." It is often associated with the *mishkan* (the Tabernacle in the wilderness) and with the Temple in Jerusalem.

Shemini Atzeret
Th eighth day of Sukkot, which holds special significance as its own holiday. Jews thank God for the harvest and ask for winter rain to prepare the ground for spring planting.

shemitah (literally "release")
In Israel, the seventh or sabbatical year when, according to the Torah, farmers must let their fields lie fallow. The *shemitah* is preset in the calendar, with each one calculated from 1257 B.C.E., the year that the Israelites conquered the tribes living in the Land of Israel. *Shemitah* would thus fall in 1250, 1243, 1236, and so on.

Shemoneh Esrei See *Amidah.*

Shevat
The 11th month of the Hebrew calendar. The holiday of Tu b'Shevat is literally the "15th of Shevat."

Shushan
Capital city of ancient Persia where the Purim story took place.

Shushan Purim
The day for celebrating Purim if a person is living in a city walled since the time of Joshua, as was Shushan. The date for Shushan Purim is the 15th of Adar, the day following the more common Purim celebrations.

spiel See *Purim-spiel.*

sufganiyot (literally, "doughnuts")
The jelly doughnuts customarily eaten on Hanukkah, especially in the State of
Israel. On this holiday, Jews eat food fried in oil to serve as a reminder of the
Hanukkah miracle.

Sukkot (literally, "Booths")
One of the three pilgrimage festivals, it occurs on the 15th of Tishrei in late
September or early October. Sukkot marks the fall harvest and commemorates the
Exodus from Egypt. The Torah says that the Israelites dwelt in "*sukkot*" (temporary
huts or booths) during their desert journey.

Ta'anit Esther See Fast of Esther.

tikun olam (literally, "repairing the world")
A phrase used by the 16th-century kabbalist Isaac Luria. It expresses the concept of
a partnership that humanity has with God to make the world a better place through
observance of commandments and through acts of lovingkindness.

Tishrei
The seventh Hebrew month of the Hebrew calendar. Rosh Hashanah, Yom Kippur,
and Sukkot all occur in Tishrei.

tsimtsum (literally, "contraction")
The kabbalistic concept of contraction and removal of God's infinite light to allow
for creation of independent realities. The primordial *tzimtzum* produced a vacant,
material vessel devoid of direct awareness of God's presence.

Tu b'Shevat (literally, "15th of Shevat")
A holiday designated by the Talmud as the New Year of the Trees. It is celebrated
when the almond trees are in bloom in Israel, a time in the calendar that
corresponds to January or February.

Tu b'Shevat Seder
A meal patterned somewhat after the Passover seder. The word seder means "order."
This seder, held on the eve of Tu b'Shevat, has no fixed ritual; but there are generally

four cups of wine and the eating of various symbolic fruits and nuts. The name of the meal in Hebrew is *Seder Layl Tu b'Shevat* (literally, "Evening Seder of Tu b'Shevat").

Vashti

First queen to King Ahasuerus in the Book of Esther. She loses her crown for refusing to show herself before the king's guests.

yetzirah

The world of formation in Kabbalah. It is the third of the four worlds in the universe, where the material is given spirit and form. It is the world from which the human soul originates.

Zeresh

The wife of the villain Haman in the story of Purim.

Contributing Authors

Bradley Shavit Artson is vice president of the American Jewish University and dean of its Ziegler School of Rabbinic Studies. A doctoral candidate in contemporary Jewish theology at Hebrew Union College–Jewish Institute of Religion, Rabbi Artson is the author of *The Bedside Torah: Wisdom, Dreams, & Visions*.

Matt Biers-Ariel, Deborah Newbrun, and Michal Fox Smart are proponents and educators of Jewish spirituality in nature. Biers-Ariel is the author of several books, including *The Seven Species, Solomon and the Trees,* and *The Triumph of Eve and Other Subversive Bible Tales.* Newbrun is the executive director of Camp Tawonga in northern California. Smart, formerly director of education for the Coalition on the Environment and Jewish Life, has written several articles on Jewish environmental ethics and has appeared in televised documentaries about the environment.

Yitzhak Buxbaum is a *maggid,* a traditional Jewish storyteller and teacher, who specializes in mysticism, spirituality, and Hasidic tales. He is the author of several books, including *A Person Is Like a Tree: A Sourcebook for Tu BeShvat; Jewish Spiritual Practices; The Light and Fire of the Baal Shem Tov;* and *Jewish Tales of Holy Women.*

Robert J. Cabelli is the rabbi of Congregation Beth Israel in Asheville, North Carolina. Ordained by the Ziegler School of Rabbinic Studies, he was previously a developmental neurobiologist and a teacher at the University of Southern California Medical School.

Gail Diamond was ordained by the Reconstructionist Rabbinical College. She lives in Jerusalem and serves as the assistant director of the Conservative Yeshiva in Jerusalem.

Wayne Dosick is the founder and spiritual leader of the Elijah Minyan and an adjunct professor of Jewish Studies at the University of San Diego. Rabbi Dosick is the author of several books, including *Dancing with God: Everyday Steps to Jewish Spiritual Renewal; The Best Is Yet to Be: Renewing American Judaism;* and *Living Judaism: The Complete Guide to Jewish Belief, Tradition, and Practice.*

Philip Goodman was born in New York 1911 and studied at Yeshiva University and the College of the City of New York. He was ordained in Israel at the yeshiva headed by Chief Rabbi Abraham I. Kook and became a congregational rabbi in New York for nine years. In 1942, he joined the staff of the National Jewish Welfare Board (JWB). During World War II he wrote and coedited a number of publications for the use of the Jewish members of the armed forces. Upon his retirement from JWB in 1976, the Jewish Book Council granted him a "Special Award for Jewish Anthology," in recognition of his cumulative efforts as the anthologist of eight volumes published by The Jewish Publication Society: seven holiday books and one on marriage (the last coauthored with his wife, Hanna). That same year, Rabbi Goodman and his family settled permanently in Israel, where he became an officer of Israel Endowment Funds, a position he retained until his death in 2006.

Theodor Herzl was born in Budapest in 1860. As an Austo-Hungarian journalist, he witnessed the notorius Dreyfus Affair in France in which a Jewish army captain was falsely accused of spying for Germany. Herzl realized that the Jewish people could be free of anti-Semitism only by living within their own country, an argument he outlined in his book *Der Judenstaat* (The Jewish State). He organized the World Zionist Organization and became its first president, a post he held until his death in 1904.

Daniel S. Isaacson was ordained by the Jewish Theological Seminary and serves as the rabbi for the Jewish Family and Children's Services of San Francisco, the Peninisula, Marin and Sonoma Counties. His environmental approach to Judaism has been documented in a number of articles about his practice of using discarded vegetable oil as fuel for operating his car.

Yehezkel Kaufmann (b. 1889–d. 1963, Russia and Israel) was a philosopher and biblical scholar who received a talmudic education in the yeshivas of Russia and a university education in Switzerland. Soon after publishing his doctoral thesis at age 21, he emigrated to Israel and began his teaching career, ultimately becoming a professor of Bible at Hebrew University in Jerusalem. The best known of his many works is the monumental *The History of the Religion of Israel*, eight volumes published from 1937 to 1956.

Lawrence Kushner is the Emanu-El scholar-in-residence at Congregation Emanu-El in San Francisco and visiting professor of Jewish spirituality at the Graduate Theological

University. He was ordained by the Hebrew Union College–Jewish Institute of Religion, where he now serves as adjunct member of the faculty. For 28 years, he was the rabbi of Congregation Beth El in Sudbury, Massachusetts. Rabbi Kushner's many books include *The Book of Letters: A Mystical Hebrew Alphabet; Honey from the Rock: Visions of Mystical Jewish Renewal;* and *The River of Light: Spirituality, Judaism, and the Evolution of Consciousness.*

Julie Pelc received master's degrees from the American Jewish University and from Harvard Graduate School of Education and was ordained by Hebrew Union College—Jewish Institute of Religion. Rabbi Pelc has been published in several periodicals, including *Spirituality and Health, Lilith, Milwaukee Journal Sentinel,* and *The Wisconsin Jewish Chronicle.* She is co-editor of the anthology *Joining the Sisterhood: Young Jewish Women Write Their Lives.*

Adam J. Raskin was ordained by the Jewish Theological Seminary and serves as the rabbi of Congregation Beth Torah in Richardson, Texas. In addition, he teaches at the Ann and Nate Levine Academy and the Florence Melton Adult Mini School in Dallas.

Lesli Koppelman Ross is a writer and communal lay leader promoting Jewish education and the Jewish Awareness movement. Her articles have been published in periodicals such as *Hadassah Magazine, The Christian Science Monitor,* and *Cosmopolitan.* Ms. Ross is the author of *Celebrate! The Complete Jewish Holidays Handbook* and *The Lifetime Guide to the Jewish Holidays.*

David Seidenberg is a scholar and teacher of eco-theology, environmental ethics, and Jewish mysticism and theology. He has a doctorate in Jewish thought focused on ecology and Kabbalah from the Jewish Theological Seminary (JTS). Rabbi Seidenberg received ordination from JTS and from Rabbi Zalman Schachter-Shalomi. His writing has been published in various collections, including *Trees, Earth and Torah: A Tu B'Shvat Anthology* and the *Encyclopedia of Religion and Nature.* He created and runs an organization called NeoHasid.

Rami Shapiro directs the One River Foundation and is an adjunct professor of religious studies as Middle Tennessee State University. A graduate of the Hebrew Union College–Jewish Institute of Religion, Rabbi Shapiro holds a PhD in religious studies from Union Graduate School. He was the founding rabbi of Temple Beth Or in Miami, Florida, and senior rabbi of Metivta, a center for contemplative Judaism in Los Angeles. Among the several books he has written are *The Sacred Art of Lovingkindness: Preparing to Practice*; *Minyan: Ten Principles for Living a Life of Integrity*; and *Proverbs: The Wisdom of Solomon*.

Elie Kaplan Spitz has served since 1988 as the rabbi of Congregation B'nai Israel in Tustin, California. In addition to being ordained by the Jewish Theological Seminary, he earlier received a law degree from Boston University. He teaches the philosophy of Jewish law at the American Jewish University. Rabbi Spitz has written many articles dealing with spirituality and Jewish law and authored the book *Does the Soul Survive? A Jewish Journey to Belief in Afterlife, Past Lives & Living with Purpose*.

Michael Strassfeld is the rabbi of the Society for the Advancement of Judaism. He was ordained by the Reconstructionist Rabbinical College and holds a master's degree in Near Eastern and Jewish Studies from Brandeis University. Rabbi Strassfeld is the author of *The Jewish Holidays: A Guide & Commentary* and *A Book of Life: Embracing Judaism As Spiritual Practice*. He is co-author of the three editions of *The Jewish Catalog* and a co-editor of a *Night of Questions: A Passover Haggadah*.

Alana Suskin is the assistant director of the American Jewish Committee, Washington Chapter. She was ordained by the Ziegler School of Rabbinic Studies at the American Jewish University. Rabbi Suskin has been published in a variety of journals, books, and anthologies, including *The Unfolding Tradition: Jewish Law after Sinai*, edited by Elliot N. Dorff.

Laurie Hahn Tapper is the director of Brandeis Collegiate Institute and Adult Programs at the Brandeis-Bardin campus of American Jewish University. She was ordained by the Jewish Theological Seminary. Rabbi Tapper focuses on engaging the Jewish community in education and spirituality through the arts, the outdoors, and alternative prayer.

Jonathan Wittenberg is the spiritual leader of the New North London Synagogue. Born in Scotland, Rabbi Wittenberg spent much of his childhood in London and was educated at Cambridge University. After being ordained, he became a leader of the Masorti movement for traditional Judaism and has authored several books, including *The Eternal Journey: Meditations of the Jewish Year*; *The Three Pillars of Judaism: A Search for Faith and Values*; and *The Laws of Life: A Guide to Traditional Jewish Practice at Times of Bereavement*.

Index

R

S

▲   ▲   ▲   ▲   ▲   ▲   ▲   ▲   ▲   ▲   ▲   ▲

About the Author and the Editor

Paul Steinberg is the rabbi and director of Jewish Studies and Hebrew at the Levine Academy: A Solomon Schechter School in Dallas. He holds master's degrees in both education and rabbinic studies and was ordained by the Ziegler School of Rabbinic Studies. He is the author of the *Study Guide to Jewish Ethics* (JPS, 2003) and several articles on Hebrew Bible and Jewish education,. He writes a monthly column on the spirit of Jewish holidays and family in the *Texas Jewish Post*. Throughout his career, Rabbi Steinberg has stressed Judaism's emphasis on the transformational power of study, as well as its approach to living a moral life.

Janet Greenstein Potter is a freelance writer and editor based in Philadelphia. Among the JPS publications she has edited are the National Jewish Book Award runner-up *Wise and Not So Wise: 10 Tales from the Rabbis* (2004); *Praise Her Works: Conversations with Biblical Women* (2005); *Zayda Was a Cowboy* (2005); and *Sarah's Journey* (2005). She was the editor and project manager for *The Kids' Catalog of Animals and the Earth* (JPS, 2006), a book about the environment and the Jewish tradition.